ESSAYS ON THE PHILOSOPHY OF GEORGE BERKELEY

SYNTHESE HISTORICAL LIBRARY

TEXTS AND STUDIES IN THE HISTORY OF
LOGIC AND PHILOSOPHY

Editors:

N. KRETZMANN, *Cornell University*
G. NUCHELMANS, *University of Leyden*
L. M. DE RIJK, *University of Leyden*

Editorial Board:

VOLUME 29

ESSAYS ON
THE PHILOSOPHY OF
GEORGE BERKELEY

Edited by

ERNEST SOSA

Department of Philosophy,
Brown University, Providence, Rhode Island

D. REIDEL PUBLISHING COMPANY

A MEMBER OF THE KLUWER ACADEMIC PUBLISHERS GROUP

DORDRECHT / BOSTON / LANCASTER / TOKYO

Library of Congress Cataloging in Publication Data

Essays on the philosophy of George Berkeley.

(Synthese historical library; v. 29)
Bibliography: p.
Includes index.
1. Berkeley, George, 1685–1753. I. Sosa, Ernest. II. Series.
B1348.E734 1987 192 86–27978
ISBN 90–277–2405–9

B
1348
.E734
1987

Published by D. Reidel Publishing Company,
P.O. Box 17, 3300 AA Dordrecht, Holland.

Sold and distributed in the U.S.A. and Canada
by Kluwer Academic Publishers,
101 Philip Drive, Assinippi Park, Norwell, MA 02061, U.S.A.

In all other countries, sold and distributed
by Kluwer Academic Publishers Group,
P.O. Box 322, 3300 AH Dordrecht, Holland.

TABLE OF CONTENTS

PREFACE

A tercentenary conference of March, 1985, drew to Newport, Rhode Island, nearly all the most distinguished Berkeley scholars now active. The conference was organized by the International Berkeley Society, with the support of several institutions and many people (whose help is acknowledged below). This volume represents a selection of the lead papers delivered at that conference, most now revised.

The Cartesian marriage of Mind and Body has proved an uneasy union. Each side has claimed supremacy and usurped the rights of the other. In anglophone philosophy Body has lately had it all pretty much its own way, most dramatically in the Disappearance Theory of Mind, whose varieties vary in appeal and sophistication, but uniformly shock sensibilities. Only recently has Mind reasserted itself, yet the voices of support are already a swelling chorus. "Welcome," Berkeley would respond, since ". . . all the choir of heaven and furniture of the earth . . . have not a subsistence without a mind . . ." (*Principles*, sect. 6). In fairness, Berkeley does play a Disappearance trick of his own – with Matter now into the hat. But his act is far subtler than any brute denial of the obvious, and seeks rather to explain than bluntly to reject. Perhaps we are today better prepared to appreciate his insights.

The present collection spans the breadth of Berkeley's thought in metaphysics and epistemology. Its table of contents shows a division by fields all under wide and active cultivation today, but already well tilled three centuries ago. The Mind-Body struggle for metaphysical supremacy serves as opening topic, followed by the notion of substance crucial to that struggle. Then come two sections on thought and reference, questions of intense contemporary interest. It is fascinating to see a philosopher of Berkeley's acumen and lucidity already struggling with them. Epistemology follows, with discussion from three different angles of that most distinctive of Berkeleian themes: his view that the best philosophy of thought and knowledge requires a metaphysics not of matter but of God. Perception gave Berkeley his start, and we turn to it next with essays on his view of its objects and its varieties. The collection closes with two scholarly papers. One offers a new view of Berkeley's Notebooks, buttressed by detailed textual support. The last paper, finally, on the reception of Berkeley's philosophy in Germany, recalls the first, which compares the phenomenalisms of Leibniz and Berkeley.

Ernest Sosa
Brown University

ACKNOWLEDGEMENTS

The Newport conference had a substantial grant from the Rhode Island Committee for the Humanities. Brown University contributed material and human resources. And the conference was hosted by St. George's School and Trinity Church in Newport. Thanks are owed to Raymond Houghton, President of the IBS, to Maureen Lapan, and to the Society of the Colonial Dames of Rhode Island and Providence Plantations, especially Mary Staley, for their enormous contribution to the success of the conference.

My warm thanks as organizer and editor to Gale Alex and Eleanor Thum for secretarial assistance; to Salvatore Fratantaro for editorial assistance; to Constance Mui for preparing the indices; to Jesus Diaz for assistance with the conference; to Suzanne Bertrand for indispensable editorial contributions; and to Matthew Kapstein for the bibliography, and for manifold editorial and scholarly help with every aspect of the book project.

CONTRIBUTORS

Robert M. Adams
*University of California,
Los Angeles
Los Angeles, California*

Margaret Atherton
*University of Wisconsin,
Milwaukee
Milwaukee, Wisconsin*

Michael R. Ayers
*Wadham College
Oxford, Great Britain*

Bertil Belfrage
*Villan
S-57020 Bodafors
Sweden*

Martha Bolton
*Rutgers, The State University of
New Jersey
New Brunswick, New Jersey*

Wolfgang Breidert
*Universität Karlsruhe
Karlsruhe, Fed. Republic of Germany*

Geneviève Brykman
*70, rue du Javelot
75645 Paris 13, France*

Phillip Cummins
*University of Iowa
Iowa City, Iowa*

Daniel Garber
*The University of Chicago
Chicago, Illinois*

A. David Kline
*Iowa State University of
Science and Technology
Ames, Iowa*

George S. Pappas
*Ohio State University
Columbus, Ohio*

Ernest Sosa
*Brown University
Providence, Rhode Island*

Ian Tipton
*The University College of Wales
Aberystwyth, Dyfed, Wales*

Margaret Wilson
*Princeton University
Princeton, New Jersey*

ABBREVIATIONS

The present volume follows John Foster and Howard Robinson, eds., *Essays on Berkeley: a tercentennial celebration* (Oxford: Clarendon Press, 1985), for most of the abbreviations here listed.

Works   *The Works of George Berkeley Bishop of Cloyne*, ed. A. A. Luce and T. E. Jessop, 9 vols. (Edinburgh: Thomas Nelson, 1948-57). References, except to the works listed below, are by volume and page number.

PC   *Philosophical Commentaries* (*Works*, vol. i). References by entry numbers (*Notebook B* = entries 1–399; *Notebook A* = entries from 400 onwards).

NTV   *An Essay Towards a New Theory of Vision* (*Works*, vol. i). References by section numbers.

TVV   *Theory of Vision Vindicated and Explained* (*Works*, vol. i). References by section numbers.

Principles   *The Principles of Human Knowledge*, Part I (*Works*, ii). Referred to by section number.

Principles, Intro. Introduction to *The Principles of Human Knowledge* (*Works*, ii). Referred to by section number.

Dialogues   *Three Dialogues between Hylas and Philonous* (*Works*, ii). References are to pages numbers.

Alc.   *Alciphron or the Minute Philosopher* (*Works*, iii). Referred to by page number.

PART ONE

METAPHYSICS:
COMPARISON WITH LEIBNIZ AND LOCKE

Margaret D. Wilson

THE PHENOMENALISMS OF
LEIBNIZ AND BERKELEY

The two great German philosophers of the early modern era, Leibniz and
Kant, overlapped Berkeley's life at opposite ends. Each was aware of
Berkeley, and had at least some knowledge of his early philosophy.
(Berkeley's *Principles of Human Knowledge* was published in 1710, when
Berkeley was about twenty-five, and Leibniz was in his sixties. When
Berkeley died in 1753, Kant was about thirty years old.) Kant's philosophy
– which he himself called "transcendental idealism" – has been linked to
Berkeley's idealism or phenomenalism through a long tradition, going back
to the contemporary Garve-Feder review of the first *Critique*. Numerous
works in English have contributed to this tradition, including several papers
of the past decade or so. Commentators have often viewed Berkeley and
Kant as united in a common concern with answering Cartesian skepticism,
and as generating their respective phenomenalisms or idealisms at least
partly in response to this concern. Some have, in effect accepted Kant's
own assessment that Berkeley embraced an extreme reductionistic subjec-
tivism only because he failed to grasp the possibility of an a priori ground-
ing of empirical knowledge in "forms of intuition" and the categories.
(Berkeley, in other words, failed to appreciate that one could mount an
idealist response to external world skepticism without giving up
"objectivity.")

Efforts to connect Berkeley's position to that of Leibniz have been
fewer, more limited, and (as far as I can determine) mostly pretty recent.[1]
Possibly Leibniz's notable *lack* of preoccupation with external world skepticism, accompanied by his uninhibited espousal of a rationalistic metaphysics, has made the comparison of his philosophy with Berkeley's seem a
less natural and inviting enterprise. Nevertheless, there are now at least
the beginnings of a tradition linking their respective "phenomenalisms."
Montgomery Furth, in an article published in 1967, proposed that Leibniz
should be interpreted as a phenomenalist, and discussed some of the relations between Leibniz's position and Berkeley's. Just as critics commenting
on the relation between Kant's phenomenalism and Berkeley's have held
that Kant does fuller justice to our objectivity concepts than Berkeley, so
Furth holds that Leibniz's special form of phenomenalism "helps to dispel
the feeling, voiced about phenomenalistic theories from Berkeley's day
down to our own, that . . . we have been swindled out of the real world of
corporeal substances . . ."[2] Furth further states that Leibniz

3

E.Sosa (ed.), Essays on the Philosophy of George Berkeley, 3–22.
©*1987 by D. Reidel Publishing Company*

> . . . perceived the essential problem set by Descartes – namely
> that of explicating the notion of a *matter of objective fact* within
> terms of objects of possible experience, much as that problem
> was later perceived by Berkeley, by Kant, and for that matter
> by C. I. Lewis.[3]

A recently published study by Robert Adams continues the discussion of
Leibniz's phenomenalism with some reference to Furth's paper. Adams
gives more detailed consideration to the relation between Leibniz and
Berkeley, stressing different issues. While Adams perceptively expounds
some major differences between Leibniz's phenomenalism and Berkeley's
position, he notes that Leibniz "did not fail to see that he and Berkeley
were fundamentally on the same side."[4] J. J. MacIntosh in a 1971 paper
has maintained that "Berkeley and Leibniz . . . held strikingly similar
philosophical views," and implies that English-speaking chauvinism accounts for the fact that this point hasn't been more widely recognized.[5]

I believe that attempts to assimilate Berkeley's phenomenalism either to Kant's position or to Leibniz's give insufficient weight to certain
fundamental and unique features of Berkeley's philosophical doctrines and
objectives – features which in fact place him in opposition to both Leibniz
and Kant. Of course, I do not deny that these three philosophers share
some common views and objectives. Certainly, each was concerned to
counter the apparently anti-religious implications of materialist philosophies
by endorsing, or leaving room for, the primacy of "spirit." Each may be
said to hold in some sense that the physical world is "mind-dependent."
Also, each was, in his own way, a critic of Newton's "transcendental realist" theory of space. And antiskeptical concerns do figure prominently in
Berkeley's philosophical writings as well as in Kant's. But Berkeley, for all
the oddities of his sensationalistic reductionism, was a "commonsense" philosopher in a way that Leibniz and Kant never were. Berkeley was a phenomenalist in the straightforward sense that he construed the appearances
of ordinary sense experience – the purple skies, "wild but sweet notes of
the birds," fragrant blooms, and warm sunshine – as *the real world*.[6] He
was deeply concerned to *deny* – in the early works, at any rate – that either science or metaphysics reveals truths about reality which provide a
corrective to ordinary sense experience. As Philonous remarks in the Third
Dialogue:

> I am of a vulgar cast, simple enough to believe my senses, and
> leave things as I find them. To be plain, it is my opinion, that
> the real things are those very things I see and feel, and per-
> ceive by my senses . . . It is likewise my opinion, that colours
> and other sensible qualities are on the objects. I cannot for my
> life help thinking that snow is white, and fire hot.[7]

Neither Leibniz nor Kant accepts this position of deliberately naive empiricism. In this important respect they follow closely in the tradition to which Berkeley most resolutely opposed himself. Both hold that materialistic science provides a *relatively* objective and true account of nature, which to some degree contrasts with that of ordinary experience. Of course; they are not strictly scientific realists, since they both hold that the scientific account of things is not a true account of things as they are in themselves, of the ultimate reality. This ultimate reality they take to lie beyond the reach of materialistic science as well as beyond the immediate data of sense. (Leibniz differs from Kant, of course, in regarding it as the appropriate subject of human metaphysics.) Still, they do both accept the view that our ordinary sensory experiences of colors and tastes are *merely* subjective; that the materialistic scientific account is *relatively* objective and real. In my opinion, this aspect of both of their positions is sufficient to place them directly at odds with Berkeley. It is true that Berkeley attributes the philosophers' distinction between the reality and the sensible appearances of things to the belief in mind-independent, material substance.[8] It does not follow, however, that he would have no objection to the distinction if it were detached from this belief (as it is, in different ways, by Leibniz and Kant). Similarly, while there are legitimate senses of "phenomenalism" (or "idealism") in which Leibniz and Kant are both phenomenalists (or idealists), it simply does not follow that their views and concerns are fundamentally similar to Berkeley's. Failure adequately to recognize this point is partly the result of insufficient attention to variations of meaning, across different contexts, of the term "phenomenalism" itself and terms commonly used in the definition or characterization of "phenomenalism" – like "perception" and "experience".

In an earlier paper I have argued this case in detail with respect to the relations between Berkeley and Kant.[9] Here I would like to develop a similar case against attempts to assimilate the "phenomenalisms" of Berkeley and Leibniz.

I

Berkeley, I have said, denies any distinction between the appearances or phenomena of ordinary, direct sense experience and the real physical world. *His* "phenomenalism" consists basically in the view that the sensory phenomena *are the real things*. (Because he identifies the objects of sense experience as "ideas," Berkeley's position may also be called an idealism.) What reasons are we given for construing Leibniz as a phenomenalist? Furth writes:

> Thus [Leibniz's] theory is a phenomenalism, for it offers a reductive explication of statements about material things as

translations or abbreviations of statements about perceptions . . .[10]

MacIntosh examines "the extent to which Leibniz moved towards phenomenalism," or to "full-blown phenomenalism";[11] he seems to take this as
much the same thing as an examination of the extent to which Leibniz
moved towards Berkeley's metaphysical position. Nowhere in his paper
does MacIntosh offer an explicit account of the meaning of
"phenomenalism." He does say, though:

> One version of phenomenalism may be plucked from the *Mona-
> dology* (1714): Monads are windowless (7) and are subject to
> change (10) resulting from an internal principle (11) which acts
> by bringing about perceptions (15). In short what is, is internal,
> and what is internal is what is perceived.[12]

In light of this comment I take it that MacIntosh's underlying conception of
"phenomenalism" is much the same as Furth's: there is no material reality
that is not in some sense reducible to "perceptions." Adams, while stressing that bodies are the *objective content* of perceptions for Leibniz, comments: "In calling [bodies] phenomena Leibniz means that they have their
being in the awareness that perceivers have of [the] story [told or approxi-
mated by perception, commonsense, and science]."[13]

    Of course, Leibniz, or any of his commentators, is entitled to his
own interpretation of the terms "phenomena" and "phenomenalism." Yet
we should be wary of attempts to assimilate Leibniz's position to Berkeley's, on the grounds that they both think that reality may be fully explicated in terms of perceivers, their wills or appetites, and their perceptions
or perceptual contents. What if the concepts of "perceivers" and
"perceptions" differ drastically between the two philosophers? And what if
there are corresponding radical differences in their conceptions of
"phenomena"? This issue arises, for example, when Adams writes:

> Part of Leibniz's point in saying that extended things as such
> are phenomena is to claim that they have their existence only
> in substances that perceive them, *and in this he agrees with
> Berkeley.* (emphasis added)[14]

Certainly there is *nominal* agreement between Leibniz on Berkeley on this
point (ignoring the question whether the archetypes of bodies in God's mind
really count as "perceptions" for Berkeley). But there is, one may point out,
nominal agreement between Berkeley and Descartes that physical things
really exist, and are different in nature from minds. Nominal agreement
may conceal radical philosophical differences. This is the case, I want to
hold, with respect to Berkeley's and Leibniz's positions on the

"phenomenal" status of bodies. What Leibniz means by "perception" is *utterly* different from what Berkeley means by "perception," and their understandings of the relations between physical reality and sensations are also sharply in conflict. I believe the difference is *so* significant that it is incorrect to say they "agree."

Before arguing this point I want to acknowledge that Adams, at least, is quite aware of the sorts of differences between Leibniz's and Berkeley's views that I am about to discuss. They are among those that he expounds in some detail. Similarly, Furth has to be aware of certain important differences: for they are to some extent preconditions of the philosophical advantage he claims that Leibniz's phenomenalism holds over Berkeley's. MacIntosh also comments on differences between the two philosophers, though not, in my opinion, as precisely as Adams. My argument here, in any case, will not hinge very much on dispute about textual details. Rather I hope that by highlighting the contrasts between more or less familiar aspects of Berkeley's and Leibniz's positions I can make clear that they are fundamentally at odds with each other with respect to both motivation and doctrine.

Let us consider first the suggestion that Leibniz and Berkeley are basically in agreement about the nature of bodies in so far as they both reduce physical things to perceptions. To evaluate this claim we surely need to ask what they respectively understand by "perceptions." To take the easier case first, it seems both evident and uncontroversial that when Berkeley speaks of perceptions he means conscious awareness. The most explicit statement of this point that I know of occurs in the early *Philosophical Commentaries*, where Berkeley notes:

> Consciousness, perception, existence of Ideas seem to be all one.[15]

Consciousness is not, as far as I can find, explicitly discussed in the *Principles* or the *Dialogues;* but I also find in those works no indication that Berkeley entertained even the possibility of unconscious mental states. In *The New Theory of Vision* Berkeley seems to reject as "incomprehensible" the postulation of unconscious mental processes.[16]

In general when Berkeley speaks of perception he means, more specifically, conscious awareness *of ideas of sense*. This is, indeed, invariably the case when he is talking about our perception of physical objects – except in the special context of "indirect perception," or association from present ideas of sense to other imagined or anticipated sensory ideas. Thus, when Berkeley says that for a physical thing to be is to be perceived, he means that a physical thing exists just in case it (or one of the sensible qualities that constitute it) is (a) the object of a conscious sensory experience for humans; and/or (b) exists in God's mind, though not as an object of sense. *Occasionally*, Berkeley will use the terms "perceive" and

"perception" – even in connection with physical objects – when he does not
have sense perception in mind: for instance, although he is clear that God
"perceives nothing by sense as we do," this does not *always* prevent him
from saying that things are "perceived by God."[17] And of course he does
hold that we know by reflection, or have notions of, ourselves as spiritual
substances, and our inner operations, such as willing:

> . . . I have a notion of spirit, though I have not, strictly
> speaking, an idea of it. I do not perceive it as an idea or by
> means of an idea, but know it by reflexion.
> . . . I know or am conscious of my own being; and that I my-
> self am not my ideas, but somewhat else, a thinking active
> principle that perceives, knows, wills, and operates about
> ideas.[18]

But, in any case, knowledge of spirits is always sharply contrasted by
Berkeley with knowledge of physical things; and when he speaks of spirits
he has in mind nothing very unusual – just you, me, other humans, God,
and perhaps animals and angels.[19]
 Before turning to Leibniz I would like to mention one further point
about Berkeley's treatment of perception. While he does sometimes say
that ideas may be more or less "clear" or "distinct," this terminology is
generally used in his system to mark the commonsense difference between
genuine sense experiences and mere imaginings or dreams:

> the ideas formed by the imagination are faint and indistinct;
> they have besides an entire dependence on the will. But the
> ideas perceived by sense, that is, real things, are more vivid
> and clear, and being imprinted on the mind by a spirit distinct
> from us, have not a like dependence on our will.[20]

I will return to this point later, in comparing Berkeley's position with that
of Leibniz.

                                    II

I now turn with a trepidation that everyone familiar with it will appreciate
to the topic of Leibniz's understanding of the term "perception." Fortunately, present purposes do not require a deep and searching analysis of
the difficulties surrounding this issue – although the *seriousness* of the
difficulties is indeed germane to my purpose.
 Leibniz, as is well known, restricts the term "perception" neither to
conscious experience nor to sense perception. He defines the term, rather
mysteriously, as "the expression of many things in one."[21] "Expression"

implies a "constant and regulated relation between what can be said of the one and of the other."[22] The "one" in which perception occurs is invariably a simple substance, or monad. Also, although not all cases of expression are perceptions, I take it that all cases of expression *in monads* are perceptions.[23] The perceptual states of monads include intellection in rational beings or spirits, sensations in spirits and animals, and states which are neither intellection nor sensations. Only the latter sort of "perceptions" occur in the bare monads, which "are wholly destitute of sensation and knowledge."[24] Further, the perceptual states of spirits and animal minds must also include subsensational perceptions, as well as sensation and (in the case of spirits) thought. For every monad "expresses the whole world from its own point of view," but Leibniz does not suppose that a human or animal mind has knowledge or sensation of everything in its world.

It should already be clear that a Leibnizian "reductive explication of statements about material things as translations or abbreviations of statements about perceptions," need be nothing *at all* like a Berkeleian one. The question indeed is whether such a purported "reductive explication," in so far as it involves appeal to "perceptions" which are neither intellectual nor sensory – and may even be states or entities that *have* neither intellect nor sense – offers us anything intelligible. I can only say that I myself can make little serious sense of this broad Leibnizian concept of "perception," and that I note that other commentators – Adams, for instance – also acknowledge its extreme obscurity.[25] One point I would particularly like to stress in this connection is that it seems very dubious practice to refer to subsensational perceptions as "awarenesses," "experiences," or even "mental events," as Furth and other commentators comfortably do.[26] It may be all right to say, "I must have experienced the closeness of the room from the moment I entered, though I didn't really become aware of it till now." But in this sort of example we are talking about a perception that has a role in a readily identified mental life, and that in fact is continuous with related conscious experiences. I do not think that the intelligibility of this sort of context shows we can talk meaningfully of the "awarenesses" or "experiences" of "mind-like substances with neither understanding nor sensation."

The point is relevant to Furth's conception of the advantage of Leibniz's phenomenalism over Berkeley's. Furth holds that Leibniz is able to satisfy a "no-residue" condition on phenomenalistic translations that Berkeley either cannot meet, or can handle only through such objectionable strategies as appeal to subjunctive conditionals or to an all-perceiving God. Leibniz, that is, "can deliver the full content of the ostensible material-thing statements in their presystematic form."[27] His advantage here lies in the fact that he doesn't stop short at any "paltry population" of observers; "every conceivable point of view in the universe is already enlisted among the monads . . ."[28] For Leibniz there is no problem of "gaps" in the population's actual experience, or "unrepresented viewpoints and interrupted

conscious histories," such as a phenomenalist of Berkeleian stripe, who
admits minds only where we normally *think* there are minds, must hope-
lessly confront.[29]

I suggest that Leibniz obtains this "advantage" at the very high
cost of leaving it quite unclear exactly what it is that bodies are being reduced to, in so far as they are reduced to "perceptions" in his system. To
the extent that Leibniz's reduction relies on the doctrine of pre-established
harmony among *all* "perceivers" – the view stressed by Furth – it simply
lets go of the more familiar conceptions of perceptions, appearances, and
experience that have been the mainstay of the more familiar forms of phenomenalism, such as Berkeley's. (For this reason I would reject Furth's
claim that Leibniz saw the problem of explicating the notion of a matter of
objective fact within "terms of objects of possible experience" in much the
same way as Berkeley – or for that matter C. I. Lewis.)

Other radical differences between Berkeley's and Leibniz's positions
relate in various ways to the one I have just been considering. For one
thing, Leibniz, as is well known, denies that we can have demonstrative
knowledge of the existence of bodies.[30] This is really a remarkable concession for a phenomenalist to make. I take it to derive precisely from Leibniz's conception of the reality of bodies as grounded in the harmonized perceptions of infinitely many "perceivers"; whereas, as individual minds, each
of us is directly aware only of (some of) our own perceptions. (The more one
thinks of Berkeley as focusing on the refutation of external world skepticism, the more deeply divided will he appear to be from Leibniz on this
point.) But Leibniz's "phenomenalism" is not only compatible with the denial of certainty concerning the existence of bodies. It is in fact tightly
bound up with a double-layered critique of the ordinary sense-conception of
bodies that Berkeley seeks to defend. The key points here are, first, that
Leibniz denies all of what he counts as "perception" is on an epistemologi-
cally equal footing; and second, that he denies that even our best perceptual
representations of bodies accurately present to us what really is. Elabora-
tion of these points will help clarify further the opposition between Leibniz's
view of "phenomena" and Berkeley's.

                                    III

Berkeley's defense of the unproblematic reality of the objects of ordinary
sense experience includes, as an essential feature, rejection of the primary-
secondary quality distinction. He holds that all the standard types of sensible qualities are equally objective and real, just as they are perceived or
experienced by us. Some have imagined that the reason for this aspect of
his position is that he overlooked the original scientific realist reasons for
the distinction (in Descartes, Locke, and numerous other predecessors), and
thus thought it sufficient to point out that primary quality perceptions are

no less perceiver-relative than secondary quality perceptions. Elsewhere I
have tried to show that this notion of Berkeley's historical ignorance and
philosophical naivete is completely unfounded.[3][1] He was in fact a well informed and intelligent – I would say deep – critic of the scientific realist
conception of the relation of bodies to our experience. His rejection of the
primary-secondary quality distinction is the cornerstone of this critique. I
will approach the comparison of his position on this issue with Leibniz's by
considering MacIntosh's attempt to establish close similarity between them.

    According to MacIntosh, Leibniz's position resembles Berkeley's
since Leibniz, too, "runs together" the primary and seconday qualities.[3][2]
MacIntosh bases his conclusion on passages like the following from Leibniz's writings:

> . . . the whole nature of body does not consist solely in exten-
> sion, that is to say in size, figure and motion, . . . there must
> necessarily be recognised in it something which is related to
> souls and which is commonly called substantial form, though it
> brings about no changes in phenomena . . . It can even be
> demonstrated that the notion of size, figure and motion is not so
> distinct as is imagined, and that it includes something imagi-
> nary and relative to our perceptions, as are also (although
> much more so) colour, heat and other similar qualities, of which
> it can be doubted whether they are truly present in the nature
> of things outside us.[3][3]
>   Concerning bodies I can demonstrate that not merely
> light, heat, colour and similar qualities are apparent but also
> motion, figure, and extension. And that, if anything is real, it is
> solely the force of acting and suffering, and hence that the
> substance of a body consists in this (as if in matter and form).
> Those bodies, however, which have no substantial form, are
> merely phenomena or at least only aggregates of the true uni-
> ties.[3][4]

    I think, however, that these passages bring out the *contrasts* be-
tween Leibniz's and Berkeley's views of qualities much more than any sim-
ilarities. Indeed, the type of "phenomenalism" that Leibniz subscribes to in
such passages is almost the opposite of Berkeley's position.

    Berkeley thinks that perceptions of secondary and of primary quali-
ties equally and adequately present to us the real qualities of bodies (bodies
themselves being only congeries of sensations). A cherry is literally red,
soft, tart-tasting, *and round*.[3][5] Or, as Berkeley expresses the point in the
Principles:

> . . . whoever shall reflect, and take care to understand what he
> says, will, if I mistake not, acknowledge that all sensible

qualities are alike *sensations*, and alike *real;* and that where the extension is, there is the colour too, to wit, in his mind . . . and that the objects of sense are nothing but those sensations combined, blended, or (if one may so speak) concreted together.[36]

The first point to be noted about Leibniz's position in this connection is that he does, in his own way, recognize and accept the traditional distinction between mere sensations in us, and their physical causes. The latter he characterizes in terms of extension, figure, and motion. Sensations like color and taste he characterizes as "phantoms," saying that they strictly merit this name, rather than that "of qualities, or even of ideas."[37] Behind this terminological precision is Leibniz's view that sensations are indecipherably blurred appearances of the figures and motions that give rise to them.[38]

Leibniz further holds, however, that *even* the primary quality perceptions have to be contrasted with the reality of things, although they are in some way less subjective than the secondary quality perceptions. As sensations like color and taste are blurred appearances of the figures and motions that cause them, so figure and extension are only ways in which infinite aggregates of unextended substances appear to our limited minds.[39] Thus size, figure, and motion are also "relative to our perception," although color, heat, and other similar qualities are "much more so."

The very fundamental opposition between Berkeley and Leibniz on the primary-secondary quality issue may now be stated succinctly. The aim of Berkeley's "phenomenalism" is to reclaim as equally "real" qualities that had come to be classified as non-objective, as *mere* subjective appearances. Berkeley, in other words, was centrally concerned to vindicate the reality of the world as presented in ordinary sense experience, against the abstractions of the philosophers and scientists of his time. Leibniz, on the contrary, agreed to the superior reality or objectivity of the physicist's conception of the world. As Adams says: "for Leibniz the universe of corporeal phenomena is primarily the object not of sense but of science."[40] But Leibniz further holds that qualities construed by physics as "real" are themselves *mere* phenomena, relative to their monadic "foundations." For him the term "phenomenon" thus carries the pejorative connotation of being in some degree subjective, unreal, or "imaginary." To quote Adams once more: "'Phenomenon' [in Leibniz's discussions] contrasts not only as intramental with 'extramental'; it also contrasts as apparent with 'real.'"[41] Thus, while both Berkeley and Leibniz construed the physicists' theory of reality as an "abstraction," they developed this notion in completely opposite directions. Berkeley construed it as an abstraction in relation to the concrete reality presented in ordinary sense experience. Leibniz thought that ordinary sense experience was still less reflective of reality, more "relative to our perception," than physical theory, but considered the latter as unreal or abstract in relation to some still more remote and basic concrete metaphysical truth.

I mentioned earlier that when Berkeley, in the *Principles* and *Dialogues*, distinguishes among perceptions in terms of clarity or distinctness he is trying to characterize in phenomenological terms the difference between normal sense perceptions on the one hand, and dreams, hallucinations, and imaginations on the other hand. Leibniz, too, sometimes draws a similar distinction in terms of "vividness."[42] Leibniz uses the characterizations of clarity and distinctness, however, in distinguishing among normal waking perceptions and states of knowledge. While his usage of these terms involves subtle and difficult issues, we may at least note here that when Leibniz speaks of a perception as relatively distinct, he is, in part, marking its relative informativeness with respect to the world of substances outside the individual perceiver, and also its relatively intellectual status.[43] His distinction among normal waking perceptions in terms of clarity and distinctness is particularly reflected in his remarks about primary and secondary qualities. On the one hand he will say, echoing Descartes: "we perceive nothing distinctly in matter save magnitude, figure, and extension."[44] On the other hand, as we've seen, he will also insist that "the notion of size, figure and motion is not so distinct as is imagined." Berkeley, however, denies that there is any world of substances external to our perceptions for our ideas to be informative about, and denies any intellectual knowledge of body superior to the sensible. Accordingly, he lacks a use for the Cartesian epistemological concept of distinctness, and for the whole rationalist framework within which Leibniz's doctrine of "perception" unfolds.

IV

In summary, we have now noted several fundamental points of divergence between Berkeley's conception of the perception-dependence, and hence the "phenomenality," of bodies and Leibniz's. First, Berkeley reduces bodies to conscious sense perceptions; but Leibniz uses the term "perception" in a far wider, and far less easily grasped way. Second, Leibniz does not interpret his position concerning our perceptions of bodies as providing a conclusive basis for the repudiation of skepticism concerning the existence of bodies – in whatever sense bodies may be said to exist. Third, Berkeley's phenomenalism is explicitly directed at denying any superiority to the "scientific," as opposed to the ordinary sensible, conception of bodies. Leibniz maintains the traditional scientific realist stance concerning the relative superiority, with respect to reality, of the scientific story (as Adams calls it). Finally, when Leibniz says that even extension and figure are phenomenal, involve "something relative to our perceptions," he is saying that even these qualities are *merely* apparent – that they are to be contrasted with the true reality of things, understood as aggregations of monads. Berkeley, on the other hand, deliberately identifies the (sensorily) perceived with the real.

Some further specific differences between their positions – touched on by Adams and MacIntosh – are closely connected with the latter two of these three fundamental ones. Thus, Berkeley's contention that nothing smaller than a minimum sensibilium is physically real, and his related rejection of "infintesimals," are not – contrary to what MacIntosh suggests – reflections of a lack of sophistication in mathematics.[45] They are consequences of his new principle that (for a physical thing) to be is to be perceived by sense. (Of course Berkeley also had other reasons for regarding the contemporary notion of infintesimals as incoherent.)[46] Leibniz's insistence on the infinite divisibility of matter correspondingly reflects his lack of empiricist or sensationalist commitments as much as his mathematical genius. Similarly, Berkeley's espousal of an instrumental interpretation of certain scientific conceptions, notably the conception of force, is closely connected with his sensationalistic criterion of physical reality. For Leibniz, who wholly lacks such motivation, physical force is at least as well founded a phenomenon as are extension and shape.

On another matter of considerable importance to Berkeley his general systematic commitments also lead him in quite an opposite direction from the one that Leibniz takes. Berkeley's opposition to skepticism, and his accompanying determination to establish that ordinary sense knowledge is perfectly in order just as it is, leads him resolutely to reject the Lockean corpuscularian notion of unknown inner constitutions.[47] The materialists, he implies, lead us into unnecessary and extravagant skepticism and doubt of our faculties by holding that:

> The Real essence, the internal qualities, and the constitution of even the meanest object is hid from our view; something there is in every drop of water, every grain of sand, which is beyond the power of human understanding to fathom or comprehend.[48]

According to Berkeley the doctrine of hidden inner natures is entirely bound up with the chimerical notion of material substance, and must happily vanish along with it. Leibniz, despite his opposition to purely material substances, has no qualms at all about hidden natures or real essences, construed as entities within the realm of *phenomena bene fundata*. It is true that he does not follow Locke in treating these constitutions as intrinsically unknowable; but he does certainly allow that they are to a large degree unknown, stressing the highly provisional and speculative status of current thought about them.[49]

V

In the paper I have often cited, Robert Adams takes up the interesting issue of Leibniz's own assessment of his relation to Berkeley. As he notes,
Leibniz's best known statement about Berkeley suggests that Leibniz was
under the common misapprehension that Berkeley's attack on the reality of
matter was intended as, or amounted to, an attack on the reality of bodies
or the objects of perception. Leibniz comments to des Bosses:

> The Irishman who attacks the reality of bodies seems neither
> to offer suitable reasons nor to explain his position sufficiently.
> I suspect that he belongs to the class of men who want to be
> known for their paradoxes . . .[50]

But Adams also quotes a less well known annotation to Leibniz's copy of
Berkeley's *Principles*, in which Leibniz gives Berkeley a bit more credit:
"Much here that's right and in agreement with my opinion *(ad sensum
meum)*."[51] It is this notation that leads Adams to remark that Leibniz saw
that he and Berkeley were fundamentally on the same side. Leibniz does
not verbally repeat the error he makes in the des Bosses correspondence, of
saying that Berkeley attacked the reality of bodies. He does, however, go on
again to accuse Berkeley of being paradoxical. And, much more to the
point, he adds an explanation of the ways that Berkeley's philosophy needs
to be corrected by the principles of Monadology that I think Berkeley would
have found hair-raising. Here is the complete notation:

> Much here that's right and agrees with my views. But too par-
> adoxically expressed. For we have no need to say that matter
> is nothing, but it suffices to say that it is a phenomenon like the
> rainbow; and that it is not a substance, but a result of subs-
> tances; and that space is no more real than time, i.e. that it is
> nothing but an order of coexistences as time is an order of su-
> bexistences. The true substances are Monads, or Perceivers.
> But the author ought to have gone on further, namely to
> infinite Monads, constituting all things, and to their preestab-
> lished harmony. He wrongly or at least pointlessly rejects ab-
> stract ideas, restricts ideas to imaginations, despises the sub-
> tleties of arithmetic and geometry. He most wrongly rejects
> the infinite division of the extended; even if he is right to reject
> infinitesimal quantities.[52]

These comments certainly indicate that Leibniz *thought* that he and
Berkeley were on the same side — to the extent of advising that what
Berkeley "needs to say" is just what Leibniz does say.[53] But Berkeley is
perhaps entitled to his own opinion of his goals. In the *Third Dialogue* he

lists "the novelties, . . . the strange notions which shock the genuine un-
corrupted judgment of all mankind; and being once admitted, embarrass the
mind with endless doubts and difficulties."[54] "It is against these and the
like innovations," he continues, "I endeavor to vindicate common sense."
The list indeed includes two or three points which Leibniz would join with
Berkeley in rejecting, e.g., "that there are in bodies absolute extensions,
without any particular magnitude or figure," and, more importantly, the
postulation of inactive matter operating on spirit. But consider some of the
other views that Berkeley lists as his primary targets:

> That the qualities we perceive, are not on the objects; that we
> must not believe our senses; that we know nothing of the real
> nature of things, and can never be assured even of their exis-
> tence; that real colours and sounds are nothing but certain
> unknown figures and motions; . . . that the least particle of a
> body contains innumerable extended parts.[55]

To a very large degree these views which Berkeley has dedicated himself to
overthrowing are views that Leibniz embraces. Who are we, and who is
Leibniz, to say that Berkeley has "no need" to reject them?

Because of the novelty of the idealist positions developed in the late
seventeenth and the eighteenth centuries, it is quite easy to see the philosophers classifiable as idealists as constituting a united front against their
materialist and dualist predecessors. It is easy to forget that Berkeley saw
himself not merely as the enemy of stupid matter, but also as the staunch
proponent of common sense, and of the unproblematic reality of the immediate objects of sense. With respect to the latter aspects of his position,
Berkeley was deeply opposed to Leibniz, even if Leibniz may himself have
overlooked or downplayed the opposition in the spirit of idealist ecumeni-
cism.[56]

Princeton University

NOTES

1. For an astute brief comparison from a work much earlier than those discussed below, see Eugen Stäbler's Inaugural Dissertation, *George Berkeley's Auffassung und Wirkung in der Deutschen Philosophie bis Hegel* (Zeulenroda: Bernhard Sporn, 1935), pp. 8-10. Herbert Wildon Carr comments even more briefly on the relationship between Berkeley and Leibniz in *Leibniz* (Boston: Little, Brown, 1929), pp. 191-92. Both Stäbler and Carr mention Leibniz's conception of bodies as *phenomena bene fundata* as a major point of difference with Berkeley. (I am indebted to Douglas Jesseph for these references, and for other valuable assistance in the preparation of this paper.)

    See also Willy Kabitz, 'Leibniz and Berkeley,' *Sitzungsberichte der Preussische Akademie der Wissenschaften*, Philosophisch-Historische Klasse, **24** (1932), pp. 623-36. In this article, which is also cited by Adams in the paper discussed below, Kabitz comments on Leibniz's reading of Berkeley, with particular reference to his marginal comments in his copy of *The Principles of Human Knowledge*.

2. Montgomery Furth, 'Monadology,' *Philosophical Review* (1967), pp. 169-200; reprinted in *Leibniz: A Collection of Critical Essays*, ed. Harry G. Frankfurt (Garden City, NY: Doubleday [Anchor Books], 1972). The passage quoted is on p. 117 of the Frankfurt edition; subsequent references are also to this edition.

3. *Ibid.*, p. 123.

4. Robert Merrihew Adams, 'Phenomenalism and Corporeal Substance in Leibniz,' in *Midwest Studies in Philosophy VIII*, ed. Peter A. French, *et al.* (Minneapolis: University of Minnesota Press, 1983), p. 222.

5. J. J. MacIntosh, 'Leibniz and Berkeley,' *Proceedings of the Aristotelian Society* (1970-71), pp. 147-63: p. 147.

6. Cf. the opening *mise en scene* of *Dialogues*, 171.

7. *Dialogues*, 229-30.

8. *Dialogues*, 229.

9.   Margaret D. Wilson, 'The "Phenomenalisms" of Berkeley and
     Kant,' in *Self and Nature in Kant's Philosophy*, ed. Allen W. Wood
     (Ithaca: Cornell University Press, 1984), pp. 157-73.

10. 'Monadology,' pp. 116.

11. 'Leibniz and Berkeley', pp. 151-52.

12. *Ibid.*, p. 151.

13. 'Phenomenalism . . . in Leibniz,' p. 218.

14. *Ibid.*, pp. 223-24.

15. *PC*, 578; in George H. Thomas' edition (Mount Union College,
     1976), p. 76. Cf. *PC*, 24 (Thomas, p. 3): "Nothing properly but
     persons . . . i.e. conscious things do exist . . ."

16. See especially *NTV*, 19.

17. See *Dialogues*, 241 and 235, respectively.

18. *Dialogues*, 233; cf. 231-32.

19. Berkeley, unlike Leibniz, has very little to say about the status of
     animals as perceivers (or non-perceivers). In *NTV*, 80 and Appen-
     dix, and again in *Dialogues*, 188-90, the perceptions of minute ani-
     mals (like mites) are invoked to make different points. In his letter
     to Berkeley dated 5 February 1730, Samuel Johnson raises a
     difficulty connected with the supposed status of animals as perceiv-
     ers (in Berkeley's system), but Berkeley fails to reply. (*Works*,
     ii. 289). (I must again acknowledge Douglas Jesseph's assistance,
     in connection with this issue.)

20. *Dialogues*, 235; cf. *Principles*, 30-33.

21. See, e.g., *Die philosophischen Schriften von G. W. Leibniz*, ed. C. I.
     Gerhardt, 7 vols. (Berlin: 1875-90), vol. II, pp. 121, 311, etc.

22. *Ibid.*, p. 112.

23. Adams suggests, however, that not all of a monad's expressions of
     a given thing count as perceptions *of that thing:* 'Phenomenalism
     . . . in Leibniz,' p. 221.

24. 'Discourse on Metaphysics,' 35, in Gerhardt, vol. IV, p. 460-61.

25. See 'Phenomenalism . . . in Leibniz,' p. 223. For a recent discussion of issues relating to consciousness in Leibniz's monadology, see Robert B. Brandom, 'Leibniz and Degrees of Perception,' *Journal of the History of Philosophy*, **XIX** (October 1981), pp. 447-79. Difficulties in understanding Leibniz's general conceptions of perception and expression are explored in the following two papers by Mark Kulstad: 'Some Difficulties in Leibniz's Definition of Perception,' in Michael Hooker, ed., *Leibniz: Critical and Interpretive Essays* (Minneapolis: University of Minnesota Press, 1982), pp. 65-78; and 'Leibniz's Conception of Expression,' *Studia Leibnitiana*, **IX** (1977), pp. 55-76.

26. Cf. Furth, 'Monadology,' p. 115; Brandom, 'Leibniz and Degrees of Perception,' p. 462.

27. 'Monadology,' p. 117.

28. *Ibid.*, p. 118.

29. *Ibid.*

30. See especially 'On the Method of Distinguishing Real from Imaginary Phenomena,' Gerhardt, vol. VII, 320-21; trans. and ed. by Leroy E. Loemker, *Leibniz: Philosophical Papers and Letters*, (Dordrecht-Holland: Reidel, 1969 (2nd edition), p. 364. See also the letter to Foucher, Gerhardt, vol. 1, 372f.; 'Discourse on Metaphysics,' 32, in Gerhardt, vol. IV, pp. 457-58; Loemker, p. 324; *New Essays* IV, ii, 14, in Gottfried Wilhelm Leibniz, *Sämtliche Schriften und Briefe*, ed. Deutsche Akademie der Wissenschaften zu Berlin, Series 6, Vol. 6 (Berlin: Akademie-Verlag, 1962), pp. 373-75. Adams provides a detailed discussion of this issue in section 4 of 'Phenomenalism . . . in Leibniz.'

31. 'Did Berkeley Completely Misunderstand the Basis of the Primary-Secondary Quality Distinction in Locke,' in *Berkeley: Critical and Interpretive Essays*, ed. Colin M. Turbayne (Minneapolis: University of Minnesota Press, 1982), pp. 108-123.

32. 'Leibniz and Berkeley,' p. 157; cf. pp. 152f.

33. Leibniz, 'Discourse on Metaphysics,' 12; MacIntosh, pp. 152-53.

34. Leibniz, 'On the Method of Distinguishing Real From Imaginary

Phenomena,' Gerhardt, vol. VII, p. 322; Loemker p. 365; MacIntosh, p. 153. (MacIntosh's reference is erroneous).

35.   Cf. *Dialogues*, 249.

36.   *Principles*, 99.

37.   *New Essays*, IV, vi, 7; Akademie ed., p. 404.

38.   Cf. 'Discourse on Metaphysics,' 33, in Gerhardt, vol. IV, pp. 458-59; also *New Essays*, II, viii, 13-15; Akademie ed. pp. 131-33. For discussion and further references see Margaret D. Wilson, 'Confused Ideas,' *Rice University Studies*, **63** (Fall 1977), pp. 127ff.; and Adams, 'Phenomenalism . . . in Leibniz,' p. 225. In *Philosophical Commentaries* Berkeley too entertains the supposition that ideas of colors contain "component ideas" that "we cannot easily distinguish & separate" (153; Thomas ed., p. 16). Berkeley particularly connects this point, as Leibniz did, with the fact that green is "compounded" out of blue and yellow. See, e.g., *PC*,502-4; Thomas ed. p. 65.

39.   Leibniz connects the "mere phenomenality" of a standard primary quality such as shape to the fact that it involves an abstraction or simplification of the infinite divisibility and complexity of nature. (Cf. Adams, 'Phenomenalism . . . in Leibniz,' pp. 225-26.)

40.   'Phenomenalism . . . in Leibniz,' p. 223. See also p. 224.

41.   *Ibid.*, p. 224. In his later discussion Adams particularly stresses Leibniz's view that bodies can have only "phenomenal" status because they lack "true unity" – are mere aggregates which owe their unity to the perceiving mind. (See pp. 241ff.) Berkeley regards the mind as responsible for unifying distinct ideas of sense – those that go constantly together – into single things; but he does not seem to see even this form of "mind dependence" as having negative implications for the reality of bodies. See, e.g., *Dialogues*, 246.

42.   Cf. 'Method for Distinguishing Real from Imaginary Phenomena,' Gerhardt, vol. VII, pp. 319f.; Loemker, p. 363. Of course, both Berkeley and Leibniz also mention other marks besides vividness for distiguishing "real" from imaginary phenomena – e.g., coherence.

43.   Robert Brandom, in the paper cited in note 25 discusses Leibniz's conception of distinctness in considerable detail with particular

emphasis on the issue of information content. Leibniz frequently links "distinctness" with the "intellectual" as opposed to the sensible: cf., e.g., 'On the Elements of Natural Science,' Loemker, p. 277. See also Wilson, 'Confused Ideas,' and Adams, 'Phenomenalism . . . in Leibniz,' pp. 223, 225.

44. 'On the Elements of Natural Science,' Loemker, p. 288. (It should be noted that this is a relatively early work, believed to have been written before the 'Discourse on Metaphysics.')

45. Cf. 'Leibniz and Berkeley,' pp. 156: "One difference [between Leibniz and Berkeley] . . . concerns infinity and infinite divisibility. It is a difference which seems to reflect the fact that Leibniz was a mathematician of genius while Berkeley was not . . ." Adams, however, points out that their difference on this issue directly reflects Berkeley's insistence that everything real is perceivable by sense, on the one hand, and Leibniz's rejection of sensationalism on the other hand. ('Phenomenalism,' pp. 222-23.)

46. See G. A. Johnston, *The Development of Berkeley's Philosophy* (London: MacMillan, 1923), chapter V.

47. For detailed discussion of Berkeley's position see Daniel Garber, 'Locke, Berkeley, and Corpuscular Scepticism,' in Turbayne, pp. 174-93, and Margaret D. Wilson, 'Berkeley and the Essences of the Corpuscularians,' in J. Foster and H. Robinson, eds., *Essays on Berkeley* (Oxford: Clarendon Press, 1985), pp. 131-47.

48. *Principles*, 101; *Dialogues*, 85.

49. *New Essays*, III, vi, 38, Akademie ed., p. 325; IV, vi, 4-8, Akademie ed., pp. 401-5.

50. The statement is found in Leibniz's letter of 15 March, 1715, in Gerhardt vol. II, p. 492; Loemker, p. 609.

51. Adams, 'Phenomenalism . . . in Leibniz,' p. 222: This notation was originally published by Kabitz, in the article cited in note 1, above. Kabitz also describes Leibniz's other marks on the copy of Berkeley, including underlining. He concludes that Leibniz gave most attention to specific passages that fit best with his own interests, and probably had not read the whole book through carefully (see p. 627).

52. Kabitz, p. 636; Adams, p. 222 (I use Adams' translation).

53. Kant sometimes takes a similarly patronizing approach in his comments on Berkeley: see *The Critique of Pure Reason*, B 71.

54. *Dialogues*, p. 244.

55. *Ibid.*

56. Cf. Stäbler's comment at the end of the passage cited in note 1: "Leibniz in seinem Streben nach Harmonie und in seiner Flucht vor Einseitigkeiten konnte an dem extrem gehaltenen System seines englishen [*sic*] Zeitgenossen nur das anerkennen, was sich als Baustein in sein universales Gedankengebäude hätte einfügen können."

Daniel Garber

SOMETHING-I-KNOW-NOT-WHAT:
BERKELEY ON LOCKE ON SUBSTANCE

There is a story we tell our students about the so-called British Empiricists. According to that story, Locke began the program by calling the notion of substance into question. His characterization of substance as a "something-I-know-not-what" that we merely suppose to underly the manifest qualities of things led Berkeley, it is claimed, to take the next step, deny that the notion of matter has any meaning at all, and in that way eliminate material substance altogether. Then Hume, seeing the ultimate implications of Locke's view, and the half-hearted way in which Berkeley extended Locke, went all the way and eliminated both mental *and* material substance. In this story, Locke and Hume are the heroes, Locke for noticing (if only confusedly) the problems with substance and Hume for seeing where Locke's position ultimately leads. But the story is not quite so flattering to Berkeley. While it makes a neat package of the British Empiricists, Berkeley's system comes out as an uncomfortable half-way house between Locke and Hume. This isn't to say that Berkeley isn't given credit for what he did. But history's judgment of Berkeley in this matter is not unlike the young Berkeley's somewhat patronizing remark about Locke: "Wonderful . . . that he could . . . see at all thro a mist y^t had been so long a gathering . . . This is more to be admir'd than y^t he didn't see farther." (*PC*, 567.)[1]

This view would have astonished Berkeley; while he did not know of Hume's work, to the best of my knowledge,[2] Berkeley *thought* that he had *rejected* Locke's account of substance in as unambiguous a way as he could. As historians of philosophy it is fitting for us to try to see the matter from Berkeley's point of view. I shall not address the Berkeley-Hume connection, a question that pertains more to Hume than it does to Berkeley. But I would like to look more carefully at how Berkeley saw his own account of substance, both substance in general and material substance in particular, in relation to Locke's. In more detail, I shall argue that Berkeley fully understood Locke's position on the notion of pure substance in general, and that he rejected it, not because we have *no* notion of substance at all, but because we have a *clearer* notion of substance than the obscure something-I-know-not-what that Locke offers us. Then I shall examine Berkeley's reflections on the emptiness of various conceptions of material substance. I shall argue that when understood in their proper context, as parts of a larger argument to establish the inconsistency of the notion of matter, these

23

E. Sosa (ed.), Essays on the Philosophy of George Berkeley, 23–42.
©*1987 by D. Reidel Publishing Company*

arguments are not an extension of Locke's view, but a direct repudiation. One cannot deny that Berkeley's account of matter in *some* sense derives from Locke. But these considerations will, I think, allow us to see the issue from Berkeley's perspective, and will allow us to appreciate the extent to which Berkeley's inspiration is fundamentally at odds with Locke's.

I. LOCKE ON SOMETHING-I-KNOW-NOT-WHAT

The project must, of course, begin with a brief review of Locke's conception of substance, the account that Berkeley either extended or reacted against, depending upon which story you prefer. Now, the matter is one of some complexity; an account of Locke on substance will involve us in an account of a large portion of Locke's program in the *Essay*. In the interest of brevity, I must pass over many important details, and present some still controversial readings of Locke without acknowledging the controversies that surround them. But, as I see it, Locke was up to something like this.[3]

The *Essay* was written for many reasons, and it would be folly to try to single out one main motivation for this long and somewhat rambling work. But one of Locke's most important goals in writing the *Essay* was to clarify some of the ideas we have in order to help settle certain important debates in the learned world, or, if not settle them, explain why they cannot be settled. (See, e.g., *Essay*, p. 10; *Essay*, III.ix.16-17, and III.x.2-13.) It is in the context of this program that we must understand Locke's project in Book II of the *Essay*, where he attempts to show how various of the ideas we have are derived from experience, from sensation and reflection. His goal, I think, is to show what various of our ideas come to by showing where it is that they came from. Now, in Book II Locke discusses a wide variety of ideas. But one of the ideas that gets the most attention, both from Locke and from later philosophers and commentators, is the idea of substance, an idea central to the thought of both ancients and moderns, to both the Aristotelians and to the Cartesians, Locke's two main antagonists in the *Essay*. It is to Locke's treatment of that idea that we must turn.

Important to Locke's account of the idea of substance is a distinction he draws between the "Ideas of particular sorts of Substances," and the "Notion of pure Substance in general." (*Essay*,II.xxxiii.1-3.) The ideas we have of particular sorts of substances are "Combinations of simple *Ideas*, as are by Experience and Observation of Men's Senses taken notice of to exist together," together with "the confused *Idea* of *something* to which they belong, and in which they subsist." (*Essay*, II.xxiii. 3.) In short, the ideas we have of particular substances are made up of a collection of sensible qualities, supposed to exist in a common substratum, and the idea of any particular substance is generated when we combine such manifest qualities in a common substratum. Obvious examples of such particular substances include man, horse, gold, and water, and the like. But the same basic account is meant to hold for spirits as well. Just as our idea of gold might include the sensible qualities of yellowness, malleability, solubility in aqua regia, etc., united in a substratum, our idea of a spiritual substance includes *"Thinking, Knowing, Doubting,* and a power of *Moving, etc."* united in a substratum. (*Essay,* II.xxiii.5.)

Our ideas of particular substance are relatively straightforward. But not so the idea of the substratum in which their manifest properties subsist. This is what Locke calls the idea of *"pure Substance in general"* (*Essay,* II.xxiii.2), an idea that gave Locke and his later commentators some trouble. Locke has relatively little to say about the derivation or content of the idea in the *Essay* itself. At one point he characterizes it as "an obscure and relative *Idea"* (*Essay,* II.xxiii.3.). Elsewhere he says that we "signify nothing by the word *Substance,* but only an uncertain supposition of we know not what . . . which we take to be the *substratum,* or support, of those *Ideas* we do know." (*Essay,* I.iv.18.) Elsewhere still he suggests that the philosopher who appeals to the notion of substance is in roughly the same position as the celebrated (but unnamed) Indian philosopher who rests the Earth on an elephant, the elephant on a tortoise, and the tortoise on "something, he knew not what." (*Essay,* II.xxiii.2; cf. II.xiii.19.) This has suggested to many that Locke thought that we had no idea at all of this substance in general, and that Locke had meant to reject the notion altogether.[4]

But Locke's view is clarified considerably in his replies to Edward Stillingfleet, Lord Bishop of Worcester, an important document for understanding Locke's views, widely consulted by 18th century readers, including Berkeley. Stillingfleet responded to Locke's account of substance by complaining that Locke had "almost discarded substance out of the reasonable part of the world." (SL, p. 5.) In replying to this criticism, the very first he discussed, Locke gave an account of what our idea of substance in general comes to, by showing how it is derived. As Locke summarized his account, the idea of substance "is a complex idea, made up of the general idea of something, or being, with the relation of a support to accidents." (SL, p. 19.) When we consider the sensible qualities of a cherry, or mental qualities like perceiving, thinking, and reasoning, we perceive "that they cannot exist or subsist of themselves." (SL, p. 21.) And "hence the mind perceives their necessary connexion with inherence or being supported." (SL, p. 19.) This idea of support is what Locke calls a relational idea, and it is, in fact, the very same idea we have when we consider the relation between a house and its foundation, or between a child and his mother's muff, when he is standing on it, to use Locke's own examples. (SL, p. 10.) "But," Locke continues, "because a relation cannot be founded in nothing, or be a relation of nothing, and the thing here related as a supporter or support is not represented to the mind by any clear and distinct idea; therefore the obscure, indistinct, vague idea of thing or something, is all that is left to be the positive idea, which has the relation of a support or substratum to modes or accidents." (SL, p. 21.) This general idea of being, derived, Locke says, by abstraction (*Ibid;* cf., though, *Essay,* II.vii.7.), is joined to the relational idea of support, derived from the mental faculty of comparison (*Essay,* II.xi.4), to produce the idea of pure substance in general, a something-I-know-not-what that supports the manifest properties of particular substances.

This, then, is the idea of pure substance. It is important to note that Locke's point in indicating the insubstantiality of this notion of substratum is *not* that we should reject either the idea or the thing. As Locke repeats over and over in the *Essay* and in response to Stillingfleet, nothing he writes is intended to undermine our confidence in the existence of underlying substances in which the manifest properties of minds and bodies inhere. (*Essay,* II.xxiii.4-6; SL, pp. 5-7.) But the doctrine does have important consequences for Locke. The true import of Locke's account of pure substance in general can be seen in one of a number of important applications he makes of that account. I noted earlier how the clarification of ideas in the *Essay* was intended to contribute to the resolution or elimination of philosophical disputes. Now, one of the most important disputes of 17th century philosophy was between those who held that minds are incorporeal substances, distinct from bodies, and those who held that they are not. But, if Locke is right about our idea of substance, a something-I-know-not-what that supports the manifest qualities of things, then this debate is in principle incapable of being settled.[5]

The point is a relatively simple one. The idea we have of a substratum for mental properties is exactly the same as the idea we have of a substratum for material properties; a mind is thus, simply a collection of mental qualities added to the idea of substratum, and a body a collection of material qualities added to that *same* idea of substratum. Or, as Locke put it, "the general idea of substance [is] the same every where." (SL, p. 33.) But if this is our idea of spirit and matter, and if we have such an obscure idea of their underlying substratum, then, it would appear, *we* can never *know* whether mind and body are made up of the same stuff or not. And so the nature of the soul is "a Point, which seems to me, to be put out of the reach of our Knowledge: And he who will give himself leave to consider freely, and look into the dark and intricate part of each Hypothesis, will scarce find his Reason able to determine him fixedly for, or against the Soul's Materiality." (*Essay,* IV.iii.6, p. 542.) Although Locke grants that it is *probable* that the soul is immaterial (SL, p. 33 (ref. to *Essay,* IV.x.16; and *Essay,* pp. 541-2), "Whether it be a material or immaterial substance, cannot be infallibly demonstrated from our ideas." (SL, p. 37.)[6]

Thus, the debate between materialists and dualists ends with a sceptical draw: the debate must end because our obscure idea of substance does not permit us to *know* one way or the other. Locke himself was not overly disturbed by this outcome. One goal of the *Essay* was, after all, to find the limits of our knowledge so that we will not let our "Thoughts wanter into those depths, where they can find no sure footing." (*Essay,* I.i.7; cf.

Essay, I.i.2-4.) As far as Locke was concerned, it mattered little whether we *knew,* in the strict sense, whether or not the soul was immaterial. It is probable that it is, and even if it isn't, revelation tells us that the soul, be it material or immaterial, is immortal. (SL, pp. 474ff.)[7] But many others shared the good Bishop of Worcester's discomfort with the sceptical position toward which Locke's view on substance led.[8] Among them, no doubt, was one George Berkeley, student of Trinity College, Dublin.

II. SUBSTANCE IN GENERAL: BERKELEY ON LOCKE ON SOMETHING-I-KNOW-NOT-WHAT

There is no question but that Berkeley knew of Locke's views on the possibility of thinking matter and disapproved of them. In the *Philosophical Commentaries* Berkeley remarked:

> If Matter is once allow'd to exist Clippings of beards & parings of nails may Think for ought that Locke can tell Tho he seems positive of the Contrary. (*PC,* 718; cf. *Essay,* IV.x.9.)

Also in the *Philosophical Commentaries* the doctrine of thinking matter is characterized as one of Locke's "dangerous opinions," (*PC,* 695), a view echoed later in the *Three Dialogues,* where the "possibility of matter's thinking" is listed as one of a list of "difficulties" that can be eliminated by eliminating matter (*Dialogues,* 258.) But while we shall return to Locke's thinking matter in connection with Berkeley's immaterialism as the paper progresses, Berkeley himself has relatively little to say about it. As is his announced procedure, the attention is not on a direct refutation of the sceptical consequences but on the underlying doctrine from which it flows. (*Principles,* Intro., 4; *Dialogues,* 167.) That doctrine is, of course, the doctrine of substance itself, the claim that our conception of substance is that of a something-I-know-not-what that supports the manifest properties of minds and bodies.

It is clear from an examination of the *Philosophical Commentaries* that problems of substance and substratum much vexed the young Berkeley. He is reasonably clear throughout these notes that matter is to be rejected, though there are some entries that occasion raised eyebrows and call for some interpretive skill. (E.g., *PC,* 80, 701.) Immaterialism appears as early as *PC,* 17-19.). However, Berkeley's treatment of spiritual substance in the *Philosophical Commentaries* is a maze of contradictions. Sometimes, as in the celebrated "Humean" entries, he rejects a mental substratum for ideas altogether (*PC,* 576-81, 587, 614-15a), sometimes he asserts that such a substratum, distinct from the ideas it supports, does or must exist (*PC,* 270, 478a, 563, 847, 863), and sometimes he is agnostic on this question (*PC,* 637); sometimes he intimates that we know the nature of the soul (when he *admits* a soul, of course; *PC*, 154, 178, 700, 704), and sometimes he appears to deny that we know the nature of the soul (*PC*, 25, 672, 702, 829, 847). And even when he admits that we know the nature of the soul, he is none too clear about just what it is, suggesting in different places thought (*PC*, 650-2; 704), will (*PC*, 478a), and even being (*PC*, 44) as that nature. The whole business is made more complicated still by the fact that throughout the *Philosophical Commentaries* Berkeley is working out his conception of an idea, and the important consequences of that conception, that there can be no idea of anything active. (*PC*, 490 seems significant here.)

Matters are somewhat clearer in Berkeley's early published writings, the *Principles* and the *Three Dialogues*, where out of the confusion and hesitation of the *Philosophical Commentaries* there emerged a clear and forceful position on substance and substrata, a direct response to Locke's view. I would like to begin examining Berkeley's position by quoting a rather long (but crucial) text from early on in the *Principles*. Berkeley wrote:

> But let us examine a little the received opinion. It is said extension is a mode or accident of matter, and that matter is the *substratum* that supports it. Now I desire that you would explain what is meant by matter's *supporting* extension: say you, I have no idea of matter, and therefore cannot explain it. I answer, though you have no positive, yet if you have any meaning at all, you must at least have a relative idea of matter; though you know not what it is, yet you must be supposed to know what relation it bears to accidents, and what is meant by its supporting them. It is evident *support* cannot here be taken in its usual or literal sense, as when we say that pillars support a building: in what sense therefore must it be taken?
>
> If we inquire into what the most accurate philosophers declare themselves to mean by *material substance;* we shall find them acknowledge, they have no other meaning annexed to those sounds, but the idea of being in general, together with the relative notion of its supporting accidents. The general idea of being appeareth to me the most abstract and incomprehensible of all other; and as for its supporting accidents, this, as we have just now observed, cannot be understood in the common sense of those words; it must therefore be taken in some other sense, but what that is they do not explain. So that when I consider the two parts or branches which make the signification of the words *material substance,* I am convinced there is no distinct meaning annexed to them. (*Principles*, 16-17; *Dialogues*, 197f.; cf. *Principles*, 68, 74; *PC*, 89, 115, 512, 517)

First I would like to remark that while the immediate target of these remarks is the "received opinion" of *material* substance, their significance is not limited to matter; the view that Berkeley presents and criticizes is not only the "received opinion" of *material* substance, but the *Lockean* conception of pure substance *in general*, the something-I-know-not-what that Locke thought stood under both mental and material substances; the account Berkeley discusses and rejects is *precisely* the account of pure substance that Locke suggested in the *Essay* and developed at some length in his response to Stillingfleet. (On Berkeley's acquaintance with the Locke-Stillingfleet exchange on this issue, see *PC*, 700). While there are some elements of this attack that pertain specifically to the *material* substratum, Berkeley means to reject the Lockean conception of this something-I-know-not-what as substratum for both mental *and* material substance. Thus Berkeley makes the following rhetorical challenge a few sections farther on in the *Principles:*

> [L]et him but reflect . . . whether he hath ideas of two principle powers, marked by the names *will* and *understanding*, distinct from each other as well as from a third idea of substance or being in general, with a relative notion of its supporting or being the subject of the aforesaid powers, which is signified by the name *soul* or *spirit*. (*Principles*, 27)

But on what grounds does Berkeley find Locke's position objectionable? One sentence of the passage I quoted earlier ties at least part of his attack to his rejection of abstract general ideas. Berkeley writes that "the general idea of being appeareth to me the most abstract and incomprehensible of all others." (*Principles*, 17). This is an illuminating way to look at what he is up to here. The problem with Locke's notion of pure substance in general, an idea that is supposed to underly both mind and matter, is that it involves the very broad notions of a bare something and a bare support, notions which Berkeley denies we have. But the problem is not merely that we have no abstract *idea* of being in general (or support in general), with "idea" understood in Berkeley's strictest sense; we can, after all, talk sensibly and in general terms about triangles or numbers or spirits without having the abstract general *idea* of a triangle or a number or a spirit, strictly speaking. The problem is more general than the problem of abstract *ideas*. Berkeley's claim is that these terms, as the Lockean wants to use them, "have no distinct meaning annexed to them" at all, as he puts it. (*Principles*, 17.)

Now, Berkeley's account of abstraction and generality is by no means unproblematic or easy to understand. But in broad outline, the view comes to something like this. Our experience acquaints us with various particulars, which, in the strictest sense, are the objects of human knowledge. These particulars are of two sorts, the ideas of sensation and imagination, and, through reflection, the notions we have of our own souls. (*Principles*, 1, 27, 89, 140, 142; *Dialogues*, 233.) But these particulars do not entirely exhaust the objects of our knowledge. In fact, Berkeley seems perfectly happy to agree, "that all knowledge and demonstration are about universal notions." (*Principles*, Intro., 15.) Berkeley, of course, denies that these universal notions designate any abstract general *ideas;* strictly speaking, there are no such things. (*Principles*, Intro., 10 - 13.) What gives general terms or names their meaning, for Berkeley, is the fact that they designate particulars; a general term is significant to the extent that it signifies ideas or notions of particular things. (*Principles*, Intro., 15, 18.) And, conversely, where a general term or name comprehends no ideas or notions of particulars, there it has no meaning at all.[9]

This account of generality is, I think, the key to Berkeley's critique of Locke's idea of pure substance in general. For Berkeley, Locke's account of substance as a bare something, a something-I-know-not-what that bears the indeterminate relation of support to sensible qualities is empty insofar as Locke attempts to abstract the notions of being and support from the ideas and notions of the particulars that give these general terms their meaning.

This view of Locke's account of substance is evident in the detailed discussions of the notions of support and being, the notions that, for Locke, combine to produce our idea of pure substance in general. The passage quoted earlier suggests that Berkeley has no trouble with the notion of support *per se*. He seems, for example, perfectly willing to grant that we understand what it means for a pillar to support a building. (*Principles*, 16; cf. SL, p. 10.) Furthermore, Berkeley claims to understand the sort of support that a spirit can provide for ideas. In a passage Berkeley added to the 1734 edition of the *Three Dialogues*, Berkeley's spokesman Philonous says: "I know what I mean when I affirm that there is a spiritual substance or support of ideas, that is, that a spirit knows and perceives ideas." (*Dialogues*, 234.) That is, specific instances of support familiar from our experience make meaningful the general relational term of "support." But, Berkeley would claim, we have no meaningful notion of support taken apart from these specific cases. In particular, Berkeley claims, again in the character of Philonous, "I do not know what is meant, when it is said, that an unperceiving substance hath inherent in it and supports either ideas or the archetypes of ideas." (*Dialogues*, 234; cf., though, p. 250.) More generally, Berkeley claims not to understand what is meant by the notion of support involved in the claim that substance is a something that *supports* the modes of extension of an extended thing or that *supports* will and intellect in a soul. (*Dialogues*, 197ff.; *Principles*, 27.) Abstracted (in a broad sense) from experience, detached from common instances of one thing supporting another, the notion of support is empty, Berkeley claims.

The case is even clearer with respect to the notion of a bare something, a being-in-general. It is one of Berkeley's most characteristic doctrines that to be is to be perceived or to perceive: *esse est percipi vel percipere;* this, in fact, is what the notion of existence *means.* That is, the notion of being, insofar as it is intelligible, comprehends two sorts of things: souls, and ideas. As Berkeley wrote in the *Principles:*

> Nothing seems of more importance, towards erecting a firm system of sound and real knowledge . . . than to lay the beginning in a distinct explication of what is meant by *thing, reality, existence. . . . Thing* or *being* is the most general name of all, it comprehends under it two kinds entirely distinct and heterogeneous, and which have nothing in common but the name, to wit, *spirits* and *ideas.* The former are *active, indivisible substances:* the latter are *inert, fleeting, dependent beings,* which subsist not by themselves, but are supported by, or exist in minds or spiritual substances. (*Principles,* 89; cf. *PC,* 228)

So the term "being" or "something" comprehends, again, only particulars with which we are acquainted: ideas and souls.[10] And, Berkeley is clear, by a spirit or soul he does *not* mean a *Lockean* complex substance, will and understanding supported by a something-I-know-not-what (*Principles,* 27); by spirit Berkeley means "one simple, undivided, active being." As for the general notion of a being, divorced from the particulars with which we are acquainted, spirits and ideas, Berkeley finds this notion unintelligible. As he wrote in the *Principles,* ". . . for any one to pretend to a notion of entity or existence, *abstracted* from *spirit* and *idea,* from perceiving and being perceived is, I suspect, a downright repugnancy and trifling with words." (*Principles,* 81.) Or, as Berkeley replied to the claim that matter is such a bare something,

> I answer, you may, if so it shall seem good, use the word *matter* in the same sense, that other men use *nothing,* and so make those terms convertible in your style. For after all, this is what appears to me to be the result of that definition [of matter as an unknown somewhat] . . . I do not find that there is any kind of effect or impression made on my mind, different from what is excited by the term *nothing.* (*Principles,* 80; cf. *Dialogues,* 222f.)

And, in this way, Locke's something-I-know-not-what is unintelligible, Berkeley claims; neither spirit nor idea, it seems to be nothing at all.[11]

And thus Berkeley rejects Locke's conception of pure substance in general. Insofar as the bare and abstract notions of being and support to which Locke appeals are without meaning, so is the notion of pure substance in general that they together are supposed to compose; Locke's something-I-know-not-what that is supposed to support the manifest properties of things in some incomprehensible way, this, Berkeley claims, is a philosopher's myth. But, it is important to note, Berkeley's aim here is *not* to *eliminate* substance, nor is it to emphasize the *obscurity* of our idea of substance. Berkeley seeks to replace Locke's "obscure and relative" notion of substance, a notion that leads Locke to sceptical conclusions, with a clear and definite conception of what there is, a conception that is intended to leave no room for Locke's scepticism. Instead of pressing the obscurity of the idea of substance in general, Berkeley's strategy is to see the obscurity of Locke's idea as a symptom of unwarranted abstraction, and to replace the obscurity with the clear and compelling vision of particulars with which we are acquainted in experience, a clear and intelligible conception of what being, support, and substance are. Berkeley intends not to reject substance, but to reject *Locke's* conception of substance; his point is not that there *is* no clear conception of substance, but that Locke has abandoned the light for the shadows. At least as far as Berkeley is concerned, there can be no greater contrast than between his view of substance and the Lockean view that he rejects.

III. MATERIAL SUBSTANCE: THE EMPTINESS ARGUMENTS AND SOMETHING-I-KNOW-NOT-WHAT

In the previous section I contrasted Berkeley's account of substance in general with Locke's, the clarity that Berkeley was trying to establish with the obscurity that Locke emphasized. At least on this issue it seems a serious misunderstanding to see Berkeley's view as deriving out of Locke's in any substantive way. But there is another intimately related issue on which Berkeley appears to be much closer to his great predecessor, the issue of *material* substance. In a number of prominent places, Berkeley takes the materialist to task, and attempts to show that a number of versions of the notion of *material* substance he offers are without coherent content. Here, one might claim, is the true locus of the Lockean inspiration. Berkeley, it might be claimed, is simply extending Locke's view on the obscurity of substance, pushing the idea of material substance from obscurity, the idea of a bare something, to nonexistence, and using the claim that we have no idea or notion of material substance to eliminate matter altogether. As Ian Tipton succinctly put it, ". . . Locke hands Berkeley the case against corporeal substance on a plate. . . [Berkeley can be seen] as completing an attack on a theory which Locke himself had done much to undermine."[1][2]

But plausible as this might seem to us, Berkeley himself could not have disagreed more. When he argued against the meaningfulness of various conceptions of material substance, his point was not to extend a conception of substance like Locke's, but to reject it; his intention was not to praise Locke but to bury him, as it were. This, in any case, is what I claim and what I shall try to establish. The story, though, is a long and somewhat complex one. The first step, as I see it, is to figure out precisely why Berkeley thought it important to establish that certain conceptions of matter are empty and without meaning in a series of careful arguments directed against specific proposals for the notion of matter that I shall call the emptiness arguments. This will turn out to be the key to seeing the matter in Berkeley's way.

Berkeley's probing examination of different conceptions of what material substance is taken to be, the skill with which he reveals the emptiness that stands behind the philosophers' conceptions of matter might lead the careless reader to believe that such discussions are, by themselves, intended to establish that there is no such thing as matter. But Berkeley's considered opinion is quite different. In an important addition to the 1734 edition of the third of the *Three Dialogues* Berkeley wrote:

> I say . . . that I do not deny the existence of material substance, merely because I have no notion of it, but because the notion of it is inconsistent, or in other words, because it is repugnant that there should be a notion of it. Many things, for ought I know, may exist, whereof neither I nor any other man hath or can have any idea or notion whatsoever. But then those things must be possible, that is, nothing inconsistent must be included in their definition . . . In the very notion or definition of material substance, there is included a manifest repugnance and inconsistency. (*Dialogues*, 232-3)

The passage is an interesting one. Berkeley declares as clearly as one could that the claim that we have no idea or notion of matter is not itself an argument against the real existence of mind-independent bodies; he freely admits that things may exist which go beyond our conceptions. But it is also interesting that Berkeley here endorses another argument, apparently in place of the one he rejects, the argument that "the very notion or definition of material substance" includes "a manifest repugnance and inconsistency."

Later I would like to look more carefully at the argument Berkeley endorses in this context, and explore the relations between the inconsistency argument, as we might call it, and the emptiness arguments that he rejects as arguments against matter. But it should be noted that while clearest in the 1734 addition to the *Three Dialogues*, this rejection of the one argument in favor of the other seems to be no late change in Berkeley's position. In a passage at the end of the 1713 edition of the second of the *Three Dialogues*, Berkeley concludes his most systematic discussion of the infirmity of various proposed definitions of matter by claiming:

> [In] all your various senses, you have been shewed either to mean nothing at all, or if anything, an absurdity. And if this

not be sufficient to prove the impossibility of a thing, I desire
you will let me know what is. (*Dialogues*, 226)

We shall have to return to this passage for a closer look. But even a superficial examination of the passage suggests that here Berkeley is not attempting to argue merely from the lack of a notion of matter to its nonexistence, and suggests, again, that the emptiness arguments are somehow
linked to the claim that matter is inconsistent. This, too, is suggested in
the *Principles,* where, following the argument showing the emptiness of
Locke's conception of (material) substance we discussed above in section II,
Berkeley breaks off that line of reasoning and writes:

> But why should we trouble ourselves any farther, in dis-
> cussing this material *substratum* or support of figure and mo-
> tion, and other sensible qualities? Does it not suppose they
> have an existence without the mind? And is not this a direct
> repugnancy, and altogether inconceivable? (*Principles*, 17; cf.
> *Principles*, 72-81, esp. 73, 76)

And while the case is not clear in the early notebooks, it should be
pointed out that Berkeley only once concerns himself directly with the emptiness of any proposed account of the notion of matter, and where he does,
there are no grounds for construing the point as an argument against the
existence of matter (*PC*, 517, cf. 22, 89). However, in those notebooks, he
often returns to the claim that it is inconsistent for an idea or a sensible
quality to exist in an unthinking thing. (*PC*, 37, 270, 280, 347, 377, 378,
597).

It is reasonably clear, then, that Berkeley does not mean to infer
the nonexistence of matter from the fact that certain conceptions of matter
are empty, and that he sees himself as having established a much stronger
claim, the claim that the notion of material substance is inconsistent. But
this leaves us with a bit of a puzzle. If Berkeley doesn't think that the nonexistence of an idea or notion of matter entails the nonexistence of matter,
then why does he expend so much effort in showing that various proposals
for the notion of matter are empty? What function *do* these emptiness arguments have in Berkeley's immaterialism? There is the hint of an answer
in the passages we have just examined. In those passages the meaninglessness of notions of matter is consistently linked with the inconsistency of
the notion of matter. To be sure, Berkeley's point is often that the one consideration is not his argument against matter, while the latter is. But perhaps exploring the connection between these two arguments will help us to
see what role the emptiness arguments play in Berkeley's scheme of things,
and eventually help us to understand the proper relation between Berkeley's arguments and Locke's.

In order to see how the emptiness arguments can contribute to the inconsistency argument, though, we must attempt a somewhat more careful formulation of the argument Berkeley endorses. The inconsistency Berkeley has in mind is, presumably, the same inconsistency that he points out over and over in his writings. Matter is supposed to be the inert and unthinking substratum of sensible qualities or their archetypes. But sensible qualities and their archetypes can only subsist in an active thinking thing. Hence, the very definition of matter is contradictory. From this it follows that matter cannot exist, since things with contradictory properties cannot exist in reality. (See *Principles*, 73, 76; *Dialogues*, 216, 234.) But this formulation will not quite do. If Berkeley is to argue that some formulations of the notion of material substance are altogether without meaning, the inconsistency claim must be elaborated to accommodate that fact, since, it seems, something without meaning cannot be inconsistent. This, indeed, is the business of a long passage from the second of *Three Dialogues*, part of which we have seen before. Hylas, trying to defend himself against the charge of inconsistency in his definition of matter tries to take refuge in an "obscure abstracted and indefinite sense" of the term, a sense that Berkeley claims is without meaning. Hylas tries to argue that insofar as he holds that conception of matter, he is safe from contradiction. The dialogue then continues as follows:

> PHILONOUS. When is a thing shewn to be impossible?
> HYLAS. When a repugnancy is demonstrated between the ideas comprehended in its definition.
> PHILONOUS. But where there are no ideas, there no repugnancy can be demonstrated between ideas.
> HYLAS. I agree with you.
> PHILONOUS. Now in that which you call the obscure indefinite sense of the word *matter*, it is plain, by your own confession, there was included no idea at all, no sense except an unknown sense, which is the same thing as none. You are not therefore to expect I should prove a repugnancy between ideas where there are no ideas; or the impossibility of matter taken in an *unknown* sense, that is no sense at all. My business was only to shew, you meant *nothing;* and this you were brought to own. So that in all your various senses, you have been shewed either to mean nothing at all, or if any thing, an absurdity. And if this be not sufficient to prove the impossibility of a thing, I desire you will let me know what is. (*Dialogues*, 225-6)

Berkeley's claim, then, is that the notion of matter is either inconsistent or meaningless. While this more careful version of the inconsistency argument appears to give the materialist a way out, the way out is cold comfort. Berkeley's claim is that the materialist cannot explain what he is advocating without uttering absurdities. The notion of matter is inconsistent in the sense that *any* attempt to formulate the notion with enough content to evaluate the materialist's claims as genuine claims rather than empty words leads to contradictions; insofar as he is saying anything at all, he is talking nonsense, Berkeley claims, and insofar as he is *not* saying anything at all, there is no position for the immaterialist to refute. If Berkeley can establish this claim, his work is clearly done; if he can establish this claim, he will have shown that where the materialist makes any genuine claim at all in contradiction to immaterialism, that claim is absurd. Berkeley seems fully entitled to the rhetorical challenge with which he ends: "if this be not sufficient to prove the impossibility of a thing, I desire you will let me know what is."

Let us now turn to the emptiness arguments Berkeley gives for the emptiness of various conceptions of matter, the arguments whose significance we are trying to discover. I will not pretend that it is always clear just what Berkeley thinks these emptiness arguments are intended to show. They are never presented by themselves as serious arguments against the existence of matter; often, particularly in the *Principles*, they appear to be mere *ad hominem* attacks against Berkeley's materialist opponents, Locke and Malebranche most visibly, arguments designed to show, perhaps, that the materialist metaphysics others have formulated is, upon closer inspection, empty and offers no real threat to the immaterialist metaphysics that Berkeley is trying to develop. (*Principles*, 16-17; 73-81.) But in an interesting passage at the end of the second of the *Three Dialogues*, the passage that precedes and concludes with the formulation of the inconsistency argument we have just examined, Berkeley presents what I take to be his considered view of the role those emptiness arguments play in the establishment of immaterialism. In this passage Berkeley, in the character of Philonous, leads the materialist Hylas through the characterization of matter as the cause of ideas (*Dialogues*, 216), matter as "an *instrument* subservient to the supreme agent in the production of our ideas," (*Dialogues*, 217), matter as an occasional cause of ideas (*Dialogues*, 219), and finally, a view intended to summarize Locke's, matter as an indefinite something, neither cause, instrument, nor occasion, that supports the "reality of things." (*Dialogues*, 221-4.) For each of the particular characterizations of matter that he considers, Berkeley attempts to push the materialist to admit that his notion of matter is either meaningless or inconsistent, insofar as it is taken to be something distinct from mind. Given the way we have seen this exchange to end, it is clear that Berkeley's arguments are in the service of the inconsistency argument. The claim that various conceptions of matter are without meaning is part of an attempt to press the materialists's notion of matter into something definite that Berkeley can show to be inconsistent. In this way the emptiness arguments to show the meaninglessness of various conceptions of matter make an essential contribution to the inconsistency argument: they show the materialist that where he is not falling into inconsistency and nonsense, he is making literally no sense at all.

This suggests at least one good reason why Berkeley may have been interested in the emptiness arguments, even though he rejected the argument from the lack of a notion of matter to its nonexistence; if my reading of the texts is right, the emptiness arguments might best be regarded as auxiliaries to a larger argument, the inconsistency argument, at least on Berkeley's considered opinion. And with this we can return to the big question I raised at the beginning of this section, the question of Berkeley's relation to Locke on material substance. If Berkeley's conception of the role played by the emptiness arguments is as I have represented it, then, I think, Berkeley's account of matter can hardly be viewed as an extension of Locke's. For Locke, as noted above in section I, the conception of substance as a something-I-know-not-what is intended as a general doctrine about the true meaning of the notion of substance. Locke does not want to eliminate the notion; his point is that the obscurity of our idea of substance, a bare something that supports qualities in some unknown way, sets important limits on the knowability of the nature of substance. But Berkeley is quite a different matter. First of all, the emptiness of the notion of matter, the doctrine that is supposedly derived from Locke, is not, for Berkeley, a general doctrine on substance, material or otherwise, from which any general conclusions about knowledge or existence are intended to be drawn. In fact, for Berkeley it is not a *general* doctrine at all, but a series of separate moves directed against specific formulations of the materialist's position, including Locke's, intended to convince the materialist that he cannot evade the general claim that Berkeley does want to make, that the notion of matter is inconsistent. But more important still, in the context of the inconsistency argument, Locke's position on substance cannot be regarded as a position in part correct, in need of further extension. Berkeley understood perfectly well that Locke was trying to give us the true notion of (material) substance, and from Berkeley's point of view, Locke's position is one of the positions that must be *rejected*. If Locke were correct in holding that we have an idea of (material) substance as a bare something-I-know-not-what, then we would have an idea or notion of matter that is neither empty nor apparently contradictory. Locke's view of substance must be rejected and shown to be empty if Berkeley's argument is to stand. The obscurity Locke emphasizes is, for us, suggestive of the arguments Berkeley uses to establish the emptiness of various accounts of matter, and it is very tempting for us to see the latter as growing out of the former. But for Berkeley, the two positions are diametrically opposed. To claim we have an obscure notion of matter is to claim that we have a coherent notion of matter, a meaningful, noncontradictory notion of matter, however thin it might be. When, in the context of the inconsistency argument, Berkeley establishes the emptiness of various conceptions of matter, it is just such a position he means to reject, not extend. From Berkeley's point of view, there is *nothing* worth saving in Locke's view of substance.

This point is an important one, and worth developing in a bit more detail from a slightly different perspective. Locke's view is that pure substance in general, that which underlies the manifest qualities of both minds and bodies, is a mere something-I-know-not-what that supports the qualities it contains in a vague and obscure way. This, as we noted in section I, has the consequence that we do not, nor can we ever know for certain whether or not mental stuff is the *same* as material stuff, whether or not mental qualities inhere in the *same* substratum as physical qualities do. But if our idea of substratum is too obscure to allow us to distinguish mental and material substrata, then it is too obscure to allow us to exclude the possibility that ideas, sensible qualities, or their archetypes might inhere in a substratum *different* in kind from that which constitutes our souls. If such Lockean material substrata exist, then they will have to be thinking substances of a sort insofar as they do contain thoughts, Berkeley would certainly insist (cf. second of the *Dialogues*). But insofar as we lack the appropriate ideas, Locke would claim, we cannot *exclude* the possibility that these hypothetical material substrata are, in their nature, as different as you like from the substrata of our souls. And so, if Locke's view on substance is correct, Berkeley's inconsistency argument cannot be; if Locke is correct in thinking we have an idea of pure substance in general as a something-I-know-not-what, then Berkeley's inconsistency argument is undermined. For this reason Berkeley must *reject* the obscure idea of substance Locke claims to have, and argue that Locke's notion of a something-I-know-not-what is, in fact, no notion at all. While this may look like an extension of Locke's position to us, Berkeley (quite correctly, I think) sees it as a repudiation, a repudiation essential for the larger point he wants to make about the inconsistency of the notion of matter.

So far in this section I have concentrated on the emptiness arguments. While suggestive of Locke's position on substance as a something-I-know-not-what, I have tried to establish that these arguments are not intended to extend Locke's position, but to refute it. But, I think, it is misleading to focus in on these emptiness arguments which, after all, are only tools in a larger argument, if my reading is correct. The superficial similarity between these emptiness arguments and Locke's position on substance has mislead many into thinking that the two philosophers are up to something of the same thing. But when we focus on the larger argument that Berkeley is pressing in those very passages where he is so anxious to show the meaninglessness of various proposals on matter, we get quite a different view. Here the contrast with Locke is clear and unavoidable. Locke's project is to emphasize the obscurity of our idea of substance, material and mental, and in that way to suspend debate over questions that, Locke thinks, are beyond our ken. Even though Berkeley emphasizes the emptiness of various conceptions of matter, his point is not to emphasize the obscurity of our ideas and notions, but to eliminate it. The obscurity of

an account like Locke's is, for Berkeley, a mask that hides either emptiness
or contradiction. Berkeley would like to remove this mask of obscurity and
show us the deep incoherence in the notion of matter. And in doing so,
Berkeley depends crucially on the *clarity* of the ideas and notions he claims
we have. It is because we know what ideas, sensible qualities are, and because we know that an idea can resemble nothing but an idea, and it is
because we know what minds are that we know that ideas, sensible qualities, and their archetypes can exist only in minds. And it is because we
know that ideas, sensible qualities, and their archetypes can exist only in
minds that we know that the notion of matter, the nonmental substratum
of sensible qualities or their archetypes is inconsistent. In this way Berkeley's position depends, in a sense, on our knowing, in contradiction to
Locke, what the nature of matter really is. Locke's claim is that we don't
know the true, underlying nature of body in general; the underlying substratum of corporeal qualities is a something, Locke thinks, but a something-
I-know-not-what, no better known to us than the foundation on which the
Indian philosopher's tortoise rests. But, Berkeley would insist, we know
perfectly well what matter is, or is supposed to be: the nonmental support
of sensible qualities or their archetypes. (See *Dialogues*, 225.) And it is
precisely because we *know* what matter is *supposed* to be that we know
that it *cannot* be.

IV. CONCLUSION

In the previous sections I have tried to emphasize some important differences between Berkeley and Locke on substance. In section II I argued that
Berkeley understood Locke's position on our obscure idea of pure substance
in general, and rejected it in favor of the clear notions we have of being,
substratum, and substance. And in section III I argued that Berkeley's
emptiness arguments are not themselves arguments against the existence
of matter. Rather, I argue, those arguments are moves in a larger argument for the inconsistency of the notion of matter, an argument inconsistent both in strategy and detail with Locke's position on the something-I-
know-not-what that constitutes our obscure idea of substance. In fact, I
claim, when Berkeley argues for the meaninglessness of various conceptions of matter in this context, he means to reject, not extend views like
Locke's. These considerations suggest just how different Berkeley's treatment was from Locke's and, to my mind at least, call into question the view
of Berkeley as derivative from Locke.

But for all of this, I don't want to deny that there is a real sense in
which Locke may have been an important inspiration to the young Berkeley, even on this issue of the notion of substance and matter. The obscurity
of Locke's definition of pure substance in general may well have led Berkeley to reflect on the obscurity of other accounts of matter and in that way

may have led him to see that all accounts of matter are either empty or inconsistent. In that way Berkeley can indeed be regarded as extending Locke's position, in a sense.

But – and this is my main point – in regarding Berkeley in this way, we are fundamentally distorting Berkeley's own view of his relation to Locke. In the Introduction to the *Principles* and, again, in the Preface to the *Three Dialogues*, Berkeley complains of the sorry state of modern philosophy:

> But no sooner do we depart from sense and instinct to follow the light of a superior principle, to reason, meditate, and reflect on the nature of things, but a thousand scruples spring up in our minds, concerning those things which before we seemed fully to comprehend. Prejudices and errors of sense do from all parts discover themselves to our view; and endeavouring to correct these by reason we are insensibly drawn into uncouth paradoxes, difficulties, and inconsistencies, which multiply and grow upon us as we advance in speculation; till at length, having wander'd through many intricate mazes, we find our selves just where we were, or, which is worse, sit down in a forlorn scepticism. The cause of this is thought to be the obscurity of things, or the natural weakness and imperfection of our understandings. (*Principles*, Intro., 1-2; cf. *Dialogues*, 167-8)

Berkeley, of course, sees himself as turning back the sceptical tide, replacing the doubt which, in his view, leads directly on to atheism, with certainty. (See *Principles*, Intro., 4.) And one of the most important moves in this project is to replace obscurity with clarity. As far as Berkeley is concerned, his system represents a fundamental break with Locke's, a replacement of Locke's complaints about the obscurity of our ideas and notions, complaints that drive Locke to scepticism, with clear and definite notions that lead us to certainty. And it is in this spirit that we should read Berkeley's arguments concerning substance in general and material substance in particular. Far from concurring with Locke or extending his position, Berkeley emphasizes in no uncertain terms the clear notions we do have of being, support and the clear contradiction he sees in the notion of material substance. From his own point of view, the project is not to press the obscurity Locke saw in these notions, but to eliminate it. From his own point of view, Berkeley is as different from Locke as clarity is from obscurity and certainty from scepticism.[13]

Department of Philosophy, The University of Chicago

NOTES

1. The primary source references are given in parentheses in the text. References to Locke's *An Essay Concerning Human Understanding* are to the text established by Peter H. Nidditch (Oxford: Oxford University Press, 1975), abbreviated by *Essay*, and given in the standard form, book, followed by chapter, followed by section. Occasionally when the passage in question is part of a long section, a page number in the Nidditch edition is given. References to the so-called Stillingfleet letters are found in volume IV of *The Works of John Locke* (London: Thomas Tegg et al., 1823), abbreviated by "SL" and given by page number in that edition.

2. See, though, Colin M. Turbayne, 'Hume's Influence on Berkeley,' *Revue Internationale de Philosophie,* no. 154 (1985), pp. 259-69.

3. My reading of Locke has been influenced by M. R. Ayers, especially his essays, 'The Ideas of Power and Substance in Locke's Philosophy,' in I. C. Tipton (ed.), *Locke on Human Understanding* (Oxford: Oxford University Press, 1977), pp. 77-104, and 'Mechanism, Superaddition, and the Proof of God's Existence in Locke's *Essay*,' *Philosophical Review* **90** (1981), pp. 210-51.

4. See, for example, Louis Loeb, *From Descartes to Hume: Continental Metaphysics and the Development of Modern Philosophy* (Ithaca: Cornell University Press, 1981), pp. 80ff.

5. It should be noted that there are a number of different varieties of materialism and antimaterialism at issue in the 17th century debates. Locke's point is most directly relevant against a view like Descartes', which attempts to establish with certainty that thoughts of any sort cannot be modes or accidents of a material substance, and must pertain to minds and minds alone. See e.g., section 10 of Descartes' *Sixth Replies*. But it is not so clear that Locke's argument is relevant against a view like Hobbes' where mentality is a function of the complex organization of a body.

6. See also Locke's remarks in a letter to Anthony Collins, 21 March 1703-4, in *The Works of John Locke* (1823), vol. X, pp. 284-5, quoted in part in Ayers, 'Mechanism, Superaddition . . . ,' p. 249. Locke does, of course, grant that the question could be settled by revelation. See *Essay,* p. 540.

7. The idea that immortality does not require an immaterial soul was

by no means unheard of in 16th and 17th century English thought. See, e.g., Norman T. Burns, *Christian Mortalism from Tyndale to Milton* (Cambridge, Massachusetts: Harvard University Press, 1972). It is interesting that though Locke grants that the soul is probably immaterial, his account of personal identity in *Essay*, II.xxvii does not presuppose an immaterial soul.

8. For some of the later reaction to Locke's doctrine, see John Yolton, *Thinking Matter: Materialism in Eighteenth-Century Britain* (Minneapolis: University of Minnesota Press, 1983), and Nicholas Jolley, *Leibniz and Locke: A Study of the New Essays on Human Understanding* (Oxford: Oxford University Press, 1984).

9. The account given in this paragraph is somewhat simplified. A more complete account of Berkeley's doctrine would have to take account of the technical use of the term "idea" introduced in the Introduction to the *Principles*, as well as Berkeley's claim in *Principles*, Intro., 20, that not every meaningful word is connected with an idea.

10. It has been claimed that for Berkeley, we are not directly acquainted with our own souls. The contrary view, with which I agree, is nicely argued in Margaret Atherton, 'The Coherence of Berkeley's Theory of Mind,' *Philosophy and Phenomenological Research*, **43** (1983), pp. 389-99. On p. 390, n. 3, Atherton gives a generous list of the recent literature on the question.

11. Berkeley's view here seems similar to the one Descartes expresses, e.g., in *Principia Philosophiae* I 63.

12. I. C. Tipton, *Berkeley: the Philosophy of Immaterialism* (London: Methuen and Co. Ltd., 1974), p. 44. See also G. J. Warnock, *Berkeley* (Baltimore: Penguin Books, 1969), p. 103.

13. Versions of this paper were presented at celebrations of the 300th anniversary of Berkeley's birth held in March 1985 in Newport, Rhode Island under the sponsorship of the International Berkeley Society and at Kalamazoo, Michigan, under the joint sponsorship of Western Michigan University and Kalamazoo College, with the help of the Machette Foundation. I would like to thank the organizers of those two meetings for giving me the opportunity to speak, and I would like to thank my commentators on those two occasions, Roger Ariew in Newport and Louis Loeb in Kalamazoo, as well as the audiences for helpful comments. Some themes from this essay will get further treatment in the introduction and notes to my forthcoming edition of Part II of Berkeley's *Principles*.

PART TWO

THOUGHT AND REFERENCE:
I. ABSTRACT IDEAS

Margaret Atherton

BERKELEY'S ANTI-ABSTRACTIONISM

Berkeley's anti-abstractionism has been most ofter presented as a theory motivated by and about Locke's inconsistent idea of a triangle. His purpose, it is assumed, was to show that Locke gave the wrong account of how a general term like "triangle" is used to stand for triangles. Berkeley's theory, so interpreted, as part of a controversy with Locke, has been much discussed; but throughout this discussion, a certain anomaly has remained. Berkeley's attack on abstract ideas was written as the introduction to his *Treatise concerning the Principles of Human Knowledge* and he regarded his anti-abstractionism as the cornerstone for all other doctrines to be found there. No account of Berkeley's anti-abstractionism can be adequate, therefore, which fails to explain its importance to Berkeley in his exposition of his theory, but the prevailing accounts that concentrate on the general idea of a triangle fail to provide such an explanation. Instead, commentators who remark on the lack of clear connection between Berkeley's immaterialism and the theory of abstract ideas they discuss, tend to see this as a problem for *Berkeley*, claiming that he exaggerated the importance of his attack on abstraction.[1] It is my view that Berkeley's anti-abstractionism can be shown to have the central role that he claims for it, but that this requires downplaying Locke's triangle in order to focus on other aspects of Berkeley's argument about abstraction.

I

Berkeley's attack on abstract ideas is usually presented, then, as being directed towards a theory of meaning often attributed to Locke.[2] Locke's claim that words are made general through the mediation of general ideas[3] is thought to amount to the claim that I am able to apply the word "triangle" to many different triangles because I have an abstract general idea of a triangle to which all particular triangles must conform. Thus, on this account, Berkeley's quarrel with Locke has to do with the way in which words apply to the world. Locke's theory is supposed to be committed to the existence of a particular kind of entity, an abstract general idea, which is used as a template or standard when identifying new instances as being of the same sort. Berkeley, in turn, is said to have thought that there can be no such entity, holding instead that words apply directly to particular

45

E. Sosa (ed.), Essays on the Philosophy of George Berkeley, 45–60.
©*1987 by D. Reidel Publishing Company*

things in the world, without the mediation of abstract general ideas.

There are several issues with respect to this approach that strike me as problematic. The first is that I am dubious that Locke in fact held such a theory of meaning or had much interest in developing one.[4] At the very least, to discuss Locke's theory almost exclusively in terms of triangles is to obscure his distinction between nominal and real essences, since triangles are examples of mixed modes, where both essences converge. But this point may not be a serious reason for rejecting an account of Berkeley, for, after all, Berkeley might have misunderstood Locke, or he might have been attacking someone else who did hold such a theory. More serious is the question how a rejection of one theory of meaning in favor of another should have had the far reaching consequences Berkeley seems to have claimed for his anti-abstractionism. The different views Locke and Berkeley are said to have had on how words relate to the world are a fairly parochial matter. They interest philosophers concerned with meaning. Progress in the sciences will remain unaffected, whether we can pick out triangles only via an abstract idea, or whether we can do it directly. The scientist will be able to say pretty much the same sorts of things on either account. Berkeley, however, views a belief in abstract ideas as having had a very detrimental effect on progress in the sciences. He identifies the belief that the mind can frame abstract ideas as one of the gravest sources of error. Berkeley therefore introduces the *Principles* with a section on abstract ideas because he believes that all the errors he intends to unmask in the body of the text depend upon the belief in abstract ideas.[5] But it is very difficult to see what Berkeley could have had in mind so long as the belief in abstract ideas is taken to commit one simply to a bad theory of meaning; for, as I. C. Tipton points out, it is surely not the case that Locke or indeed anyone believes in the continued existence of unperceived objects because of a theory of meaning.[6]

Thus, if Berkeley's attack on abstract ideas is treated as part of a theory of the meaning of general terms, it could only be tangential to his overall aims. But throughout the body of the *Principles*, Berkeley is careful to tie the topics he plans to take up with the issue of abstract ideas. Berkeley's central principle, that the being of a sensible thing lies in its being perceived, rests on an argument in *Principles*, 4-6 that depends on anti-abstractionism. In *Principles*, 5, he says: "If we thoroughly examine this tenet, it will, perhaps, be found at bottom to depend on the doctrine of *abstract ideas*. For can there be a nicer strain of abstraction than to distinguish the existence of sensible objects from their being perceived, so as to conceive them existing unperceived?" In *Principles*, 10, Berkeley's argument that primary qualities are on a par with secondary qualities relies on anti-abstractionism. He says: "But I desire any one to reflect and try, whether he can by any abstraction of thought, conceive the extension and motion of a body, without all other sensible qualities." And summing up on *Principles*, 11, he says: "Thus we see how much the tenet of extended movable substances extisting without the mind, depends on that strange doctrine of *abstract ideas*."[7] He returns to this theme in an important summary passage at *Principles*, 99, where he says:

> So likewise, when we attempt to abstract extension and motion from all other qualities, and consider them by themselves, we presently lose sight of them, and run into great extravagances. All which depend upon a two-fold abstraction: first, it is supposed that extension, for example, may be abstracted from all other sensible qualities; and secondly, that the entity of extension may be abstracted from its being perceived. But whoever shall reflect, and take care to understand what he says, will, if I mistake not, acknowledge that all sensible qualities are alike *sensations*, and alike *real;* that where the extension is, there is the colour too, to wit, in his mind, and that their archetypes can exist only in some other *mind*: and that the objects of sense are nothing but those sensations combined, blended, or (if one may so speak) concreted together: none of all which can be supposed to exist unperceived.

Thus, Berkeley's anti-abstractionism can't be removed from the center of the *Principles*.[8] Among the innumerable errors created by the mistaken belief in the mind's ability to frame abstract ideas must be numbered those errors to which Berkeley is directing attention most specifically in the *Principles*. As the passage just quoted makes clear, Berkeley regards both his immaterialism and his idealism as supported by his anti-abstractionism.

II

The difficulty, then, is that the standard account of Berkeley's attack on abstraction describes him as motivated by issues that are peripheral to his concerns, whereas Berkeley himself regards the attack as central. What is needed is a better understanding of what Berkeley thinks is revealed by his attack on abstraction. The assumption that Berkeley's focus is on the means by which we classify, and hence, that he is worried about meaning, stem from the prior assumption that what Berkeley principally finds objectionable are abstract *general* ideas, such as the abstract general idea of a triangle. What is crucial to notice, however, is that Berkeley is not opposed to generalizing or to generality but only to abstraction. "And here it is to be noted," he says, "that I do not deny absolutely there are general ideas, but only that there are any *abstract general ideas*." (*Principles*, Intro., 12.)[9] Abstraction, that is, analyzing or separating qualities, properties or attributes from each other, should be distinguished from generalizing, from taking such properties or attributes to be shared by many different instances, if it is abstraction alone that Berkeley finds to be problematic.

It has often been observed that the passages in the Introduction at 7-10 in which Berkeley first discusses the issue of abstract ideas do not limit themselves to general ideas, and indeed, the question of how many different kinds of ideas Berkeley discusses in this passage has been regarded as controversial.[10] But I think this question is misleading. What we find Berkeley discussing is an illegitimate process, that of abstraction, together with several applications or accounts of its illegitimate use. Section 7 introduces the process Berkeley wants to reject. He says: "It is agreed on all hands, that the qualities or modes of things do never really exist each of them apart by it self and separated from all others, but are mixed, as it were, and blended together, several in the same object. But we are told, the mind being able to consider each quality singly, or abstracted from those other qualities with which it is united, does by that means form to it self abstract ideas." The examples that he gives in the passage have to do with separating one particular quality from another. What is illegitimate, Berkeley is saying, is to suppose that we can abstract a particular quality from the rest of the supporting conditions or qualities among which that quality exists, so as to suppose that we can have an idea of what, for example, extension or color is like, all on its own "exclusive of the rest."

In section 8, Berkeley discusses a different sort of illegitimate attempt to separate sensible qualities one from another. In section 7, Berkeley had talked about attempts to separate one quality from another, while in section 8, his examples are attempts to separate one quality from its sensory determinates. He first takes up the case of extension: "Again, the mind having observed that in the particular extensions perceived by sense, there is something common and alike in all, and some other things peculiar, as this or that figure or magnitude, which distinguish them one from another, it considers apart, or singles out by it self that which is common, making thereof a most abstract idea of extension, which is neither line, surface, nor solid, nor has any figure or magnitude but is an idea entirely prescinded from all these." Thus, the example Berkeley is dealing with is now clearly a general idea, but the mistake involved is the same, that of supposing we can frame an idea of a sensible quality in isolation from the qualities which embody it. What has gone wrong in this instance is that it has been supposed possible to get an idea of what extension is like exclusive of all of the different ways of being extended.

Section 9 discusses a second application of this principle, this time to ideas of compounded beings, as man, animal and body. The mistakes involved here resolve themselves into those discussed in the previous section, section 8, since these abstract ideas will be compounds of various qualities as color, or motion, each of which will have been isolated from the conditions in which they actually exist. Since the idea of a triangle is an example of an idea of this sort, whatever errors Berkeley thinks we fall into when we think we can frame an abstract general idea of a triangle will presumably be similarly resolvable into errors about the illegitimate abstraction of its various components.

In section 10, Berkeley distinguishes this illegitimate process of abstraction from one that he considers to be perfectly appropriate. "To be plain, I own my self able to abstract in one sense, as when I consider some particular parts of qualities separated from others, with which though they are united in some object, yet, it is possible they may really exist without them. But I deny that I can abstract one from another, or conceive separately, those qualities which it is impossible should exist so separated; or that I can frame a general notion by abstracting from particulars in the manner aforesaid. Which last are the proper acceptations of *abstraction*." In this passage, the examples Berkeley gives are quite clear cut. I can have an idea of just a hand, or just a foot or just an eye, without including the rest of the body to which these parts are typically attached, but I can't have an idea of an eye that has not some determinate shape and color, nor could I have an idea of what a color would be like, all by itself, if no other qualities, like shape or size, were present.[11] These ideas Berkeley regards as inconceivable. It is worth noting that, even though, in this passage, Berkeley speaks of two uses of abstraction, one of which involves the creation of abstract general ideas, he is also clear that this second use resolves itself into the first. The issue of abstraction, then, is motivated by Berkeley's conviction that separate ideas of qualities which don't exist in separation are ideas that are inconceivable.

III

The difficulty that remains, of course, is that of understanding exactly why it is that such abstract ideas are inconceivable. This difficulty is especially acute since Berkeley usually justifies this claim, not with an argument, but with a challenge to perform a thought-experiment. That abstract ideas are inconceivable seems to mean to Berkeley that, if I attempt the process of framing one, I will find myself unable to do so; no idea of the relevant sort will emerge into my consciousness. (Willis Doney has called this an argument from Inconceivability.[12]) What has proved especially problematic has been to get clear on the reason why Berkeley can feel so sure that such abstract ideas will not be found. One suggestion is that Berkeley has some intuitions about entities or states of affairs, the existence of which is impossible, and has concluded that ideas of such impossible entities or states of affairs are inconceivable.[13] Doney has cast doubt on this line of reasoning, however, for this sort of procedure would seem to make nonsense of the use to which Berkeley puts his anti-abstractionism in the body of the *Principles*. That is, if Berkeley already has to know which states of affairs are impossible, in order to know that ideas of these states of affairs are inconceivable, then he can't also urge us not to accept claims about certain sorts of states of affairs, as, to regard them as impossible, because they involve abstractions. If he wants to argue in the *Principles* that some things are impossible, because they are inconceivable, then he can't identify ideas that are inconceivable through states of affairs that are impossible.

Some of these difficulties can be avoided if we take into account the ways in which Berkeley's arguments are limited to ideas and to the nature of ideas. His claims are about the impossibility of abstract ideas, rather than about the impossibility of what these ideas are supposed to be of,[14] and he supposes, therefore, that the impossibility of ideas can be understood by thinking about our mental faculties and about the sorts of processes that go on when we frame or conceive ideas. Berkeley begins his discussion, as is very often his practice, with a claim that he says is "agreed on all hands": in this case it is that "qualities or modes of things do never really exist each of them apart by it self, and separated from all others, but are mixed, as it were and blended together, several in the same object." (*Principles*, Intro., 7.) We do not experience isolated qualities, but rather chunks of things in which qualities are all mixed up together.[15] Thus, when we have experiences, even in the case of a single sense modality, like vision, our visual experience is simultaneously, for example, extended and colored. To frame an abstract idea of any one of these qualities, say, extension, would require us to start from the visual experience of a colored expanse and first peel off from this any way in which the expanse is colored, and then any way in which the extension of this expanse can be distinguished from any other extension. Berkeley denies that we can follow these directions and be left with an idea that has any content. If we take away all ways in which the expanse is colored, we have also taken away all ways in which it can be visually extended, because the way to take up visual space is by being colored. Being colored is a determinant of visual extension. You can't remove the color and have any visual taking-up-space left. We can of course pay selective attention to one quality or another, that is, think about the extension of an object without thinking about its color, but this is not the same as thinking about extension in the absence of color, what extension would be like if color were annihilated. This is what the directions for framing an abstract as opposed to a merely separated idea requires us to do: they tell us to remove some quality from a way in which that quality is determined in our experience. Our abilities to frame ideas of qualities are limited to the conditions of perception under which we experience them, and, thus, which qualities can or cannot be separated one from another depends upon the way in which we experience them.[16] "Being sweet-smelling," to use another of Berkeley's examples, can be separated from the rest of the ideas we have of the rose, not because it isn't impossible for a rose to be scentless, but because the smell is not a determinant of any other way of perceiving the rose.

For similar reasons, Berkeley holds that we cannot frame an abstract idea of extension-in-general. Such an abstract idea of extension would be one that contains only those qualities that apply to all instances of extension. To frame an abstract idea of extension, therefore, requires us to remove or peel off all qualities that differentiate one instance of extension from another. Berkeley's point is again that these directions can't be followed, for, when you have removed all ways in which an instance of extension can be distinguished from all other instances of extension, you will also have removed all the ways in which it can be extended.[17] Given the nature of our experience, there is no way for us to have ideas with the content these abstract ideas are supposed to have. Since these ideas are inconceivable, they are of course, as ideas, impossible, for the way for an *idea* to exist is to be conceived, but Berkeley is not deriving his argument from any general claims about which things are or are not impossible. The only general premise he uses is the one he says is uncontroversial, namely, that things, as it happens, consist of qualities blended together, and this, then, is how we experience them.

When Berkeley's anti-abstractionism is taken in this light, as a statement of the inconceivability, or the contentlessness of abstract ideas, then it becomes clear why he took the attack on abstraction to be basic to his important aims. His rejection of the notion of unperceived existence, of the distinction between primary and secondary qualities, and of the concept of extended, movable substance, all of which occur in rapid succession in the early pages of the *Principles*, can all be seen to depend upon the principle that abstractions are inconceivable. Thus, when Berkeley says that sensible qualities can't exist unperceived, this is a special case of the claim Berkeley could expect to regard as having been already established, that it is impossible to conceive separately what isn't experienced in separation. (That Berkeley expects us to apply this right away to thinking things, which surely can't be imaged, shows, I think conclusively, that he is not depending on any assumptions that ideas are images.) We can be assumed to be able to understand that ideas of unperceived sensible qualities lack content and so are inconceivable. This depends upon the recognition that sensible qualities occur only as determinants of perception or as ways of being perceived, and so can't be intelligibly separated from this context. Sensible qualities, such as red, warmth, or pain, are ways in which perceivers take things to be, and so exist only in the condition of our perceiving or being aware of them. So it is unintelligible to suppose we can separate ways of being aware from acts or states of awareness and to claim we have ideas of red, warmth or pain as they exist unperceived. Berkeley spells out this argument in much greater detail in the first of the *Three Dialogues between Hylas and Philonous*, where Berkeley has Philonous convince Hylas that he can't have ideas of sensible qualities such as heat except in the context of someone's feeling or being aware of them. The argument depends upon the admission that we can only know what qualities like heat are like as they are felt. To try to separate heat from its embodiment so as to be able to talk of heat in an unfeeling body is to try to frame an idea without legitimate content. Thus the argument of *Three Dialogues* is not a new argument, but a more detailed version of an argument that in the *Principles* talks simply about abstraction.

The argument against the distinction between primary and secondary qualities depends in the same way on this principle, that sensible qualities that are not experienced in separation can't be conceived to exist in separation. Since there is no way in which I can frame a contentful idea of extension, an alleged primary quality, exclusive of the idea of color, an alleged secondary quality, there is no way in which I can give content to a claim that I know what it would be like for a body to have a mind-independent quality like extension, but not a mind-dependent quality like color. This argument about primary and secondary qualities is in itself important for undermining the claim that our ideas depend upon and are the result of extended movable, material substances. Berkeley calls as well upon conclusions which he can again expect to have already gained – in this case, that ideas of extension-in-general and motion-in-general, independent of any sensible determination, are contentless – as part of his rejection of the materialist account of extended, material substance.

It is important, again, in order to see exactly what Berkeley is up to, to appreciate the extent to which the conclusions he is prepared to draw are limited to the nature of the ideas we can have. While he is intending to reject the claims of those who want to assert that the world contains qualities like extension existing in separation from others like color, this is not because he thinks he can show that it is impossible for objects as they exist unperceived to have primary but not secondary qualities. He is not trying to show anything about the nature or existence of unperceived objects. His point is that we can't conceive of such objects, and hence can't flesh out or make sense of the claims of the materialists that such objects exist. Berkeley's claim will inevitably look circular if we take what he says about our experience of sensible qualities to be a direct denial of the materialist claims about mind-independent qualities. Rather, what he seeks to establish in the Introduction to the *Principles* is that several of the ideas important to materialist theorizing are actually inconceivable, and what he goes on to conclude in the *Principles* itself is that the materialist who claims to have been able to isolate ideas of primary qualities, and to use these ideas to describe a mind-independent world is speaking, not falsely, but unintelligibly.[18]

Thus, in the end, it is not, in fact, unreasonable for Berkeley to have supposed that the attack on abstract ideas would be relevant to the undermining of the theory of materialist mechanism, resting as that theory does, as Berkeley points out in *Principles*, 99, on a twofold abstraction. The reductive impulse of materialist mechanism requires the assumption that appeal to entities possessing a small number of properties, as extension and motion, will be adequate to account for the full range of our experience. And this presupposes that it be possible to separate off or abstract some of the ideas we are aware of from others in order to be able to argue that some

ideas provide a description of an extramental reality, which is responsible
for the rest of our ideas. This presupposition, in turn, rests on the assumption that at least some of our ideas, some of the ways in which we are
aware, can be abstracted from the context of awareness in which they occur, so that they can be used to describe this extramental reality which is
said to have been responsible for the ideas we have. Berkeley's motivation
in his arguments about abstract ideas is provided, not in any direct sense
by Locke's triangle,[19] but rather by passages such as this one from Descartes' *Principles of Philosophy*:

> Thus, for example, figure cannot be understood except in an
> extended thing, nor can motion except in an extended space;
> nor can imagination, sensation, or will, except in a thinking
> substance. But on the contrary, extension can be understood
> without figure or motion, and thought without imagination or
> sensation and so on; as is obvious to anyone who pays attention
> to these things.[20]

But what Berkeley prefers to think attention will reveal is that
"Mathematicians treat of quantity, without regarding what other sensible
qualities it is attended with, as being altogether indifferent to their demon-
strations. But, when laying aside the words, they contemplate the bare
ideas, I believe you will find they are not the pure abstracted ideas of extension." (*Dialogues*, 193.) Berkeley's arguments are directed at and relevant to any position which entails that it is possible for the mind to arrive
at an idea of extension, whose content would be exclusive of any sensory-
based qualities or determinations.[21]

IV

Although Berkeley's target in his attack on abstract ideas was, as I have
argued, materialist mechanism, and not a theory of meaning exemplified by
Locke's triangle, he did of course suppose that some sort of lesson, in fact a
"killing blow," could be derived from a consideration of Locke's triangle.
Locke's passage about the abstract general idea of a triangle (notoriously)
runs as follows:

> For example, Does it not require some pains and skill to form
> the *general Idea* of a *triangle* (which is yet none of the most
> abstract, comprehensive and difficult,) for it must be neither
> Oblique, nor Rectangle, neither Equilateral, Equicrural, nor
> Scalenon; but all and none of these at once. In effect, it is
> something imperfect, that cannot exist; an *Idea* wherein some
> parts of several different and inconsistent *Ideas* are put

together. (IV.vii.9.)

Berkeley has standardly been taken to have read Locke as claiming that in
order to be able to recognize any triangle as a triangle, whether it be equilateral or scalene or whatever, we must have a general idea which includes
all these inconsistent properties. Berkeley's refutation is then supposed to
be that such a monster can't be pictured. But, as Kenneth Winkler has
argued, if we look at the range of references Berkeley makes to Locke's
triangle, and in particular to those in *A Defence of Free-Thinking in Mathematics*, it seems that Berkeley understands precisely how Locke intended
the idea of a triangle to be framed, namely, by omitting distinguishing features of a particular triangle, and not by adding them together.[2 2] What,
then, is the killing blow? Winkler finds Berkeley faced with a difficulty here,
since there seems to be no reason to believe that an idea formed by omitting parts of perfectly consistent ideas would be one that is contradictory.
And yet Berkeley is unequivocal, on at least some occasions,[2 3] that the
reason why we can't frame abstract general ideas is that they are contradictory. The problem here, as I have argued, is that the illegitimacy of the
abstract general idea of a triangle has nothing to do with the way general
ideas of things are put together. It derives entirely from the illegitimacy of
the ideas of the qualities that go to make up these general ideas. The
"killing blow," then, Berkeley perceived was Locke's admission that the
abstract general idea of a triangle was "something imperfect, that cannot
exist."[2 4] Locke's triangle is imperfect because it omits particular charac-
teristics that distinguish one triangle from another, as some determinate
length to its lines, and it can't exist, because it can't have common charac-
teristics like length, except by virtue of having some determinate characteristic, some particular length. Berkeley's point rests again on the inconceivability of the idea we are supposed to be able to frame.
    There are those who want to claim that Locke, like Berkeley, only
wanted to say that general ideas are formed by paying attention selectively
to resembling aspects of experience. If this account of Locke is correct, then
perhaps Berkeley can be accused of taking advantage of exaggerated language in paying as much attention as he did to the triangle that is
"something imperfect, that cannot exist." Berkeley is certainly not intending to be quarrelling with anyone who takes general ideas to be formed by
selective attention or by a partial consideration of some but not other sensible qualities. He is careful to point out this is not the use of abstraction
against which he is arguing and added a passage to the Introduction in the
second edition which makes this clear:

> And here it must be acknowledged that a man may consider a
> figure merely as triangular, without attending to the particular
> qualities of the angles, or relations of the sides. So far he may

abstract: but this will never prove, that he can frame an abstract general inconsistent idea of a triangle. In like manner we may consider Peter so far forth as man, or so far forth as animal, without framing the forementioned abstract idea, either of man or of animal, inasmuch as all that is perceived is not considered. (*Principles*, Intro., 16.)

Berkeley's argument acknowledges that we can frame ideas just by ignoring or overlooking features of the perceptual situation. His argument is not directed, therefore, against anyone who wants to generalize about ideas as we experience them, but only with those who want to, as he sees it, illegitimately extend the reach of our ideas beyond the conditions of perceiving.

In *Alciphron*, Berkeley talks about the extent to which we can generalize or universalize:

> Now, these rules being general, it follows that they are not to be obtained by the mere consideration of the original ideas, or particular things, but by the means of marks, and signs, which being so far forth universal, become the immediate instruments and materials of science. It is not therefore, by the mere contemplation of particular things, and much less of their abstract general ideas, that the mind makes her progress, but by an apposite choice and skillful management of signs: for instance, force and number, taken in concrete, with their adjuncts, subjects and signs, are what everyone knows; and considered in abstract, so as making precise ideas of themselves, they are what nobody can comprehend. (*Alc.*, 304.)

Thus the issue to which Berkeley is calling our attention is a particular theory of what progress in the sciences is like. He is opposed to those who think they can take a concept like force, which Berkeley regards as useful and appropriate within its proper context, and apply it, independent of sensible bodies and their sensible effects to some of underlying reality. So long as we resist this temptation, laws concerning force are intelligible and beneficial. It is equally appropriate, Berkeley would think, for a scientist to describe things too small to see, such as the corpuscles of materialist mechanism, so long as one is doing no more than using visible things as a model. As Berkeley says:

> We substitute things imaginable for things intelligible, sensible things for imaginable, smaller things for those that are too great to comprehend easily, and greater things for such as are too small to be discerned distinctly, present things for absent, permanent for perishing, and visible for invisible. Hence the use of models and diagrams. (*Alc.*, 306.)

What is inappropriate is to abandon the terms of the model or to imagine that, in some cases, instead of speaking metaphorically, we have uncovered something about the underlying nature of things. Thus Berkeley's "corpuscles" would differ in a number of ways from those of many materialists, most notably, they would be characterized by secondary as well as primary qualities.

It should be clear that, once the issue about abstraction is identified in this way, then the extent of Berkeley's agreement or disagreement with Locke can't depend simply on what Locke says about how we frame ideas of triangles, but on Locke's far more complicated views on the nature of reality. Adjudicating on this issue would take me much too far afield.[25] It is not even clear that there is a single answer to the question, do Berkeley's arguments about abstraction apply to Locke? It is possible, for example, that Locke's talk of primary qualities which resemble our ideas of them involves nothing more than ideas framed by selective attention, and hence they are not a target of Berkeley's strictures against illegitimate abstractions, but that Locke's talk of substance is intended to be included among the ideas Berkeley wants to rule out. One of Berkeley's letters to Johnson, for example, makes clear that what he finds troublesome in Locke with respect to abstraction is Locke's tendency to speak of Being-in-general, on which Locke's willingness to assert the existence of a mind-independent material substance depended.[26] For the issues to which Berkeley's anti-abstractionism calls attention, and which, as he sees it, have impeded progress in the sciences are those which involve abstracting from the conditions of perception to give a description of an underlying extramental reality.[27]

I have been arguing that the prevailing tendency to see Berkeley's anti-abstractionism as concentrating on Locke's triangle produced a distortion of Berkeley's claims that hides the overall shape and thrust of his theory. To see Berkeley's principle concern as that of undermining what he found in Locke can result in overlooking other or more general targets. I should add that this tendency to set Locke and Berkeley at odds with one another is not only perhaps unfair to Berkeley, as I have been arguing, but may not always be helpful in our understanding of Locke, inasmuch as it also tends to bury aspects of Locke's theory that may, in fact, be quite Berkeleian.[28]

University of Wisconsin, Milwaukee

NOTES

1. David Armstrong, for example, in his introduction to his edition of the *Principles*, says: "The long Introduction, with its attack on the doctrine of Abstract Ideas, is probably not as important for his main thesis as Berkeley believed it to be" (p. 41). Others have supposed that Berkeley is using the issues surrounding abstract ideas as an illustration of more general problems concerning the abuse of language. Kenneth Winkler, who is especially sensitive to this issue, suggests in his editor's introduction that Berkeley wants us to be aware that relations among words can't be taken as guides to relations among things, so that we will not be inclined to insist, for example, that just because existence and perception are two different words, that they must stand for two different and separable things (p. xxxvi). But I find this kind of approach too fails to do justice to the clear importance Berkeley attaches to the issue of abstract ideas throughout the text of the *Principles concerning Human Knowledge*.

2. For some examples, see G. J. Warnock, *Berkeley* (London: Penguin, 1953); David Armstrong, Introduction to *Berkeley's Philosophical Writings* (London: Collier-Macmillan, 1965); I. C. Tipton, *Berkeley: The Philosophy of Immaterialism* (London: Methuen, 1974); George Pitcher, *Berkeley* (London/Boston: Routledge and Kegan Paul, 1977).

3. *An Essay Concerning Human Understanding*, III.iii.6. All references are to the Clarendon edition of the *Essay*, edited by P. H. Nidditch (Oxford: Oxford University Press, 1975).

4. I have expressed my doubt on this issue in 'The Inessentiality of Lockean Essences,' *Canadian Journal of Philosophy*, **XIV**, 2 (June 1984), pp. 277-93.

5. In section 6 of the Introduction, Berkeley says: ". . . but the unravelling this matter leads me in some manner to anticipate my design, by taking notice of what seems to have occaisioned innumerable errors and difficulties in almost all parts of knowledge. And this is the opinion that the mind hath a power of framing *abstract ideas* or notions of things." See also *Principles*, Intro., 17, *Principles*, 97, 118.

6. I. C. Tipton, *Berkeley, op. cit.*, pp. 152-3. A similar sort of complaint is made by John Mackie in *Problems from Locke* (Oxford: Oxford University Press, 1976), p. 121.

7. In addition, in *Principles*, 13, he dismisses unity as an abstract idea, in *Principles*, 17, being, and in *Principles*, 97-8, he says that difficulties with the concept of time stem from attempting to derive an idea that is abstracted from the succession of ideas in the mind.

8. When Berkeley draws out the implications of his views for physics, mathematics, and psychology in the remainder of the *Principles*, he returns repeatedly to the theme of errors introduced by abstract ideas.

9. Berkeley stresses this point in *A Defence of Free-Thinking in Mathematics*. He rejects any suggestion that he thinks there are no general ideas, saying: "But I hold the direct contrary, that there are indeed general ideas, but not formed by abstraction in the manner set forth by Mr. Locke." (Sect. 45, *Works*, iv. 134.)

10. See Kenneth Winkler, 'Berkeley on Abstract Ideas,' *Archiv fur Geschichte der Philosophie*, **65**, 1 (1985) 63-80.

11. Later passages relax the idea of the kind of abstraction I can perform still further, by drawing attention to a kind of abstraction by selective attention. I discuss this matter further below.

12. Willis Doney, 'Berkeley's Argument against Abstract Ideas,' in Peter A. French, Theodore E. Uehling, Jr., and Howard K. Wettstein, eds., *Midwest Studies in Philosophy VIII* (Minneapolis: University of Minnesota Press, 1983). Doney has also discussed these issues in 'Is Berkeley's a Cartesian Mind?' in Colin M. Turbayne, ed., *Berkeley: Critical and Interpretive Essays* (Minneapolis: University of Minnesota Press, 1982).

13. Kenneth Winkler and George Pitcher have argued along these lines. It seems undeniable that Berkeley uses *an* argument of this sort as at *Alc., 333-34 (i.e. Seventh Dialogue, sect. 6, of the* 1st and 2nd eds.). The question, therefore, is whether this is Berkeley's only argument.

14. Martha Bolton, in her contribution to this volume, also points out that Berkeley's arguments are about ideas, what she calls idea-objects, and not about the objects of ideas.

15. Doney has mentioned the presence of this premise, but has found it puzzling, in part, I think, because he has failed to take account of its generality. What is agreed by all is not that there are *some* qualities which it is impossible to separate from each other, even

though there are others which can be so separated, but that all qualities exist in blended chunks.

16. This is what I take Berkeley to be saying in *Principles*, 5, where he says: "But my conceiving or imagining power does not extend beyond the possibility of real existence or perception." Since he is talking about sensible objects, he is identifying perception with the conditions of real existence.

17. Berkeley spells out this objection most clearly in the first occasion where he introduces his argument against abstraction in *NTV*, 122-3, where he writes: "We are therefore to understand by extension in abstract an idea of extension, for instance, a line or surface intirely stript of all other sensible qualities and circumstances that might determine it to any particular existence; it is neither black, nor white, nor red, nor hath it any color at all, or any tangible quality whatsoever, and consequently it is of no finite determinate magnitude. For that which bounds or distinguishes one extension from another is some quality or circumstances wherein they disagree. (123) Now I do not find that I can perceive, imagine, or any wise frame in my mind such an abstract idea as is here spoken of. A line or surface which is neither black, nor white, nor blue, nor yellow, etc., is perfectly incomprehensible."

18. Berkeley is not, therefore, behaving in a manner inconsistent with his claim in *Dialogues*, 232, that "Many things, for ought I know, may exist, whereof neither I nor any other man hath or can have any idea or notion thereof."

19. In *A Defence of Free-thinking in Mathematics*, Berkeley complains of having been misread in this way: "This doctrine of abstract general ideas seemed to me a capital errour, productive of numberless difficulties and disputes, that runs not only throughout Mr. Locke's book, but through most parts of learning. Consequently, my animadversions thereupon were not an effect of being inclined to carp or cavil at a single passage, as you would wrongfully insinuate, but proceeded from a love of truth, and a desire to banish, so far as in me lay, false principles and wrong ways of thinking, without respect of persons." (Sect. 48, *Works*, iv. 136.)

20. *Principles of Philosophy*, translated by Valentine Roger Miller and Reese P. Miller (Dordrecht: Reidel, 1983), pr. 53, p. 24.

21. In the course of the discussion of primary and secondary qualities in *Dialogues*, 193-4, Berkeley expressly considers whether it might be

possible to arrive at the relevant abstractions by means of the pure
intellect alone, so that it is clear that he intends his arguments to
hold against such a position as well as against those who hold that
ideas of primary qualities are abstracted from sense experience. He
has two things to say about this. The first is that he has grave
doubts about such a use of a pure intellect, since he thinks that
whatever information we have about bodies comes from the senses.
The second is that it is nonetheless impossible to "frame the idea of
any figure, abstracted from all particularities of size." The idea of a
figure of no size whatsoever cannot be framed, the directions can't
be followed, however we are alleged to come by our idea of figure.

22.   Winkler, 'Berkeley on Abstract Ideas,' p. 68.

23.   As *Alc.*, 293-95.

24.   This connection as well emerges especially clearly in *A Defence.*

25.   See Nancy L. Maull, 'Berkeley on the Limits of Mechanistic Expla-
      nation,' Margaret D. Wilson, 'Did Berkeley Completely Misunder-
      stand the Basis of the Primary-Secondary Quality Distinction in
      Locke?,' I. C. Tipton, 'The "Philosopher by Fire" in Berkeley's *Al-
      ciphron*,' Daniel Garber, 'Locke, Berkeley and Corpuscular Scepti-
      cism,' all in C. M. Turbayne, ed., *Berkeley: Critical and Interpretive
      Essays*; Barry Stroud, 'Berkeley v. Locke on Primary Qualities,'
      Philosophy, **55** (April 1980); and Margaret D. Wilson, 'Berkeley and
      the Essences of the Corpuscularians,' in John Foster and Howard
      Robinson, ed., *Essays on Berkeley* (Oxford: Clarendon Press, 1985).

26.   "He holds an abstract idea of existence exclusive of perceiving and
      being perceived. I cannot find I have any such idea, and this is my
      reason against it." (*Works*, ii. 293.)

27.   Martha Bolton also points out that Berkeley's arguments are di-
      rected against the idea that science progresses by relying on what
      she calls "partial conceptions."

28.   I am very grateful to Robert Schwartz, John Koethe, and Fabrizio
      Mondadori for their help in writing this paper, and to James Van
      Cleve and Rhoda Kotzin, who served as commentators.

Martha Brandt Bolton

BERKELEY'S OBJECTION TO ABSTRACT IDEAS AND UNCONCEIVED OBJECTS

1. According to Berkeley's famous theory of perception, we see, feel and otherwise perceive nothing but ideas; the whole of the sensible world with its trees and rocks, sun and stars, consists of nothing but idea sequences. The oddity of the consequence, that we eat, drink and clothe ourselves in ideas, seems to have discredited this theory for the first two hundred years. But in this century, the theory has been applauded for its elegant economy and the daring way it cuts off speculation about the existence and nature of the sensible world. Many other early modern philosophers regarded sensory ideas as only the means by which we perceive other sorts of things; for them, ideas were instruments which, even if fully known in themselves, offer at best partial knowledge of objects that exist in the sensible world. Berkeley's stunningly simple move is to identify objects we apprehend by sense with aggregates of ideas, while still maintaining that ideas are fully accessible to the mind that has them. This is *inter alia* a thesis about the intentional objects of perceptual states. We do not perceive objects by means of ideas, because ideas do not *represent* other things. By identifying ideas and sensible things, Berkeley robs minds of cognitive access to perceptual objects that are not fully accessible to consciousness.

Recent admiration for Berkeley's theory of perception in matched, however, by widespread dismay over another aspect of his theory of ideas, his denial of the possibility of abstract ideas.[1] Strategically placed in the introduction to the *Principles*, the attack on abstraction is said by Berkeley to "anticipate the design" of the whole work. It exposes a general source of error which, Berkeley thinks, plays a more particular part encouraging the mistaken opinion that matter exists independently of mind (*Principles*, Intro., 6, 5).

This anti-abstractionist part of Berkeley's philosophy has been severely attacked on several counts.[2] For instance, even the most sympathetic commentators doubt that the attack on abstraction has the direct relevance to immaterialism Berkeley claims.[3] In contrast, however, I think one only needs to understand Berkeley's general theory of ideas to see that it does and that the case is just as Berkeley's prefatory handling of the doctrine of abstraction suggests. At the outset of the *Principles*, he suggests (mainly by presupposing it) a *general* theory of ideas as they function, not only in sense perception, but also in derivative modes of thought: memory, imagination, dreams and reveries, the practice of geometry and other

61

E. Sosa (ed.), Essays on the Philosophy of George Berkeley, 61–81.
©*1987 by D. Reidel Publishing Company*

sciences. In this broad theory of ideas, Berkeley makes the same sort of move he makes, more famously, in the case of sense perception. That is, Berkeley takes the objects of various modes of cognition, objects his contemporaries typically regarded as things *represented* by ideas, simply *to be* ideas. Because Berkeley agrees with those who thought ideas are fully known, the result is strictly to limit the class of objects we are able *to think about* to things of a type we adequately know. Now this general theory of ideas is diametrically opposed to the view of ideas as instruments by which we think of other sorts of things and by which we have a partial knowledge of them. I will contend that Berkeley's theory of ideas is the basis of his rejection of abstraction.

My aim in this paper is to vindicate Berkeley's treatment of abstract ideas in the introduction and early sections of *Principles*. I do not want to defend the truth of Berkeley's account of ideas, but rather to defend him against familiar charges of misusing the rejection of abstract ideas in certain arguments and especially the charge of misjudging the *relevance* of the doctrine of abstraction. Far from being irrelevant, I want to show, Berkeley's anti-abstractionist theory of ideas grounds the unintelligibility of mind-independent sensible things. Berkeley's "Idealism" claims not just that sensible objects *are* mind-dependent collections of ideas, but further that it is *incoherent* to think sensible objects are independent of mind. Thus, Berkeley agrees with other "anti-realist" philosophers that it is incoherent to suppose there are things in the sensible world outside the scope of possible knowledge. But what exactly is Berkeley's basis for such a view? Some commentators suppose he means to argue that expressions like "unperceived matter" are meaningless, due to the Empiricist demand that significant noun phrases be linked with items of sense experience.[4] But, as other scholars have shown, Berkeley does not hold that theory about language.[5] My contention is that what grounds Berkeley's claim that mind-independent sensible things are unintelligible, and gives his Idealism its special stamp, is his anti-abstractionist theory of ideas, in particular his views about the intentional objects of ideas.

Let me explain before proceeding that of course ideas, or sensible things, are not the only objects of thought and knowledge Berkeley recognizes. There are also "notions": minds, their actions and relations (see, e.g., *Principles*, 2, 27, 89, 142). My concern here is only with various modes of thinking about bodies or what exists in the sensible world. Berkeley holds notions and ideas to be mutually exclusive categories. Thought about bodies involves ideas, but not notions, whereas thought about minds concerns notions, not ideas. So, it is, I believe, possible to discuss his views about cognition of sensible objects with only passing mention of minds and other notions.

2. As a first step toward understanding Berkeley's attack on abstract ideas, it is useful to look at his view of the history of the unfortunate doctrine. He ranks it chief among the false principles responsible for confusion, uncertainty and absurdity in logic and metaphysics, mathematics and other sciences (*Principles*, Intro., 4-6; Draft Intro. 17). He took the doctrine to be central to all the main traditions regarding the theory and practice of the sciences, for he ascribes it to Aristotle, Locke, "ancient [and] modern logicians and metaphysicians," to the Scholastics and, indeed, "all other philosophers" (Draft Intro. 17; Letter to Johnson, *Works*, ii. 293). This last is presumably an overstatement, but surely it indicates that Descartes, Malebranche and Arnauld are among the "masters of abstraction."

It is not easy to identify a relevant view shared by this heterogenous group of philosophers. Surely they did not all hold to a single theory of ideas.[6] But Locke and others such as Arnauld and Nicole took abstract ideas to be the means by which we think about kinds and the basis of all knowledge of general truths (e.g., *Essay* III.iii, and IV.vi; *Logique*, I.v). Berkeley links abstract ideas with genera and species (Draft Intro. 7; *PC*, 566, 703) and with accepted views about "science" and the "demonstration of general propositions" *NTV*, 124; *Principles*, Intro., 15). His target seems to be a view I call "Essentialism" about knowledge of general propositions. The tenets of this view are: that essences determine kinds in that the things that belong to a kind are distinguished from others by having the essence of the kind; that the essence is the "source" of the features shared by all members of the kind; that, in addition to the essence and the features derived from it, members of the kind have various "accidental" features in which they do, or can, differ from one another; and, most important for Berkeley's purposes, knowledge of the essence is required for science or knowledge of universal propositions about a kind. Now I have purposely constructed this set of tenets so generally that they ignore a wide range of deep and important topics of dispute, including: the status of universals, the nature of essences, how (and whether) essences can be known, the objectivity of the distinction between essence and accident, the role of species-essence in the identity of individuals, how properties "flow from" essences, the semantic connection between essences and general terms. But it requires a broad doctrine that arches over these issues that had divided philosophers to sustain Berkeley's charge of responsibility for a continuing history of error in the sciences going back to Aristotle.

Berkeley objects particularly to one tenet of the Essentialist view: an account of essence gives a perspicuous, but only partial, characterization of particular things. It is incomplete relative to the things to which it applies, because it omits all features accidental to the kind. It is this assumption that we can conceive a partial characterization, and thereby have (partial) knowledge of all things that conform to it, that Berkeley rejects. Conceptions of essences would be abstract ideas, and they are among Berkeley's targets:

It is indeed a tenet, as well of the modern as the ancient philosophers, that all general truths are concerning universal abstract ideas; without which, we are told, there could be no science, no demonstration of any general proposition . . . (*NTV*,
124; see also *Principles*, Intro., 15.)

Now the abstractionist model for understanding general propositions by a
partial characterization to which any number of particulars may conform
can be separated from other principles of Essentialism. But the model is
embedded in that traditional view, and I think it is in that role that Berkeley supposes it had pernicious effects upon the sciences.

    Berkeley's descriptions of the abstractions he opposes clearly show
that abstract ideas are incomplete characterizations (relative to things that
conform to the ideas) and that abstract ideas include conceptions of essences of kinds.[7] There are two types of abstract ideas, he explains in
Principles, Introduction (see also *Principles*, 99). In the first, "singling"
type, the mind forms an idea of a single quality abstracted from other
qualities which it cannot exist without, for instance, an idea of color or
motion without extension. Notice that anything that conforms to the idea of
color will have extension, so the idea of the "singled" quality conforms to
the pattern of abstract ideas. The second type of abstract idea includes the
features shared by several particular things and omits their various differences. The idea of extension abstracted from all particular sizes and shapes
is one example; for another:

    . . . the mind having observed that Peter, James and John
resemble each other in certain common agreements of shape
and other qualities, leaves out of the complex or compound idea
it has of Peter, James, and any other particular man, that
which is peculiar to each, retaining only what is common to all
and so makes an abstract idea, wherein all the particulars do
equally partake. (*Principles*, Intro., 9.)

This favors a Lockean view of the (nominal) essences of human beings,
rather than an Aristotelian or Cartesian one, but ideas of essences of any
sort would be abstract ideas of this second type.

    Finally, Berkeley allows that he can form abstract ideas of things of
qualities that can *exist* apart:

    Thus, I imagine the trunk of a human body without limbs, or
conceive the smell of a rose without thinking on the rose itself.
So far, I will not deny I can abstract; if that may properly be
called *abstraction* which extends only to the conceiving separately such objects as it is possible may really exist or be actually perceived assunder. (*Principles*, 5; see also Intro., 10.)

I will later have something to say about the use of this "test" for possible
abstractions. For the present, I want only to suggest that the conceptions
Berkeley allows are *not* partial characterizations of the objects that conform
to them. A limbless body is part of a natural whole and a rose's scent, part
of the collection of qualities that belong to a rose; but the object that conforms to an idea of a limbless body is not the natural whole, nor is the object of the idea of a rose's scent the rose. Compare the abstract idea of red
that omits extension or a specific shade; any particular instance of red,
anything that conforms to the idea, will be extended and determinate in
shade. It is that type of partial characterization of things that conform to
an idea that Berkeley rejects.

   In light of his rejection of abstract ideas, Berkeley thinks it necessary to explain himself particularly on two topics: the signification of general terms and the knowledge of general propositions. Detailed discussion is
impossible here, but a brief account is necessary background for Berkeley's
main arguments. Locke urged that words acquire meaning by association
with ideas, that a general term signifies an abstract idea of the things to
which the term applies (e.g., *Essay*, III.iii). Berkeley maintains that a general term stands, not for one abstract idea, but for many particular ones;
that is, in case the general term names sensible things, it signifies many
particular things, i.e. ideas. (Commentators have noted that, unlike Locke,
Berkeley seems unconcerned with explaining how general terms are linked
to the particular things they name.) Further, it is not necessary that on
every occasion that a word is used, it should raise in the mind of those who
use it the idea of what it stands for (*Principles*, Intro., 18-20).

   As for the knowledge of universal propositions, Berkeley maintains
there are no universal conceptions, but a particular conception is "rendered
universal" by coming to represent other particular things. For instance, to
demonstrate a general theorem about triangles, one proves it of a particular
triangle which "doth equally stand for and represent all . . . triangles
whatsoever" (*Principles*, Intro., 15). How can we be sure that a property
known to belong to one particular triangle belongs to others that are not
exactly like it? Because, Berkeley replies, one sees that the proof does not
depend on any feature peculiar to that triangle as opposed to any other. He
adds:

> And here it must be acknowledged that a man may consider a
> figure merely as triangular, without attending to the particular
> qualities of the angles, or relations of the sides. So far he may
> abstract. But this will never prove that he can frame an ab-
> stract, general, inconsistent idea of a triangle. (*Principles*, In-
> tro., 16.)

As many commentators have observed, Berkeley gives no clear account of
what determines the features common to all things in a kind, for instance,

no explanation of what is supposed to distinguish the things a particular triangle "stands for and represents" from those it does not. Still, something can be gleaned. One main point is that what an idea represents is not intrinsic to the idea, but rather the idea is "rendered universal" by the use to which it is put. Further, the account strongly suggests that one idea might represent quite different things in different circumstances: a right triangle would represent all triangles if shown to have interior angles equal to two right angles, but would represent only right triangles if shown to be inscribed in a semicircle, and so on. What the particular represents is a function of human activity (also see *Alc.*, 303-308). Although Berkeley gives no full account of how actions establish a relation of representation between one idea and others, it seems to have something to do with our ability to attend selectively to certain features of an idea. This view about the basis of distinctions of kinds, which I have only sketched, is central to Berkeley's alternative to "Essentialism."

3. Why is the doctrine of abstract ideas a "false principle"? Berkeley's main argument seems intended to apply generally to all abstract ideas and to show that they are impossible on logical grounds.[8] The argument is actually made in a quoted passage from Locke's *Essay*, in which Berkeley seems to think the author so clear and candid that he reveals the absurdity of his own doctrine. Locke's example is the abstract idea of a triangle. It includes being a figure with three sides and angles, for these features are common to all triangles, but it omits angles and sides of any definite size or mutual relation, because triangles differ in these respects. Locke expresses the surprising view, which Berkeley eagerly endorses, that it is an idea of a triangle that ". . . must be neither oblique nor rectangle, neither equilateral, equicrural, nor scalenon; but *all and none* of these at once." But, the argument goes, such a figure is logically impossible, and so the idea of it is impossible; or, as Locke writes of the idea: ". . . it is something imperfect that cannot exist, an idea wherein some parts of several different and *inconsistent* ideas are put together" (*Principles*, Intro., 13, quoting *Essay*, IV.vii.9). It has by now become a familiar point that there are two main objections to this argument. In the first place, why should we think an idea is impossible just because its object is? A triangle that is both right-angled and not right-angled is impossible, but why should it follow that an idea of such a thing is impossible? And in the second place, what entitles Berkeley to conclude that the object of the abstract idea *is* impossible? In particular, why should we agree that its object is neither obtuse, acute nor right angled? Of course, if its object is a triangle, it must be one of these, but why must it also be none of them? Berkeley assumes that the features *omitted* from the idea are *lacking* from its object, but there seems no need for this. It seems an idea of a triangle may simply fail to specify the length of a figure's sides without specifying that the figure has sides of no particular length. Why should we agree that an abstract idea must be formed in this second way and that its object must be supposed to have features it also lacks?

No doubt the generally accepted view is correct that Berkeley relies on a peculiar theory of ideas which perhaps need not be accepted by an advocate of abstraction. The problem is to say just what Berkeley's theory of ideas is. Neither of the two lines of thought dominant in the secondary literature seems to me entirely correct.[9]

One view ascribes to Berkeley a more or less deliberate tendency to think that an idea *has* the features of what it is the idea *of:* the idea of a triangle is triangular.[10] This answers our first question, why Berkeley assumes an idea to be impossible if its object has mutually incompatible features; the idea must have the incompatible features of its object. But it does not answer the second question, why the object of an abstract idea *is* impossible. In particular, it does not explain why the abstract idea of a triangle represents a triangle that is neither acute, obtuse nor right-angled, nor *a fortiori* why it is "all and none of these." The principle that the idea of F *is* F simply does not explain why the idea of F that *omits* G should be thought to be the idea of an F that is *not* G. For that, we should need two further principles: (i) that an idea that omits G is itself not G; and (ii) that an idea that *is* F and not G is the idea *of* an F that is not G. (The latter is needed, if the initial proposal is understood to be the conditional: if I is the idea of F, then I is F. It is not needed, if the proposal is understood to be biconditional: I is the idea of F if and only if I is F.[11]) A further problem with this attempt to explain Berkeley's position on ideas is that it fails to say why Berkeley should have adopted the rather implausible thesis that an idea of F is itself F; for instance, the idea of motion is moving, the idea of heat is hot. Berkeley does think an idea has the features of its object, and only those features, but the key point is that he does so *because* he deliberately identifies ideas and objects.

It is often said that Berkeley's reasoning is explained by the fact that he takes ideas to be images of things, i.e. mental reconstructions of what it is like to see some thing, hear it, etc.[12] This may also explain why an idea is impossible if its object is. For, we say an image has the features of what it is an image of (although this may not be the best way of speaking[13]), so the image of something with inconsistent features might be said to have those features; moreover we do seem unable to form images of things with incompatible properties. Indeed, we seem unable to make images corresponding to a large number of abstract ideas, for instance, that of a triangle which is neither acute, obtuse not right-angled. But this image view of ideas does *not* explain Berkeley's general objection to abstract ideas, for images typically do, and perhaps must, omit some details of their objects; the image of a scalene triangle need not exactly specify the sizes of angles or sides.[14] Furthermore, although the image theory explains why we cannot have ideas that omit certain features of their objects, it does not account for the assumption crucial in Berkeley's actual argument, that if an idea does *omit* a feature it is an idea of something that *lacks* that feature.

Berkeley took for granted that to think about an object is to have an idea in mind, but he maintains that the object *is* the idea. He wrote in the early notebooks: "By Idea I mean any sensible or imaginable thing" (*PC*, 775; also see 101 and 808). Thus, we sense and imagine ideas. He continued to regard ideas (or collections of ideas) as the objects of our cognitive activities, for he frequently asserts that we perceive ideas (e.g., *Principles*, 1, 4, 5, 7, etc., and especially 38 and 39); and sometimes he writes that ideas are objects of knowledge (*Principles*, 1), objects of geometrical demonstration (*Principles*, Intro., 12), and the things named by general terms for objects (*Principles*, Intro., 11, 18). Other idea theorists habitually write of ideas as *representing* the objects of cognitive acts, for instance, Arnauld and Nicole: "When I consider a body, the idea of it represents to me a thing or substance, because I consider it as a thing that subsists by itself . . ." (*Logique*, I.2; also, e.g., 5 and 6).[15] On this view, an idea must be an idea of something else, for the idea just is the instrument by which thought is directed toward that other thing. Berkeley also uses the expression "idea of," but whereas other idea theorists mean by it "idea that represents," he typically means "idea, namely."[16] When Berkeley writes that someone who perceives something triangular has an idea *of* a triangle, he means the person perceives an idea that *is* a triangle. So, we can say that for Berkeley an idea is its own object; if there is an idea of *x*, then *x* itself is that idea.

It is fundamental that an idea is its own object, but there is more to Berkeley's theory of ideas than that. Although the intrinsic object of an idea is just the idea itself, Berkeley holds that an idea can *come* to represent something else, or as I shall say, it can have an "acquired" object. We saw earlier that one idea comes to represent another idea, only by the actions of a mind and only if the first idea (object) shares selected features with its acquired object. Berkeley's view departs markedly from that of Arnauld and Nicole, for whom each idea has an intrinsic object other than itself, and has it in virtue of features the conception "includes" rather than features the idea has. The notebooks show Berkeley's dissatisfaction with the standard account of the intentional objects of ideas:

> Properly speaking Idea is the picture of the Imagination's making this is ye likeness of & refer'd to the real Idea or (if you will) thing. *PC*, 657a.

> The referring Ideas to things wch are not Ideas, the using the term, Idea of, is one great cause of mistake, as in other matters, so also in this.[17] *PC*, 660.

> Whoever shall cast his eyes on the writings of Old or New Phi-
> losophers & see the Noise is made about formal & objective
> Being Will etc.[1][8] *PC*, 781.

> The distinction between Idea & Ideatum I cannot otherwise
> conceive than by making one the effect or consequence of
> Dream, reverie, Imagination the other of sense & the Constant
> laws of Nature. *PC*, 843.

(Also see *PC*, 230, 523, 657, 672, 684, 823.) Berkeley deliberately asserts
that an idea of F is itself F, because he cannot understand the notion of the
"objective being of F" or an idea that intrinsically represents F. (One would
like to know more about Berkeley's objection, but I have been unable to find
a basis for more than speculation about this.) So, Berkeley rejects the view
that an idea represents things in virtue of features the idea includes (vs.
has) and the view that an idea has an object independently of the action of
a mind. If a mind sets an idea up to represent something else, the idea
must share certain features with its acquired object. Berkeley draws from
this the important conclusion that the acquired object must be another idea
(see, e.g., *Principles*, Intro., 15-16, 8, 9, 25, 27).

Now Berkeley does share with many other idea theorists the view
that an idea is fully accessible to the mind that has it:[1][9]

> As long as I confine my thought to my own ideas, divested of
> words, I do not see how I can easily be mistaken. The objects I
> consider, I clearly and adequately know. (*Principles*, Intro., 22;
> also see *Principles*, 25 and *PC*, 606.)

He also writes about ideas that "since they and every part of them exist
only in a mind, it follows that there is nothing in them that is not perceived" (*Principles*, 25; also 87). Two qualifications need to be made, however. Berkeley does not suppose it is impossible to err about your own
ideas, but just that care and attention suffice to avoid it. Further, the
"adequate" knowledge we have of an idea does not extend to its relations to
other things (e.g., *Principles*, 89); perhaps this enables Berkeley to explain
why one who has the idea of a triangle may not easily apprehend all theo-
rems about triangles. For Berkeley, then, a mind not only "clearly and
adequately" knows its ideas, but also adequately knows the (intrinsic) objects of those ideas, for the objects are identical to the ideas. In contrast,
according to the instrumental view of ideas, what may be completely known
is the features ideas "include" or how they characterize their objects, and
typically the characterization is incomplete. So, here we have Berkeley's
characteristic move: while maintaining that ideas can be adequately known,
he collapses the ontological distinction between an idea and its (intrinsic)
object, and thereby arrives at the position that the (intrinsic) object of an

idea is adequately known.[20]

This theory of ideas fully explains, I think, the argument against abstraction. If an idea has been identified with its own object, then evidently the idea is impossible if its object is, and the properties of the idea coincide exactly with those of its object. The abstract idea of a triangle omits any specific angular size, and so any particular size is "omitted" from the triangle; but this can only mean that the triangle lacks angles of any particular size. Presumably, however, any triangle must have determinate angles, so the object of the abstract idea is a triangle that both does and does not have angles of some particular size. The same reasoning applies to any abstract idea: an abstract idea is its own object and thus has all the properties its object does; but it must also lack some of those properties, because it is supposed to omit some properties of its object(s). Thus all abstract ideas are logically impossible.

Abstract ideas are possible on the view that ideas have objects in virtue of their intrinsic representational content, the features they "include." Berkeley's attack against abstract ideas presupposes an alternative theory of ideas and their intentional objects. Berkeley's ideas do not "include" and "omit" features of their objects. An idea simply is an object of cognition. Moreover, an idea has no fixed representative function; but if an idea does acquire an object, a mind selects some features the idea has as basis of representation.

In his unfortunate account of the abstract idea of a triangle, Locke seems to have a foot in both camps.[21] He clearly does *not* suppose the idea has a content, since on that view it simply includes triangularity and omits any specific ratio of sides. He seems rather to adopt the view that the idea is an object of cognition and represents by features it *has*. His predicament stems from the assumption that *all* features of the idea have an equal role in determining what the mind represents. Unlike Berkeley, he does not base representation on a mind's *selection* of certain features. Thus, he says the idea that represents all triangles cannot be, for example, a scalene triangle, because it represents triangles that are not scalene; but then the idea also must be a scalene triangle in order to represent those triangles that are. A general idea of a triangle is impossible, if the idea is supposed to represent a figure if and only if it has exactly the features the idea has. Berkeley must have thought Locke was only recognizing the truth in adopting the view that an idea represents in virtue of features it has (vs. includes). He must also have thought Locke erred in continuing to think of the general idea of a triangle as *abstract*, as intrinsically (vs. by activity of mind) providing a partial characterization to which all triangles conform.[22] Locke's passage perfectly illustrates Berkeley's contention that ideas are objects which, although they may come to represent, cannot be abstract.

4. Having clarified Berkeley's objection to abstraction, we are in a position to consider the uses to which he puts the impossibility of abstract ideas. He maintains that the false doctrine of abstraction lends support to the opinion that material things exist unperceived, and further he uses the impossibility of abstract ideas as a positive argument for the mind-dependence of sensible things. Unlike many others, I think Berkeley is correct about this pair of connections. I think that, with one possible exception, his arguments are successful *if* he is granted his theory of idea-objects.

One of Berkeley's appeals to the doctrine of abstract ideas occurs in *Principles*, 5, and it is important to remember what he has already accomplished in the earlier sections. In swift order, he has established (as he supposes) the main tenets of immaterialism: sensible objects are collections of sensible qualities; sensible qualities are ideas; ideas cannot exist without a mind (*Principles*, 1, 3 and 4). Then Berkeley turns to the "opinion strangely prevailing among men" that trees, mountains and other sensible things have an existence distinct from a mind that perceives them:

> If we thoroughly examine this tenet it will, perhaps, be found at bottom to depend on the doctrine of *abstract* ideas. For can there be a nicer strain of abstraction than to distinguish the existence of sensible objects from their being perceived, so as to conceive them existing unperceived?

The conception of existence abstracted from perception seems not to fit the paradigms of abstract ideas, in which some *features* of a thing are abstracted from others. However, Berkeley thinks he has shown that sensible qualities are ideas which depend upon perception; for example, the particular color a mountain has depends on how it is perceived. Given that doctrine, a mountain abstracted from the perception of it is taken apart from all its determinate sensible qualities. As Berkeley complains, "For my part, I might as well divide a thing from itself." It seems an unperceived sensible thing *must* have determinate sensible qualities; but given the assumption that sensible qualities depend on perception, it *cannot* have any determinate qualities. The idea of an unperceived mountain is abstract and logically impossible for the same sort of reason the abstract idea of a triangle is.

It is a mistake to think Berkeley offers this as an argument for the conclusion that is is impossible for a mountain, etc., to exist unperceived.[2][3] That conclusion does not appear in the text, nor was that conclusion to be expected from the opening remark that suggests the strangely prevailing opinion is *supported* by the doctrine of abstraction (the argument would "deny the antecedent"); moreover, the mind-dependence of sensible qualities is presupposed in showing that the idea of an unperceived sensible thing is abstract. Then why does Berkeley bother to point out that the idea is abstract? In part, I think, to help explain why the view of the sensible world he claims is false has not always been recognized as such: it came under the protection of abstraction and the traditional model of scientific knowledge. In addition, Berkeley probably wanted to illustrate (vs. establish) the absurdity of unperceived sensible things by showing it to involve the inconsistencies already shown to plague abstract ideas.

Elsewhere, however, Berkeley does appeal to the impossibility of certain abstractions as a premise for arguing that sensible things cannot exist unperceived. In the most familiar case, the strategy is used against those who think figure, motion and other primary qualities exist unperceived although colors, heat and cold are sensations that depend on a mind:

> But I desire any one to reflect, and try whether he can, by any abstractions of thought, conceive the extension and motion of a body without all other sensible qualities. For my own part, I see evidently that it is not in my power to frame an idea of a body extended and moving, but I must withal give it some colour or other sensible quality, which is acknowledged to exist only in the mind. In short, extension, figure, and motion, abstracted from all other qualities are inconceivable. Where, therefore the other sensible qualities are, there must these be also, to wit, in the mind and nowhere else. (*Principles*, 10; also 11-13; also *Dialogues*, 193f.)

This argumentative strategy has been sharply criticized on logical grounds.[24] The problem turns on how Berkeley can support the claim that an idea of body without color or other sensible quality is impossible. Clearly, the fact that Berkeley, you or I try to frame an idea and fail does not prove the point, because future attempts may succeed and other minds may be better at forming ideas than we are. Berkeley needs something better than the "try and fail" test to establish impossibility of an idea. He does sometimes offer the principle that it is possible to form an idea of A without B if and only if it is possible for A to exist without B (assuming here that A and B are sensible qualities or things; e.g., *Principles*, Intro., 10, 5). But critics point out it is circular to appeal to this principle in the context of the present argument, where the impossibility of a certain abstract idea is invoked to prove that certain qualities cannot exist apart. In this context, is Berkeley able convincingly to show that the crucial idea is indeed impossible?

Furthermore, a critic can ask what is supposed to follow if it *is* impossible to conceive, say, a figure without color or other sensible quality. If the idea is merely beyond our conceptual powers, that does not show the object cannot exist. Surely, there may be things inconceivable to us. Nor does the impossibility of the idea show that an expression such as "unperceived figure" is meaningless; no Lockean in the theory of language, Berkeley admits meaningful expressions that are not linked with an idea of what they name (e.g., *Principles*, 2). Did he misjudge the *significance* of the impossibility of the idea?

Understanding Berkeley's attack on abstract ideas helps clear up these difficulties, because it supplies an argument against the possibility of certain putative ideas. Granted Berkeley's theory of ideas, any abstract idea is logically impossible; a description of its features is a formal contradiction. This is directly relevant to Berkeley's anti-materialist claims, because a Berkeleian idea is identical to its object. Berkeley does not rely on the weak "try and fail" test alone to establish that an idea-object is impossible.[25]

In some cases where Berkeley appeals to the impossibility of abstractions to establish the impossibility of mind-independent sensible things, it is quite clear that he can rely on the logical argument against abstract ideas (e.g., *Principles*, 11-13). However, it is not clear to me that it is *completely* successful against the ideas of primary qualities central to the argument quoted above. It is true that a *visible* or *tangible* figure must have some determinate color or tactile "feel"; thus, an abstract idea of visible figure without color would be a figure that has a determinate color and does not have one. But it begs the question against the Cartesian idea of intelligible extension to assume a figure must be visible, tangible or otherwise perceivable. Perhaps Berkeley assumes in *Principles,* 10, that figure, motion and extension are *sensible* qualities and his argument there is not meant to show that the idea of *intelligible* extension is impossible. Or perhaps he thinks he can show there is no such idea by the meager gambit of "try and fail." However, I doubt that he used that weak argument without having in reserve a more compelling objection to the idea's logical consistency. A passage in *Three Dialogues* shows clear appreciation of the logical requirements of the case:

> . . . I do not deny the existence of material substance, merely because I have no notion of it, but because the notion of it is inconsistent. Many things, for ought I know, may exist, whereof neither I nor any other man hath or can have any idea or notion whatsoever. But then these things must be possible, that is, nothing inconsistent must be included in their definition . . . (*Dialogues*, 232.)

Berkeley's general attack on abstract ideas fits perfectly into this lucid picture of his strategy against materialist doctrines.

5. The rejection of abstract ideas enters most fully into Berkeley's metaphysics in what has been dubbed "the master argument."[26] In *Principles,* 22-23, Berkeley boasts he is "content to rest the whole" question whether sensible things can exist without the mind on a single test: whether the reader can *conceive* such a thing to exist unperceived. You cannot do so, he argues, because if you conceive, say, books in a closet with no one standing

by perceiving them, still you *do* conceive the books, and so you do not conceive something that is unconceived (*Principles*, 22-23; also see *Dialogues*,
200).[27] This astounding argument does not mention abstract ideas, but I
think that the rejection of abstraction is behind it.[28] Indeed, I think, the
main thesis of Berkeley's metaphysics is an almost immediate consequence
of his model of conception. What he is rightly "content to rest the whole
upon" is the theory that identifies ideas and their objects and precludes
abstraction.

   It seems Berkeley makes a glaring error by overlooking the difference between what one conceives and the circumstances necessary for conceiving it. Pitcher offers the comparison of someone who denies it is possible
to perform a play about Robinson Crusoe, stranded on a desert island, because of the presence of the audience. Of course, I can see a play "about" a
man (in that he is a character in the plot) who is not thereby seen by me
(as part of the plot); similarly, it seems I can conceive of a woman who is
not (as part of the conception) conceived by me. Berkeley may be right that
I cannot conceive books which are not thereby conceived, but that does not
force me to include their being conceived in my conception. It does not show
that a conception of books that leaves out their being conceived is logically
impossible.[29]

   Berkeley's attack against abstract ideas gives him a devastating
reply to this very natural objection. The "manifest contradiction" of supposing the books you conceive are not conceived, the objection goes, is no
barrier to a conception of books that leaves out their being conceived. But
given Berkeley's theory of ideas, this is a case of illegitimate abstraction.
An idea of books that omits their being conceived is logically impossible; it
would be books that are conceived (by you) and not conceived (being conceived is omitted from the idea-object). Berkeley undoubtedly thought the
most compelling objection to his argument would take this form, and his
general argument against abstract ideas provides the response to it. Of
course, there may be further objections formulated in terms of other alternatives to his theory of idea-objects,[30] but Berkeley's attack on abstraction
addresses the main historical competitor to his view. I am not attempting
here to defend Berkeley's theory of ideas, but I do want to bring out that
the shocking "master argument" is nothing more than a clever, unexpected
application of his theory of cognition. According to that theory, there is no
ontological difference between an idea and its (intrinsic) object and thus an
idea does not "include" features that partially characterize its object.[31]

   The master argument does not show that unconceived books are
logically impossible, but only that it is logically impossible to conceive books
that are unconceived. The former thesis, of course, does not follow from the
latter. Nevertheless, Berkeley proclaims that the argument decides the case
for immaterialism. The point is, I think, that we are unable to secure
something (i.e. something sensible) as an object of thought unless it is an
idea-object and an idea-object cannot exist unconceived on logical grounds.

That is, I think, the characteristic thesis of Berkeley's Idealism. An unconceived, mind-independent sensible object is literally *unthinkable*. Either a mind fails in attempting to think *about* a sensible object or the mind has an idea of the sensible object and, in the latter case, it is logically impossible that the sensible object is unconceived. One cannot think about books that are not conceived. It might seem, nevertheless, that the books you succeed in thinking about might have existed even if they had not been conceived, but the reply is that you cannot *think* so. To think that books exist unconceived, you must form an idea of unconceived books and that idea is impossible on logical grounds.

Can we escape the conditions Berkeley lays down as necessary for cognitive contact with an object in order to examine the logical status of the object itself? Perhaps language offers means of referring to the object that circumvent Berkeley's identification of *idea* and object. In the section of *Principles* immediately following the "master argument," Berkeley responds to this attempt to evade his theory of cognition:

> It is very obvious, upon the least inquiry into our own thoughts, to know whether it be possible for us to understand what is meant by the *absolute existence of sensible objects in themselves*, or *without the mind*. To me it is evident those words mark out either a direct contradiction, or else nothing at all. (*Principles*, 24.)

When using the words "unconceived books," either I succeed in referring to an object (thinking about it) or I do not. In the former case, the conditions are created which make it logically impossible that the books in question are not conceived. In the latter case, the words are not used to "mark out" anything for thought, and I can make no judgement about the logical possibility of unconceived ideas. In sum, language does not secure reference when ideas do not. The argument comes around again to the demands of Berkeley's theory of idea-objects.

Berkeley's main metaphysical doctrine is thus a consequence of his revolutionary theory of ideas. That theory seems to have been motivated, at least in part, by obscurities in the established view that ideas have intrinsic representational contents; however, I have only hinted at Berkeley's place in the development of the theory of ideas and their intentional objects. The point I hope to have made is that his theory of ideas is central to both his attack on abstract ideas and his Idealist metaphysics. Abstract ideas are incompatible with the account of ideas Berkeley adopts. If that theory is granted, it follows that abstract ideas are logically impossible. That vindicates Berkeley's use of the attack on abstraction in some arguments against materialist claims. Moreover, abstract ideas form part of a theory of intentionality that countenances mind-independent objects of cognition. Thus, the attack against abstraction can be turned against the claim to be able to conceive sensible things that are unconceived, as in the "master argument." Berkeley's anti-abstractionist theory of ideas limits things that can be secured as objects of cognition to things that are conceived, and that is the basis of Berkeleian Idealism.[3] [2]

Rutgers University

NOTES

1. See, e.g., Monroe C. Beardsley, 'Berkeley on "Abstract Ideas,"' *Mind*, **52** (1943); E. J. Craig, 'Berkeley's Attack on Abstract Ideas,' *Philosophical Review*, **77** (1968); Jonathan Bennett, *Locke, Berkeley, Hume: Central Themes* (Oxford: Clarendon Press, 1971), ch. 2; George Pitcher, *Berkeley* (London: Routledge and Kegan Paul, 1977), ch. 5; Willis Doney, 'Is Berkeley's a Cartesian Mind?' in Colin Turbayne, ed., *Berkeley: Critical and Interpretive Essays* (Minneapolis: University of Minnesota Press, 1982); J. O. Urmson, *Berkeley* (Oxford: Oxford University Press, 1982), pp. 23-31; Kenneth Winkler, 'Editor's Introduction' to Berkeley, *A Treatise Concerning the Principles of Human Understanding* (New York: Hackett, 1982), pp. xviif.

2. Compare the praise of David Hume, *Treatise*, I.i.7. The reversal in appraisals of the attack on abstract ideas and the doctrine of immaterialism was noted long ago by A. A. Luce, *Berkeley and Malebranche* (Oxford: Clarendon Press, 1934), p. 126.

3. See M. R. Ayers' introduction to George Berkeley, *Philosophical Works* (London: Dent, 1975), p. xx. Also Bennett, sect. 8; I. C. Tipton, *Berkeley* (London: Methuen, 1974), p. 157.

4. See especially Urmson, pp. 15-20; also Bennett, sect. 10.

5. The crucial point is that we have no ideas of spirits and other "notions," but Berkeley clearly holds that there are words that name these things (see, e.g., *Principles*, 2); see especially Luce, pp. 20ff., on the importance of this thesis in the development of Berkeley's philosophy.

6. There was, however, a tradition regarding abstraction or the cognition of universals; see Julius Weinberg, *Abstraction, Relations and*

Induction (Madison: University of Wisconsin Press, 1965), pp. 5-13.

7. Berkeley does not deny that we use and understand linguistic expressions that are incomplete *descriptions*. He opposes partial *conceptions* and denies that one who understands a partial description of a thing has in mind a partial characterization of it (see, e.g., *Dialogues*, 193).

8. Compare Craig, who maintains that the argument made in Locke's passage does not apply to the "singling" or the "common properties" types of abstract ideas. When the argument is correctly understood in terms of Berkeley's theory of idea-objects, however, it is clear that it holds for all abstract ideas. Throughout this paper, I mean by "abstract idea" abstractions of the sort Berkeley rejects, ideas that partially characterize objects that intrinsically (vs. by activity of a mind) conform to them.

9. Two main commentators who seem to me correctly to understand Berkeley's theory of ideas do not discuss its application to the attack on abstraction: Luce (see pp. 126-47 on abstract ideas) and Desirée Park, *Complementary Notions* (The Hague: Martinus Nijhoff, 1972), pp. 36-53 on ideas, and pp. 100ff. on concepts.

10. See, e.g., Bennett, sect. 6; Craig, pp. 435f.

11. One might reconstruct the reasoning this way: once an idea is reified, *all* its features have representational significance. If the abstract idea of a triangle had right angles, then it would be the idea *of* a right-angled triangle. The idea of a triangle (regardless of angle size) must then be a triangle, but cannot have angles of any particular size. I think this is the reasoning that ensnared Locke (see below, p. 000). Notice, however, that *this* argument does not depend on the thesis that the idea of F is F (i.e. if I is the idea of F, then I is F), but rather on the thesis that an idea represents whatever has *all* the features the idea has.

12. See, e.g., Craig, p. 430; Pitcher, pp. 70f; Urmson, pp. 28f; Tipton, pp. 142ff. Contrast Ayers' brief suggestion (p. xx) about *Dialogues*, 193; also Kenneth Winkler, 'Berkeley on Abstract Ideas,' *Archiv für Geschichte der Philosophie*, **65** (1983), pp. 75f.

13. See Bennett on "how not to reify ideas," sects. 5 and 7.

14. The point is made by Bennett, p. 22; Pitcher, p. 70; Tipton, pp. 144f.

15. Also *Des vraies et des fausses idées*, pp. 209-10. Descartes also regards ideas as representations of their objects, comparing ideas to images and pictures, and writing that they "exhibit" or "represent" other things to mind; see, e.g., Haldane and Ross, pp. 159-65, *passim*.

16. See also Park, pp. 43ff.

17. The question here is our having no idea of spirit, as Berkeley sees it, because there is no resemblence between active spirits and passive ideas.

18. See, e.g., Descartes, ed. Haldane and Ross, vol. 1, pp. 162f.

19. Locke held that with attention we can completely know any of our own ideas, but it is not clear Descartes took this view of confused and obscure ideas. See, e.g., *Meditations*, III, on "false ideas"; also compare *Principles*, I, 45, and *Essay*, II.xxix, on confused ideas. Jessop's note to *Principles*, 25, oversimplifies the case.

20. In case a mind has an idea A that represents another idea B, the mind has adequate knowledge of A, but presumably may only know that B has those features in virtue of which it resembles A and is represented by it. Still, B *is* an idea and, Berkeley will claim, it cannot exist without *some* mind for which it is an intrinsic object and by which it is adequately known. All ideas are "in principle" knowable, but all ideas are not knowable to a given finite mind.

21. I do not want to discuss here Locke's settled views on abstraction. Berkeley's understanding of *Essay*, IV.vii.9, seems to me natural. Of course, it should not be taken in isolation from other passages as giving an accurate account of Locke's position, but I doubt that Berkeley takes it that way. I think he thought it recorded a lucid moment in which Locke briefly saw part of the truth about ideas and how ideas represent.

22. Some others have pointed out that an idea theorist can avoid Berkeley's attack either by strictly adhering to a doctrine of representational content or by agreeing with Berkeley that the representative function of an idea depends on the features it has plus the interpretive activity of the mind; see C. C. W. Taylor, 'Berkeley's Theory of Abstract Ideas,' *Philosophical Quarterly*, **28** (1978), sect. 5; Winkler, 'Berkeley on Abstract Ideas,' p. 74. It is a further question whether either of these moves would be fully consistent with Locke's actual doctrines.

23. Compare Doney, p. 279.

24. See Beardsley, sect. 4; Doney, sect. 2.

25. Also see Weinberg, pp. 13-24; but compare Willis Doney, 'Berkeley's Argument against Abstract Ideas,' *Midwest Studies in Philosophy*, **8** (1983).

26. André Gallois, 'Berkeley's Master Argument,' *Philosophical Review*, **83** (1974).

27. The text presents a puzzle, because Berkeley sets out to show that a sensible object cannot exist *unperceived* and ends with the conclusion that a sensible object cannot exist *unconceived*. Some critics have complained that at best the conclusion would not establish what Berkeley wants to show, that the existence of objects depends upon perception. I think, however, that Berkeley's conclusion suffices for his purposes. Berkeley's identification of ideas and their objects implies that an object *exists* if an idea of it exists; as he noted in *PC*, 473, he has a more inclusive conception of existence than the ordinary one. What distinguishes idea-objects that are part of the actual world from other objects that exist, but are only imagined or conceived, is roughly that the actual idea-objects are related to other idea-objects in the steady, general ways dictated by the laws of nature. Thus, we can say that an object is *perceived* if and only if (a) it is an intrinsic (vs. acquired) object for some mind and (b) it is related by appropriate laws of nature to other objects (idea-objects).

   Berkeley asks the reader to conceive books existing without the satisfaction of condition (a). For, if the reader conceives books actually existing, then automatically the object of conception meets (b). The contention that it also meets (a) rests on the point that the reader *conceives* the books. For the reader, the books are acquired (vs. intrinsic) objects of conception; but by Berkeley's account of ideational representation, the acquired object must be an idea-object and thus must be an intrinsic idea-object for some mind. Thus, the fact that the reader *conceives* books actually existing suffices to show that some mind must be conceived to *perceive* them.

28. See also Pitcher, p. 63; Gallois, pp. 64f.; J. J. Thomson, 'G. J. Warnock's *Berkeley*,' *Mind*, **65** (1956).

29. See, e.g., Gallois, pp. 56ff.; Pitcher, pp. 112ff.; Urmson, pp. 45ff. Also, A. N. Prior, 'Berkeley in Logical Form,' *Theoria*, **21** (1955), p. 122.

30. E.g., someone might phrase an objection in terms of some sort of "causal theory" of the intentional objects of cognition. This is not entirely unknown to Berkeley's predecessors: Locke, at least, suggests that ideas caused by secondary qualities refer the mind to the qualities that cause them (although he never writes of these ideas as ideas *of* secondary qualities); see *Essay*, II.xxx and xxxi.

31. Critics have suggested that the "master argument" proves too much, for I cannot conceive books which are not conceived by *me* and conceived *when* I do so; it should follow by Berkeley's reasoning that books cannot exist unless conceived by me, etc. The sting of this objection is removed, I think, by Berkeley's theory of ideational representation. Presumably I cannot now have an idea from the past, or one which belongs to another mind. But suppose I have an idea A which represents such an idea, B. Must the fact that *I conceive* A be part of the basis of the representation of B? I do not see that Berkeley is forced to say it must. B is represented by A in virtue of salient respects that may *not* include being conceived by me at a certain time. This means of thinking about B poses no threat to the thesis that I cannot conceive (even representationally) something that can exist unperceived, for the object represented by one idea must be another which, according to Berkeley's principles, cannot exist without a mind.

32. I want to thank Robert Bolton and Peter Klein for helpful comments on a draft of this paper. I benefitted a great deal from conversation with participants in the Newport Conference, and this is reflected in some revisions made afterwards. I am especially grateful to Robert Sleigh, who commented on the paper, Michael Ayers, George Pappas and Kenneth Winkler.

BIBLIOGRAPHY OF WORKS CITED

Antoine Arnauld and Pierre Nicole, *La Logique ou L'Art de Penser*, repro-
  duced from the 1662 Paris ed. (Hildesheim: Georg Olms,
  1970).

Antoine Arnauld, *Des vraies et des fausses idées*, in *Oeuvres de Messieur
  Antoine Arnauld*, vol. 38 (Paris, 1683), pp. 177-365.

John Locke, *An Essay Concerning Human Understanding*, ed. P. H. Nidditch (Oxford: Clarendon Press, 1975).

The Philosophical Works of Descartes, trans. Elizabeth S. Haldane and
  G. R. T. Ross, 2 vols. (Cambridge: Cambridge University
  Press, 1970).

The Works of George Berkeley Bishop of Cloyne, ed. A. A. Luce and T. E.
  Jessop, 9 vols. (Edinburgh: Thomas Nelson, 1948-57).

PART THREE

THOUGHT AND REFERENCE:
II. IMAGINATION AND ARCHETYPES

Ian Tipton

BERKELEY'S IMAGINATION

In *Principles*, 22-3, and in a parallel passage in the *Dialogues*,[1] Berkeley presents an argument that is important in his eyes because he thinks, or appears to think, that it is sufficient to establish his immaterialism. He is, he says, "content to put the whole" upon the issue of whether his reader can "conceive it possible for one extended moveable substance, or in general, for any one idea or any thing like an idea, to exist otherwise than in a mind perceiving it." The reader, or Hylas in the *Dialogues*, has only to look into his own thoughts to find the answer. To be sure, one can frame the idea of books or trees without framing the idea of any onlooker, but that does not do the trick. ". . . it only shows you have the power of imagining or forming ideas in your mind; but it doth not shew that you can conceive it possible, the objects of your thought may exist without the mind: to make out this, it is necessary that you conceive them existing unconceived or unthought of, which is a manifest repugnancy."

Most commentators, including me, have not been impressed, though some have been more sympathetic than I was in my book, not necessarily arguing that what Berkeley says should convince us, but that it is certainly less silly than is sometimes suggested, or, alternatively, that if he does not establish what he thinks he does, he has at least got on to something of interest.[2] The debate continues, and it raises complex issues. It emerges that it is far from clear what the argument *is*.[3] It therefore remains unclear how it should be answered. In this paper I want to examine a number of the approaches to it, and I hope we shall learn something on the way. I do not, however, expect to come up with much that is startlingly original. Indeed I would like to think of this paper as defending what some will take to be an orthodox interpretation. If I dwell on commentators with whom I disagree, this is in part to show that the orthodox needs a defence. That is what I shall be doing in my first three sections.

I

There is, first of all, what I think of as the brusque approach, represented by J. O. Urmson who quotes a large chunk of *Principles* 23, but devotes only eight lines to dismissing the argument as "surely fallacious."[4] For him, all Berkeley is entitled to is the proposition that "it is not possible that

E. Sosa (ed.), Essays on the Philosophy of George Berkeley, 85–102.

a body be conceived of and at the same time both exist and not be conceived of," a proposition that is of no more significance than a claim that I cannot kick a chair that is at the same time unkicked. It does nothing to support the contention that the concept of an unperceived object is logically deficient. Arthur Prior and J. L. Mackie have argued at greater length, bringing formal logic to their aid,[5] but their conclusion is similar. Putting it simply, Berkeley's mistake will be comparable to that of supposing that because, quite obviously and uncontroversially, I cannot answer the challenge to "think of a number" without thinking of a number (the number 12 perhaps) that is, at that moment, thought of by me, I cannot make coherent sense of the notion of a number that is not thought of by me. Indeed, this parallel points to what both Mackie and Prior see as a further weakness in Berkeley's argument. Not only does it prove too little – that I cannot think of a tree without thinking of it, rather than that I cannot conceive that a tree might be unthought of – it also "proves" too much. As Mackie puts it (and he is rather more impressive here than Prior): "Since the choice of *material* things, trees and houses, as what Hylas tries to conceive existing unconceived plays no special part in the argument, it would, if sound, show equally that no one can coherently postulate the independent existence, out of his own mind, of other human minds or of God."[6]

I called this the brusque approach, but not to be insulting. I concede that the line of thought Urmson, Prior and Mackie attack can be abstracted from what Berkeley actually says, and would argue only that there must be more to be said if we are to understand the relevant passages and, in particular, how it is that Berkeley can think that his argument supports the claim that the *esse* of sensible things is *percipi* rather than *concepi*.[7] This will presumably involve attending to another feature of Berkeley's argument, which stands out in the *Principles* but is there in the *Dialogues* too, this being the suggestion that getting at the truth requires "looking into your own thoughts" and considering what goes on there when you think of trees or other sensible objects: an exercise of introspection that would hardly be necessary to come up with the truism that I must conceive what I conceive. The relevant feature stands out in the *Principles* where it occurs in Berkeley's own presentation of his argument, while in the *Dialogues* it is presented almost as an afterthought, and by Hylas rather than Philonous. But it needn't worry us that it is the *materialist* who makes the crucial move. At this point Hylas is yielding, and in fact giving Philonous just what he needs. Indeed it is interesting that while Philonous makes no mention of *perceiving* during the relevant exchanges, consistently referring to *conceiving* (or to what is "in the mind"), it is Hylas who brings us back to *esse/percipi*. He cannot, he allows "conceive a tree as existing unperceived or unthought of."[8]

Too often, it seems to me, critics of Berkeley's argument ignore this aspect and, what is crucial, the fact that readers of the *Principles* at least have been alerted to the importance of drawing "the curtain of words" as an aid to reaching truth.[9] As a result, they sometimes give the impression of talking *past* Berkeley, who certainly doesn't accept that contradictions and repugnancies are necessarily discoverable at the level of sentences or linguistic utterance. The point isn't new of course: not long before Prior's paper was published in 1955, W. H. Hay had stressed that "if our purpose were to refute Berkeley . . . we should have to revise his account of language, and not merely ignore it,"[10] and his critical eye was on G. Dawes Hicks's examination of the argument over twenty years earlier. But the point remains important. Nor is there really any excuse for forgetting the strictures Berkeley issued towards the end of his introduction. There he had urged that we should contemplate "bare ideas." But in the first edition version of *Principles*, 24, he issued a reminder. "Cou'd men but forbear to amuse themselves with words, we shou'd I believe, soon come to an agreement in this point."

II

I'd like to think that a natural move here would be towards an approach that did make a clear link with the Introduction to the *Principles* and the attack on abstraction and which, frankly, took a critical line on that basis. But what I in fact want to do now is to look at a highly original interpretation proposed by Désirée Park[11] that conflicts with the sort of approach I would support just as much as it does with that of Urmson, in that while the Urmson approach is abstemious, Park allows Berkeley considerable resources that would in fact allow for a defence of his argument against most of the objections that have been made to it. In my third section I shall try to make a link between her interpretation and what Michael Ayers says about Berkeley's argument in his introduction to the Everyman edition of Berkeley's works.

    A feature of the Park approach is her insistence that Berkeley's argument should be taken in its context, an insistence that leads her to lay great stress on the fact that what Berkeley is trying to show is that we cannot conceive any particular *sensible* thing existing unperceived. Now an obvious consequence of this is that though in the *Dialogues* (and Park concentrates on the *Dialogues* version) Philonous argues that it is a contradiction to talk of conceiving "a thing" which is unconceived, thus apparently inviting the Prior-Mackie observation that this would apply to minds as well, it must be assumed that Berkeley still has sensible things in view. He might as well have had Philonous point out that it is "a contradiction to talk of conceiving a *sensible* thing which is unconceived"; and he might actually have resisted an interpretation that made this simply a consequence of a more general claim about conceiving "things." It might be something about sensible things that matters, and the relevant consideration might not apply to minds.

This, Park holds, is in fact the case. She believes that if Berkeley did hold that his crucial claim applied to sensible things, he would not accept that the *same* claim could be applied to minds, this on the ground that, for him, minds and ideas have nothing in common apart from the name "thing."[1] [2] But she also takes it that Berkeley did have a special reason for applying it to sensible things, for she holds that Berkeley is working with the background assumption that sensible things are *ideas* "of the peculiarly Berkeleian sort." Thus:

> . . . an idea for Berkeley must conform to the single condition which he states; that is, any idea must be perceived. This means at least that it is imagible. Indeed a test for a putative Berkeleian idea is whether it can be captured as a mental picture, of whichever sense one pleases. It may be added that each idea is wholly present, momentary and therefore is strictly unrepeatable.

This must not be forgotten when we consider the passage in the *Dialogues*. So, given the context – that is, given that the discussion concerns *sensible* things; that sensible things are *ideas* "of the peculiarly Berkeleian sort"; and indeed that "by definition" no Berkeleian idea can exist unperceived – it is hardly surprising if Philonous takes it for granted that we cannot conceive a sensible thing existing "otherwise than in a mind."

That at least is Park's view, and though I can't accept it I should perhaps point out that it might seem to have certain advantages. For example, and if I understand it correctly, the interpretation would give Berkeley an easy answer to one objection that I and others have levelled at him in the past, this being the objection that, even when restricted to sensible things, his line of argument must be too strong in that it would lead to the conclusion that no individual can coherently suppose that any object can exist that *he* does not perceive. Berkeley's answer would be this. Hylas supposes that he can imagine an unperceived tree. That is, he can frame an image of a tree and need include no perceiver in his mental picture. And, on this basis, he concludes that an unperceived tree must be a possibility. But it is Hylas who has made the mistake. All he has offered is an idea, in this case an image, that he himself perceives. This has no tendency to show that a sensible tree can exist unperceived, for on Berkeley's general theory any sensible tree will remain a collection of mind-dependent ideas. There is no solipsism. All Hylas has to recognize is that any mental picture anyone forms is dependent on the mind of whoever it is that forms it, while any sensed idea remains dependent on some mind, though of course not necessarily on *his* mind.

Rather similarly, the Park interpretation would enable Berkeley to answer the stock objection that he is guilty of confusing a thought-vehicle with the object of thought,[1] [3] because now (and again if I have got it right) if anyone is guilty of that confusion it will be Hylas. Not for one second need Berkeley relax a firm grip on the distinction between the mind-dependent ideas that are constitutive of physical reality and those feebler ideas we can form when exercising our imaginations. The thought will merely be that though we can of course form the image of a tree without a perceiver, this carries no implication that trees can exist unperceived. Even the image is perceived, by the imaginer, while for any sensible object, *esse* is *percipi*. That is the background assumption.

It seems to me, however, that the Park approach is not acceptable, and this for two different but connected reasons. The first, and perhaps this isn't an objection in itself, is that it downgrades the importance of the argument by making it do much less work than is normally supposed. Thus there is no doubt that philosophers such as Prior, Mackie and Bernard Williams,[14] who would not consider themselves Berkeley scholars, have given the argument the attention they have because, along with most scholars, they have taken it that Berkeley believes himself to be justifying, not presupposing, the *esse/percipi* thesis. And if that isn't an objection in itself, it seems to become one when joined with the second point which is that it is Berkeley himself who leads us to expect a lot from this argument. Thus it is Philonous who introduces the *Dialogues* passage by saying that Hylas can "pass by all that hath been hitherto said, and reckon it for nothing, if you will have it so," claiming that he will "put the whole" on what follows. And of course there is a similar grand claim in the *Principles*. Commentators have taken the invitations in both works seriously, and I think that they are right to do so.

The objection is a serious one, even if it is not decisive. For even if it is countered that we may not be expected to pass by literally *all* that has been said but only what has been said on some particular point or issue, Berkeley's wording must mean that *some* things he would take himself to have established can be disregarded, and that in turn must place *some* limit on what Park can appeal to and accuse others of overlooking. Thus, in general, it won't do to *assume* that acceptance of *p* must be presupposed if *p* has already been argued for or asserted,[15] given that we are to pass by some things and that *p* may be one of those things. And, to turn to a concrete case, it won't do to object to Bernard Williams's reading of the *Dialogues* passage that it has been "conceded some pages before . . . that anything which Hylas can see . . . must be an idea," given that Philonous is responding to Hylas's failure to take earlier points on board. Philonous's response is, admittedly, to allude to the arguments Hylas has forgotten or misinterpreted, but then he sets them aside. We can "pass by" that material.

Unfortunately Park doesn't tell us what she thinks Hylas is being allowed to pass by,[16] and I do think that that is a serious weakness in her paper. But I think that more must be involved than she can recognize, and certainly that her charge against Bernard Williams is not fair. To see this, we should look at the context.

When the *Dialogues* open, Hylas assumes that sensible qualities exist "without the mind," and Philonous sets out to convince him that they are mind-dependent. He does this by running through what are in fact the secondary qualities, arguing that colors, tastes and so on, as Hylas perceives them, are not external to the mind. Then, when Hylas draws a distinction between primary and secondary qualities, Philonous claims that similar arguments apply to the supposed primary qualities. Indeed, there is another point. The ideas of extension and motion cannot be separated off from other sensible qualities, even in thought.[17] Consequently, "where the one exist, there necessarily the other exist likewise." On p. 194 (in the standard edition) Hylas concedes that "all sensible qualities are alike to be denied existence without the mind," and this means, though Berkeley doesn't actually use the word here – that they are mind-dependent *ideas*. Given that this concession comes six pages before the argument we are concerned with, it might *seem* that Berkeley can take it for granted at the later stage. It must be this that Park thinks Williams has overlooked.[18]

What Park has herself overlooked, however, is the fact that though Hylas does make the concession, it is followed by a series of exchanges in which he attempts to retrieve the situation, a quite proper procedure given that his acceptance of the earlier arguments was a qualified one. Thus when he accepted that extension was ideal, he reserved "a right to retract my opinion, in case I shall hereafter discover any false step in my progress to it." And this qualification is generalized on p. 194:

> You need say no more on this head. I am free to own, if there be no secret error or oversight in our proceedings hitherto, that all sensible qualities are alike to be denied existence without the mind. But my fear is, that I have been too liberal in my former concessions, or overlooked some fallacy or other. In short, I did not take time to think.

What follows is a series of attempts by Hylas to locate some "error or oversight" and show that, after all, sensible qualities are *not* Berkeleian ideas. Whatever he comes up with, Philonous cannot answer him by appealing to the concession that Hylas is now attempting to withdraw.

The argument we are concerned with has to be set in this context. At the bottom of p. 194 Hylas attempts to locate "one great oversight" in their failure to distinguish the *object* of perception from the mind-dependent *act* of perception; and then on p. 197 he claims that when he thinks of sensible things as modes or qualities, "I find it necessary to suppose a material *substratum*, without which they cannot be conceived to exist." Philonous responds by collapsing the distinction between the perceiving and the object, and by showing that we have no adequate conception of a "support" of qualities. And in each case Hylas concedes. But he is still looking for "some fallacy or other" in the earlier reasoning. Our passage follows.

Locating what he now takes to be "the ground of all our mistakes," what Hylas points to is their procedure of running through the qualities individually, for, as he now sees it, this leads only to the conclusion that "each quality cannot singly subsist without the mind." It remains possible that "blended together" they can. Viewed in that way we need not consider them Berkeleian ideas. That is the move, and it exasperates Philonous who reminds Hylas that the earlier arguments were not designed to show that qualities cannot exist singly without the mind, "but that they were not *at all* without the mind."[19] But it is at this point that Philonous makes his generous gesture. Hylas can "pass by all that hath been hitherto said, and reckon it for nothing, if you will have it so." To say the least, it is difficult to avoid the conclusion that this means just what it seems to mean. Hylas is being allowed to withdraw his earlier concession, even though he has found no ground for doing so. It can play no part in what follows.

III

Park attempts to defend Berkeley by allowing him very generous resources. On the face of it, Michael Ayers's treatment of the argument, which is offered within the context of a more general treatment of Berkeley's strategy, looks very different,[20] though as already noted, I think the two approaches can be linked. I should state at the outset, though, that, unlike Park, Ayers concentrates on the *Principles* version.

What Ayers does is to focus attention on what is undoubtedly Berkeley's main *target* in the *Principles*, this being the notion of a physical reality conceived in "a *sense-independent* way"; and Ayers certainly thinks that if we consider what he writes in *Principles*, 23, in that light we can see that what he is after is the not implausible point that "to think and talk of the table in an unoccupied room is still to think and talk of the potential perception of it, of how it would look, feel and so on." Again:

> if . . . I "imagine trees . . . in a park or books existing in a closet, and nobody by to perceive them" [a quotation from *Principles*, 23, of course], I merely imagine how it would be to perceive them myself. I do not conceive of Locke's "particular constitution which everything has within itself, without any relation to anything without it."

"The strength of this argument," Ayers observes, "should be obvious to anyone who has felt the temptations of phenomenalism." Ayers concedes that we should not applaud too loudly and that the argument as Berkeley actually presents it has a feature that has given it "an unjust notoriety." But this feature, to which I shall return, is said to be "inessential" to the basic point. It "does not affect the main contention that neither imagining a tree nor anything else can count as conceiving of a tree 'as it is in itself.'" Ayers's treatment of the argument is brief, and it is perhaps possible that I have misunderstood him. But I think my summary of his position is fair.

If it is, Ayers's interpretation will have the obvious merit that it focuses attention on what nobody could doubt is Berkeley's main target in the *Principles:* the broadly Lockean notion that our senses do not reveal things as they are in themselves, and indeed (as Berkeley interprets the view) that they do not really acquaint us with the "real" things at all. Against that, Berkeley can plausibly claim that he cannot conceive a tree that is not perceivable. The best I can do in thinking of unperceived objects is to "imagine how it would be to perceive them myself," and this means that I must, after all, think of them as perceivable, and as having the familiar qualities that I find in them when I do actually perceive them. This would give us something like what is often labelled "common-sense realism." Add the assumption that to imagine how a tree would look to me is to imagine a possible sensation and we are coming round to phenomenalism. It all begins to look rather impressive.

But it also begins to look rather disappointing. As in the case of the Park approach, it will turn out that the argument is doing less work than is commonly supposed. Helping ourselves to a tag introduced by A. A. Luce,[21] it seems that the conclusion we might be led to is that *esse* is *percipi aut posse percipi*, not *esse* is *percipi*. I am reminded of the passage in the *Third Dialogue* where Philonous appeals to "the common sense of the world" for the truth of his notion, drawing attention to the view that real things are perceivable, only to be met with the understandable protest that there is a gap between "being perceivable" and "being actually perceived."[22] At that stage Philonous is able to help himself to the premise that nothing is perceivable but a mind-dependent idea, and it would seem to be that premise that Berkeley will need on the Ayers interpretation of *Principles*, 23, given, that is, that Berkeley is to be seen as offering clinching support for idealism, and not just as opposing what is after all, just one possible alternative to it. But if that is correct, Ayers's position will be quite close to that of Park, in that the premise Berkeley will require will be the one that Park gives him as an assumption. Perhaps it is significant, then, that Ayers and Park react to more orthodox critics in much the same way. As already noted, Ayers refers to an "inessential" feature that has given Berkeley's argument "unjust notoriety." And Park strikes a similar note. She refers to a "notorious" argument that is, she claims, "not Berkeley's argument."

So far as Ayers is concerned, however, I do have to be a little more conciliatory than I was in the case of Park, and in particular to concede that it is easier to defend this sort of interpretation with our eyes on the *Principles* version, for the immediate context is different and, in general, Berkeley is readier to help himself to assumptions he shares with his philosopher opponents, including the assumption that we perceive only ideas. It follows that he *could* be resting on that assumption in *Principles*, 23, and that his demonstration of his doctrine "in a line or two" does depend upon it.

If I am not convinced, this is partly because the argument does recur in the *Dialogues*, and, for reasons already given, I find it impossible to accept this sort of interpretation of the later occurrence, but also because the feature of the argument that Ayers takes to be "inessential" to it does seem to me to be so well calculated to support the strong conclusion that Berkeley appears to want. In Ayers's words, that feature is found in the assumption that "imagining or conceiving of a sensible quality [is] *perceiving* a recalled idea or image." It is perhaps worth quoting Berkeley's own words:

> When we do our utmost to conceive the existence of external bodies, we are all the while only contemplating our own ideas. But the mind taking no notice of itself, is deluded to think it can and doth conceive bodies existing unthought of or without the mind; though at the same time they are apprehended by or exist in it self. A little attention will discover to any one the truth and evidence of what is here said, and make it unnecessary to insist on any other proofs against the existence of material substance.

The context makes it quite clear that, when the object concerned is not present to my senses, the idea will be one I frame and, as Ayers says, an image. But that notion is, surely, highly significant, and it is difficult to believe that it is idling. For if Berkeley does take the notion seriously he will have an argument that will lead him directly to *esse/percipi*. Putting it simply, if to conceive of a sensible quality (or a tree) is to contemplate or perceive an image I frame, then the only object involved will be mental. That should be uncontroversial. After all, as Berkeley noted in *Principles*, 3, that "ideas formed by the imagination" do not exist without the mind, "is what every body will allow."

IV

Now of course there is nothing original in the suggestion that this or something very like it is what lies behind the argument we are considering, and Pitcher for example is one commentator who seems to interpret Berkeley in this way, being as a result very critical of him for confusing a thought-vehicle (or image) with the object of thought (or what is imagined).[2][3] What Pitcher does not do is to make any attempt to link the disastrous move to its wider historical context, or to Berkeley's strictures in the Introduction to the *Principles*. In broadest outline, there are two things we need to bear in mind. The first is that Berkeley was strongly influenced by the notion that, to avoid talking nonsense, we should be prepared to "draw the curtain of words" and attend to the ideas we find in our minds. And the second is that he was highly critical of others for not following their own advice. Berkeley's rigor in this area may lead to a strange result, but it is hardly fair to see it as a quirky aberration in his thought. We are on to something central.

Approaching Berkeley in this spirit we get one immediate result, in that we can well understand his assumption that to determine the coherence of the generalized notion of an unperceived object we should be prepared to consider any one object chosen at random – a tree perhaps – and consider whether we can conceive *it* existing unperceived. That challenge does not seem grossly unfair in itself; but it is backed up by the assumption that to think in general terms is not to have an abstract idea in one's mind, but rather a determinate idea which can represent many particulars. Nor is it surprising that when Berkeley sets the word "tree" aside, all he finds is an image. A test on any first-year student, or on oneself, is likely to produce the same result. And this gets us very quickly to the argument we are concerned with. Look at a tree. Then close your eyes and try supposing that it is unperceived. That involves attending to what is in your mind: the image. Given that you are now allowed to entertain thoughts about *that* object, there is one thought that you cannot coherently entertain, this being the thought that it is not mind-dependent. It is, after all, your image.

If this line of thought seems just too absurd, that is not the way it looks to Ian Hacking, one writer who is commendably sensitive to the historical context. As he notes:

> Descartes' *Rules for the Direction of the Mind* are famous because of their author, but are entirely typical of the manuals in circulation at the time. The gist of the advice is that to avoid error we must train ourselves to "scrutinize" our ideas "with steadfast mental gaze." Stop speaking and start looking, looking inside yourself. What is one to look *at*? The answer is given by that code word "idea."[24]

In this tradition, ideas need not be images, but they are, it seems, mental. Indeed, to suppose that one can cast the eye of thought on something that is not mental, that is not, as Hacking puts it, "an object of thought," can easily appear nonsense. That is the notion that Berkeley needs, so it is significant that Hacking's sensitivity to the context goes along with the uncommon judgment that Berkeley's argument is "very impressive." As he puts it: "Within the conceptual scheme in which it is formulated, the steps seem to me cogent (not incontestable, of course, but cogent)."[25] And one can accept this without suggesting that Pitcher and other less sympathetic commentators have got the story straightforwardly wrong. We do not share the relevant conceptual scheme; nor should we. And the position it leads to *is* flawed. Hacking shows *how* Berkeley got where he did. It does not follow that we should take Berkeley's route.

V

It might seem that this paper could end there, and so it could were it not that there is a residual puzzle, a puzzle I can introduce by returning briefly to Ayers, who does note in passing that the feature of Berkeley's argument that he sees as "inessential" can also be seen as "a natural consequence of its historical context." This hints at the Hacking approach, though it only hints at it, both because Hacking regards the feature as crucial, and because, in elaborating, Ayers refers only to Locke, noting that "[Berkeley's] move may be open to objection, in that Locke . . . would not treat imagining a tree as perceiving a tree but as perceiving an idea *of* a tree" (my emphasis).[26] This perhaps suggests that Berkeley may have been a little bit careless, but it in fact raises a real difficulty facing the believer in what Hacking describes as "purely mental discourse": the issue of the "aboutness" of thought.[27] The problem may not appear pressing to a philosopher who is either very vague about "ideas," or who supposes that in some sophisticated fashion he can build "aboutness" into them,[28] but I think that it is pressing for Berkeley.

To bring this out it will perhaps help if we start by taking our cue from Hacking and consider the historical context. For if we start from the received notion that to think of X is to have an idea in one's mind, and then ask ourselves how philosophers in this period could live with that notion, I think the answer that emerges, or at least part of the answer, is that they were often very vague about what an idea *is*. And it does seem that the basic notion often appeared truistic precisely because to say that "A has the idea of X" was to say little more than that A is thinking *of* X (or even that he has the capacity to think of X). Significantly, this position tended not to go along with an "imagist" view of ideas. For Berkeley, however, an idea formed by the mind is always an image, and this has important consequences. Let me illustrate.

It can appear to be a truism that to think of God is to have in one's mind the idea of God. Clearly that seemed evident to Descartes, but then (as he in fact observed to Hobbes)[29] he did not hold that an idea is (at least necessarily) an image. Hobbes, on the other hand, denied that we can have an idea of God, but then, he was an imagist. Berkeley denied it too, for the same reason, but for him this went along with a revision of the received view that to think of X is to have an idea of X. At best this was true of *sensible* things, things that can be pictured. For *other* things, Berkeley has to tell a different story. And of course he does. As it happens the point is obscured from Hacking, because he makes the unfortunate mistake of supposing that Berkeley "acknowledges plenty of ideas of which we can form no images, God and the will, for example,"[30] but it remains important. For this is not the only area where Berkeley's insistence that any idea we frame must be an image *has to* lead to a revision of received notions about thought.[31]

With that in mind, we can turn our attention away from the received notion that to think of X (whatever X may be) *is* to have an idea of X to the more restricted notion that to think of a *sensible* thing is to perceive an image, for it seems to me, not only that this is an unsatisfactory notion, but that this should have been obvious to Berkeley himself. It should have been obvious precisely because, for wholly understandable reasons, Berkeley is determined to distinguish between the ideas *we* frame (ideas of the imagination) and those sensed ideas, imprinted from without, which he claims constitute a genuine, though still ideal, "real" world. I suggested earlier that one apparent merit of the Park approach as I understood it was that it would allow Berkeley to retain a firm grip on this distinction. On what I would take to be the correct interpretation, that firm grip is lost. On this interpretation Berkeley does confuse an image and the "real" thing, when he, above all, should not.

In this connection it may help if I draw attention to one entry in the *Commentaries* which suggests that Berkeley was quite capable of avoiding the confusion. For in entry 657a he writes:

> properly speaking Idea is the picture of the Imagination's making this is ye likeness of & refer'd to the real Idea or (if you will) thing.

I think, incidentally, that Park mishandles this in her *Complementary Notions* when she sees it (together with the corresponding recto entry) as saying that "perceived ideas are simple and depend for their existence and meaning on being related by spirits or minds to something *unlike* themselves" (my emphasis);[32] but she is quite right to see Berkeley as recognizing that "so-called 'real' ideas or 'things' are distinguishable from the ideas or pictures referred to them." But this only highlights *my* problem. For the entry suggests that Berkeley was indeed quite capable of seeing that thinking of the sun, say, must involve *more* than attending to an image, and that the "picture" (or thought-vehicle) must, as he puts it, be "refer'd to the real Idea," which will be what I am thinking *about*. But of course this is not a problem *for Park*. It is the rest of us who should be puzzled. For it is the more orthodox commentators who have it that Berkeley does confuse the image with the object of thought; and even Ayers has him holding that conceiving something *is* perceiving "a recalled idea or image no different from an idea of sense except in its immediate origin, context and vivacity." Against this, it might be argued that the philosopher who penned *PC*, 657a, could never have made *that* mistake.

VI

I see the position differently. For one thing it seems to me that it is very difficult to read *Principles*, 23, without seeing Berkeley as confusing the image with the object of thought;[33] and, for another, it could hardly be argued that Berkeley did come round to a clear and consistent view on the relevant relationship. I find *Principles*, 36, particularly interesting in this connection. For it seems very significant that here, where Berkeley is explicitly addressing himself to the *distinction between* those "faint, weak, and unsteady" ideas we form and those ideas which "are not fictions of the mind perceiving them" but which do constitute "real" beings, he also claims that "the sun that I see by day is the real sun, and that which I imagine by night is the *idea of* the former" (my emphasis). And what is significant, of course, is the fact that it is supposed here that the sun which I imagine by night is a "faint, weak, and unsteady" image which I form, and that, on the face of it, Berkeley is explicitly committing himself to the view that I cannot imagine "the real sun" at all. Now I am sure that this is a slip, in the sense that Berkeley would not want to commit himself to the view that the very thing that is sensible is not also imaginable, but it is not an unimportant slip. It reveals that Berkeley *is* confused, and for a quite understandable reason. That is, he is more or less taking it for granted (in the spirit of the "received" view) that a person who has the idea of the sun in his mind is imagining – thinking about – *the sun;* but this is difficult to reconcile with the independently tempting view that the only object available is a "picture." And if *Principles*, 36, provides clear evidence that Berkeley had not achieved a satisfactory reconciliation, the "notorious" argument we have been considering is, it seems, simply a dramatic consequence of that failure. For he faces a dilemma. In short, it is only if the object I imagine is distinct from any image I frame that Berkeley can hold that I am imagining "the sun that I see by day" (or trees); but it is only if the object is the image – "the sun . . . which I imagine by night" – that the object is obviously mind-dependent. In fact, it seems Berkeley wants both.

Clearly this is a most unsatisfactory position to leave Berkeley in, but I suspect that it may be where we have to leave him if our interpretation is not to go wildly awry. I concede, however, that it would be a service to Berkeley scholarship, and to Berkeley, if someone could show that his apparent confusion is apparent only, and that, underlying even *Principles*, 23, there is some clear grasp of what the object of the imagination *is*. But I am not optimistic. I don't believe that Berkeley has a clear and consistent view even on the nature and status of ideas *of sense;*[34] and it will hardly be surprising if his attitude to the ideas of the imagination was equally Janus-faced. And, again, the problem of the "aboutness" of thought has been perennially troublesome. It will hardly be surprising if Berkeley was unsound on it. Finally, it will not be surprising if Berkeley's mishandling of the issue led to one argument that continues to puzzle us.

University College of Wales, Aberystwyth

NOTES

1. *Works*, ii. 200.

2. Christopher Peacocke, for example, opens his 'Imagination, Experience, and Possibility: A Berkeleian View Defended' (in John Foster and Howard Robinson, ed., *Essays on Berkeley*, Oxford University Press, 1985) by observing: "Bishop Berkeley had a gift for making clear, crisp statements of doctrines that are also unbelievable. His doctrine that it is impossible to imagine an unperceived tree is often taken as a prime example of this gift. I will argue here that, on the contrary, there is an important sense in which the doctrine is true." It is significant, however, that Peacocke offers his own argument for the conclusion, and makes it quite clear that he does not accept Berkeley's. And Peacocke supports Berkeley's doctrine only in so far as it concerns the imagination. He does not agree that we cannot conceive of an unperceived tree.

3. As just noted, Peacocke is concerned to support a Berkeleian view, not the Berkeleian argument, which he deals with only in a footnote. That footnote is interesting, however, in that it confirms that there is some haziness over what Berkeley is up to. Thus: "Mackie . . . regards Berkeley as having misused a self-refutation argument . . . There is some support for Mackie's reading . . . But it may be that an even cruder, and totally indefensible, argument was influencing Berkeley . . ." Textual support is given for *both* readings.

4. J. O. Urmson, *Berkeley* (Oxford University Press, 1982), p. 45.

5. Arthur Prior, 'Berkeley in Logical Form', *Theoria* **21** (1955); and J. L. Mackie, *Problems from Locke* (Oxford University Press, 1976), pp. 52-54.

6. What Mackie brings out rather more clearly than Prior is the ten-

dency towards solipsism. Hence his observation that the line of argument should show that nobody can conceive of anything at all existing "out of his own mind." Prior is content to point out that the argument would make *everything*, including minds, dependent on thought. The trouble is that, put in *that* way, Berkeley might find the supposedly absurd conclusion broadly acceptable.

7. It has even been thought that Berkeley changes tack in *Principles*, 23. J. O. Wisdom takes it that the crucial argument is contained in the thirteen words he quotes – "you conceive them existing unconceived or unthought of, which is a manifest repugnancy" – and dismisses the point as "entirely specious and not worth a moment's academic discussion." He does however observe that "Berkeley has shifted his ground, and replaced his doctrine of *Esse percipi* by *Esse concepi.*" (J. O. Wisdom, *The Unconscious Origin of Berkeley's Philosophy*, The Hogarth Press, 1953, pp. 8-9.) Prior, Mackie and Urmson don't actually make that criticism, but their reading of Berkeley would seem to justify it.

8. It could I suppose be argued that the wording here might allow the suggestion to be that we can only conceive an object as existing when perceived or, if not perceived, then thought of. That reading would at any rate be implausible, but a comparison with *Principles*, 22-23, virtually rules it out.

9. *Principles*, Introduction, sects. 21-25.

10. W. H. Hay, 'Berkeley's Argument from Nominalism,' *Revue internationale de philosophie*, **VII** (1953): p. 25.

11. Désirée Park, 'Prior and Williams on Berkeley,' *Philosophy*, **56** (1981).

12. The reference is to *Principles*, 89.

13. See for example George Pitcher, *Berkeley* (Routledge and Kegan Paul, 1977), pp. 113-5; my *Berkeley: The Philosophy of Immaterialism* (Methuen, 1974), pp. 165-66; and (though not in his discussion of the argument we are concerned with) Urmson's *Berkeley*, pp. 30-31.

14. Bernard Williams, 'Imagination and the Self,' a British Academy lecture reprinted in his *Problems of the Self* (Cambridge University Press, 1973).

15.   It does strike me as odd both that Park nowhere hints at *any* limit to what can be appealed to, and that she refers so readily to what Berkeley has *stated* in the *Dialogues*, and indeed elsewhere. For example: ". . . in Berkeley's account there are no grounds for supposing that a thing which one does not perceive is like a thing which one does perceive. In fact he expressly states that they must be different." The reference she gives here is to *Principles*, 8, and entries in the *Commentaries*.

16.   It can't be much. In evaluating Berkeley's argument we are to bear in mind that: "It is simply inconsistent to speak of a Berkeleian idea as if it were absent for the moment, but none the less somehow poised in the wings of future quietly awaiting its cue. In short, it cannot be insisted on too much that an absent idea is not an idea *in absentia*, but no idea whatever." Even more clearly, Park tells us that in order to give force to his argument: "[Berkeley] needs to bring into play some of his claims about the relations between minds and ideas . . . Not least among these relations is the rule [!] that *esse* is *percipi*, with its full complement of implications."

17.   The thought-experiment Hylas is challenged to perform here is of course comparable to the one that is central to the argument we are concerned with.

18.   Park does in fact refer to p. 194, though she quotes only Philonous's statement that: ". . . thus much seems manifest, that sensible things are only to be perceived by sense, or represented by the imagination" (see her notes 7 and 21). I am far from clear that conceding *this* would amount to conceding that any sensible thing is "an *idea* of the peculiarly Berkeleian sort." .

19.   This point is made in relation to the supposed *secondary* qualities in particular. Philonous notes that in discussing figure and motion it was indeed argued that these are mind-dependent because "it was impossible even in thought to separate them from all secondary qualities, so as to conceive them existing by themselves." "But then," Philonous adds, "this was not the only argument made use of upon that occasion."

20.   See his introduction to *George Berkeley: Philosophical Works* (Dent, 1975), pp. xii-xiii.

21.   A. A. Luce, 'Berkeley's New Principle Completed' in Warren E. Steinkraus (ed.), *New Studies in Berkeley's Philosophy* (Holt, Rinehart and Winston, 1966). I examine Luce's use of this tag in my

Berkeley, pp. 101-2 and 114-20.

22. *Works*, ii. 234.

23. See the reference in note 13 above. What we have here is, basically, the "even cruder, and totally indefensible" notion that we found Peacocke suggesting "may" have been influencing Berkeley (note 3, above).

24. Ian Hacking, *Why Does Language Matter to Philosophy?* (Cambridge University Press, 1975), pp. 17-18.

25. *Ibid.*, p. 41.

26. This formulation is in fact not unproblematic, though no doubt it captures a vagueness in Locke's own mind over whether ideas have "of-ness" built into them. In *Essay*, IV.xi.1, he urges that "the having the *idea* of anything in our mind no more proves the existence of that thing, than the picture of a man evidences his being in the world." It is the analogy that poses the problem. *If* we take it seriously (more seriously than *perhaps* Locke intended) we find ourselves wondering, not simply how we can know that there is something corresponding to the picture, but how perceiving the picture can amount to thinking of the thing.

27. This is the term used by Anthony Kenny in his 'Aquinas: Intentionality,' in Ted Honderich (ed.), *Philosophy Through Its Past* (Penguin Books, 1984). Kenny shows how Aquinas tried to account for the *sense* our thoughts have in terms of the presence to the mind of abstract "forms"; but he sees his attempt to account for reference to *individuals* as marred by an erroneous understanding of sensory imagination and the role of "phantasmata" in thought. For all Berkeley's attack on the abstract notions of the schoolmen, I don't see that he has a superior understanding of the imagination.

28. Thus, if a philosopher is vague about "ideas" he can take it as just obvious that when I think of John and Jim I must have two different ideas in my mind, and it needn't worry him if John and Jim are identical twins and there happens to be no difference in my images. Again, the champion of abstract ideas or "forms" will hold that universality is "built in" to at least some ideas.

29. Hobbes, of course, wrote the third set of objections to the *Meditations*. Descartes's observation comes in his reply to the fifth objection there.

30.   Hacking, *op. cit.*, p. 40.

31.   I have in mind, in particular, Berkeley's account of general ideas. Thus, once it is clearly recognized that an idea is an image, it becomes clear that having an idea in one's mind can't *be* thinking in general terms of, say, man. For Berkeley, it is the mind that contributes generality by *using* the idea in a certain way, so that it is "rendered" universal. I don't think that Berkeley is at all clear on how this happens, but obviously this is one context where what I am thinking *about* cannot be identified with what I am thinking *with*.

32.   Désirée Park, *Complementary Notions* (Martinus Nijhoff, 1972), p. 34.

33.   Note in particular the suggestion that it is the idea *we* frame that we "call" *books* or *trees*, for it does seem that it is only on the assumption that the referent of the word in each case is the image that the argument goes through. The trouble is that the idea we frame should only be a "copy" of a supposed "real" or sensible thing (cf. *Principles*, 33, for example), and yet Berkeley clearly thinks that he is demonstrating something, not of images, but of things.

34.   Thus it is certainly not clear whether a Berkeleian idea of sense is "private" or "public." It is not particularly controversial to suggest that, in different contests, it is *both*.

Geneviève Brykman

BERKELEY ON "ARCHETYPE"*

To see that the title of this paper is polemical, imagine another title:
'Berkeley on Archetypes.' Since a long tradition has kept the word
"archetype" in current use in philosophy, this other title would probably be
considered just as acceptable, and long since justified by commentaries on
immaterialism. However, Berkeley made a point of showing that some men
with a name for learning merely fooled themselves with fine words and
scholastic jargon. I shall argue: (I) that "archetypes," contrary to what is
often said, play no role in immaterialism; (II) that Berkeley used the term
"archetype" only in response to his adversaries; and (III) that he uses this
term, in any account of his own view, only when compelled to by objections
made to his philosophy.

I. A TRADITIONAL MISCONCEPTION OF
BERKELEY'S USE OF "ARCHETYPES"

Let us look, for example, at a famous French dictionary, Lalande's *Dictionnaire du Vocabulaire Technique et Critique de la Philosophie*, which reminds
us that the word "archetype" has been employed in various ways. We may
chiefly keep in mind two senses of "archetype," each of which played a different role in seventeenth century usage. One is a sense Lalande calls
"metaphysical," and is in keeping with the etymology of the word (from
ἀρχε, "first," and τύπος, "stamp"). In this sense "archetype" is used to
refer to the ideal prototype of things. Such would be the ideas of Plato, the
eternal and immutable Forms of things, standing in contrast to sensible
appearances that are ephemeral and ever in flux. The other sense Lalande
calls "psychological and empirical." Here the archetype is any idea capable
of serving as a model for something else, either as sensations that are
models for images, or as notions that are freely constructed to serve as
labels in a system of classification.

----

* Translation and adaptation of 'La notion d'"archétype" selon Berkeley,'
published in *Recherches sur le XVIIème siècle*, no. 7 (Paris: Éditions du
Centre National de la Recherche Scientifique, 1984), pp. 33-43.

E. Sosa (ed.), Essays on the Philosophy of George Berkeley, 103–112.
©*1987 by D. Reidel Publishing Company*

Lalande points out that the meaning of the term "archetype" that is attributed to Plato is met with again in the seventeenth century, in Malebranche to designate God's Ideas. It is true that from 1678 on – in his famous tenth *Éclaircissement* and then in his later work – Malebranche will more and more tend to oppose the obscurity of our modes of consciousness to the clarity of Ideas (particularly the clarity of the Idea of intelligible extension[1]), which are contained in the "Universal Reason" which is God. Lalande rightly points out that, according to Malebranche, it is absolutely necessary that God have in himself the ideas of all things he has created; otherwise he could not have brought them forth.

To such a use of ideas as archetypes in God of created things, Lalande thought one could link, in Berkeley: (A) "Ideas of all things as they exist before creation" – such ideas or "archetypes" allow it to be said that, even once material substance is excluded by Berkeley, two minds perceive the *same* thing; and (B) an altogether auxiliary proposition, according to Lalande, is to be added, namely that Berkeley "also uses the word [archetype] to designate material things existing without the mind, of which thing he denies the reality." Now these observations need to be corrected. And the order of importance assigned to (A) and (B) should be reversed. If we look at the occurrences of the word "archetype" in Berkeley, we shall find that he uses it chiefly in the second sense (B), taking up the terminology of a language he does not understand. And if he reluctantly agrees to make use of the other sense (A) in the context of problems related to creation, it is a concession that, according to Berkeley, adds nothing to what he thinks can be said of the power of God.

II. BERKELEY'S POLEMICAL USE OF "ARCHETYPES"

When Berkeley uses "archetypes" polemically, what he understands by them is the "material thing" of the new philosophers. Descartes had given a new status to the word *idée*. And by saying that ideas are like images of things (*Meditations*, III), he made archetypes fall from heaven to earth. Archetypes were traditional models from which God had created the world. Now material things would stand as models or archetypes of ideas. Thus, it is in the context of materialism that Berkeley took up "archetypes": it is chiefly as a material model that the term is encountered in his writings. he thought that immaterialism would allow him to reconcile the claims of philosophers and the naive realist language of common sense. Common sense is persuaded that the things we perceive immediately are the real things; but philosophers hold that behind fleeting and changeable sensible appearances stands the only reality worth the name, the reality of "material things" or "material substance," of which our sensations are only various and perishable copies. By showing that the word "matter" is without meaning and leads to contradictions, immaterialism was to imply that what we call "things," in ordinary language, are always reducible to a congeries of sensible ideas, which cannot exist without the mind that perceives them. It is in this framework of an assimilation of things to a congeries of sensible ideas that "archetypes" are, in the *Principles*, the target Berkeley takes aim at. Whatever the disciples of Descartes or Locke may think, there are no material archetypes for our ideas to be more or less good "reproductions" of.

For Descartes, that our ideas are like images of things was an index of optimism about our power to know and master the world. It was no longer thus in Locke, who made his *Essay concerning Human Understanding* an examination of the limits of our power to know. Our knowledge, Locke says, is *real* only so fas "as there is a conformity between our *ideas* and the reality of things." Again "to make our knowledge *real* it is requisite that the *ideas* answer their *archetypes*" (*Essay*, IV.iv.3 and 8). Locke had before made an inventory of simple and complex ideas, to see how far these ideas could be adequate (*Essay*, II.xxxi). He had observed that simple ideas are always adequate, because they necessarily correspond to the powers that produce them in us: the sweetness experienced when sugar is tasted, for instance, comes from the natural power of sugar to produce the simple idea of sweetness. Likewise always adequate are complex ideas that are "voluntary collections of simple ideas, which the mind puts together, without reference to any real archetype or standing patterns existing anywhere." These complex ideas are themselves "archetypes" in the sense that they are "made by the mind to rank and denominate things by" (*Essay*, II.xxxi.3). However, complex ideas of substance give rise to a thornier problem: "There is another sort of *complex ideas*," Locke says, "which being referred to *archetypes* without us, may differ from them, and so our knowledge about them may come short of being real" (*Essay*, IV.iv.11). On the other hand, as Locke axiomatically allows that adequate knowledge could be thought of as a kind of "faithful image" of reality, he observes that our ideas of substances can never be adequate. With complex ideas of substances we are no longer able to know whether the idea is true to its "archetype." "For there desiring to copy things as they really do exist; and to represent to ourselves that constitution on which all their properties depend, we perceive our *ideas* attain not that prefection we intend" (*Essay*, II.xxxi.3).

From such a confession of imperfection, together with Locke's insistence on making substances the archetypes of our ideas, Berkeley launches his criticism of material substance. Intended to abolish the model/copy relationship generally assumed between ideas and substance, the argument will consist in asserting, throughout the *Principles*, that *an idea can be like nothing but an idea.*

To his basic thesis that things (congeries of ideas) cannot be without being perceived, Berkeley imagines an objection which should be prior to any other:

> . . . you will say that though the ideas themselves do not exist
> without the mind, yet there may be things like them whereof
> they are copies or resemblances . . . I answer, an idea can be
> like nothing but an idea; a colour or figure can be like nothing
> but another colour or figure . . . Again, I ask whether those
> supposed *originals*, or external things, of which our ideas are
> the pictures or representations, be themselves perceivable or
> no? If they are, then they are ideas, and we have gained our
> point; but if you say that they are not, I appeal to anyone
> whether it be sense to assert a colour is like something which is
> invisible; hard or soft like something which is intangible; and so
> of the rest. (*Principles*, 8)

Not only does Berkeley reject the widely held theory that ideas are "like
images of things," but, in keeping with the account he gives in *An Essay
towards a New Theory of Vision* on the complete heterogeneity of the five
senses, he goes so far as to say that an idea can be like nothing but another
idea of the same sense: red can only be like red, or at least like some color
or other. It is only playing with words to say that red is "like a picture or
image" of matter. Berkeley adds that the distinction proposed by modern
philosophers between secondary qualities and primary qualities by no
means gives the ideas of primary qualities the privilege of being "fair copies" of reality: "neither they [ideas] nor their archetypes can exist in an
imperceiving substance" (*Principles*, 9).

Because of its reduction of things to congeries of ideas, immaterialism alone can make an end of scepticism:

> Colour, figure, motion, extension and the like, considered only
> as so many *sensations* in the mind are perfectly known, there
> being nothing in them which is not perceived. But if they are
> looked on as notes or images, referred to *things* or *archetypes*
> existing without the mind, then we are involved all in scepti-
> cism . . . Things remaining the same, our ideas vary, and
> which of them, or even whether any of them at all, represent
> the true quality really existing in the thing, it is out of our
> reach to determine. (*Principles*, 87)

Material archetypes in Locke were to guarantee permanence and identity of
sensible things. Berkeley secures this permanence and identity by recourse
to divine benevolence: the associations among all ideas are regular and
predictable; they may be called "laws of nature," on the understanding
that, in mankind, the need to survive and the desire for happiness predom-
inate in any concern for knowledge. For want of such "laws of nature" we
would go astray, but not at all for want of a "material substance." According to Berkeley, then, some constancy in the laws of nature, once things are

reduced to ideas, allows the granting of a single valid and very limited sense to the word "archetype": sensible ideas are archetypes of the ideas of the imagination since, in this case, we have direct experience of faithful reproduction of the sensible given in the imagination (*PC*, 823; *Principles*, 33). Here alone do we know what is meant by talk of a "picture" or "image" or "model."[2]

III. BERKELEY'S CONCESSIONS

Once this single meaning of the word "archetype" had been settled on in 1710, the divine guarantee of the sensible world, as construed by Augustine, Malebranche, or Norris, is not in the *Principles* described in terms of archetypes, but merely in terms of divine ideas.

Having described occasionalism without attributing it to any particular philosopher, Berkeley lays out the presuppositions of such a doctrine: "The question is . . . whether there are not certain ideas, of I know not what sort, in the mind of God, which are so many marks or notes that direct him how to produce sensations in our minds, in a constant and regular method." Such a conception of matter, obscurely reduced to divine ideas, "seems," he writes, "too extravagant to deserve a confutation" (sect. 71). "It is an extraordinary instance of the force of prejudice, and so much to be lamented, that the mind of man retains so great a fondness . . . for a stupid thoughtless *somewhat*, by the interposition whereof it would . . . screen itself from the providence of God and remove him farther off from the affairs of the world" (sect. 75). Now, saying that matter is, in the mind of God, the occasion of the producing of sensible ideas in us comes down to saying that there are, in the mind of God, certain ideas, unknown to us, which move him to act (sect. 75). "Whether . . . there are such ideas in the mind of God and whether they may be called by the name *matter*, I shall not dispute" (sect. 76). In the *Principles*, then, all discussion about "archetypes" considered as "divine ideas" is closed beforehand – before it has been half-opened in terms that Malebranche could recognize.

The reserve shown by Berkeley in not discussing Malebranche's philosophy as such was shaken by the reception given the *Principles*. Taken for a disciple of Malebranche and Norris,[3] then labelled "malebranchiste de bonne foi,"[4] Berkeley undertook a more direct critique of Malebranche in the *Three Dialogues between Hylas and Philonous* (1713). Now "archetype" takes on some ambiguity,[5] but remains a term in Berkeley's adversaries language until Hylas cautiously declines to use it, and Philonous allows its use *in extremis* for what is, anyhow, mysterious "on any hypothesis whatsoever."[6]

At the end of the first dialogue, which is devoted to the critique of material archetypes of which our ideas might be "images," Hylas concedes that an idea can be like nothing but an idea and that no idea can exist without the mind. The second dialogue deals much more directly with the question of the relation between God and sensible thing. Treating this question, Berkeley also gives an original proof of the existence of God: "I say sensible things do really exist, and if they really exist, they are necessarily perceived by an infinite mind; therefore there is an infinite mind or God" (*Dialogues*, 212). But Hylas asks: what should we understand by a "divine perception of sensible things?" This is now the difficulty to clear up, one that the *Principles* brushed aside.

More than once Philonous remarks that the sensible ideas we perceive are our *own* ideas, individual and momentary successions whose regularity and correspondence depend on the providence of God.[7] The universal harmony between the series of ideas by which creatures are affected forms this network we call the "laws of nature." However, such a network should not be thought of as the same as Divine Wisdom or Divine Ideas in Malebranche's sense. In Berkeley, God is the cause and not the seat of ideas. As Philonous point out, our ideas, which are "altogether passive,"[8] can be no part of the substance of God. And to Hylas's objection that, on Philonous's view, pain would be in God, hence God would suffer pain, Philonous replies that God knows what pain is without suffering it. Human understanding is never altogether separable from what it receives from the senses; by contrast, the Almighty cannot be affected by anything whatever (*Dialogues*, 240-241).

An unhappy word of Philonous merits some further attention (*Dialogues*, 239). While Hylas is at pains not to describe causality in terms of archetypes, Philonous seems, just at this point, to admit "divine ideas": "That we are affected with ideas from without is evident," Hylas allows, "and it is no less evident that there must be (I will not say archetypes, but) powers without the mind, corresponding to those ideas. And as these powers cannot subsist by themselves, there is some subject of them necessarily to be admitted, which I call *matter* and you call *spirit*." This is all the difference between us, Hylas says, a difference in the choice between these two words. To which Philonous answers that common usage never attributes power save to what is supposed to be naturally active (therefore, in his own view, spiritual). "What can be plainer," he adds rather unfortunately, "than that a thing which hath no ideas in itself cannot impart them to me?"[9]

At just this point Hylas detects a contradiction: to admit ideas in God is to admit in God passivity, imperfection, and so − why not? − pain and uneasiness. And at just this point Berkeley's attitude vis-à-vis archetypes turns from criticism to concession: since we do not know what it is in God that corresponds to our sensible ideas, the word "archetype" can be left to do the job. Earlier, Berkeley had made a first concession (*Dialogues*, p. 231): in contrast with a strict use of "idea" to mean "sensation," he had allowed a larger sense of the word to point out the doubly imperfect knowledge we have of God. Doubly imperfect because: 1) if it be granted that there can be no (passive) idea of an (active) spirit, then I have an idea neither of my spirit, nor of the spirit of any other; 2) since God is infinite and my soul finite, the knowledge of God that my soul can furnish me with will be extremely inadequate. Hence, all discussion about God will be vitiated by an inescapable anthropomorphism. This is why Berkeley here casually admits the principle of which he had denied the validity in his notebooks: "nothing can give save what it possesses." He admits it to apply to the production of ideas: God has to *have* some ideas to *give* ideas to creatures, even in a sensible form that is not his own. Further on, Philonous sets himself to distinguish finite sensible ideas, passive effects of the power of God, from the power that is their source. That is why he then introduces the word "archetype," which Hylas has been at pains to set aside: "Not to mention your having discarded those archetypes," Philonous points out, "so may you suppose an external archetype on my principles; *external* I mean to your own mind; though indeed it must be supposed to exist in that mind which comprehends all things." Here speaking of the archetypal status of a divine design for creation, Berkeley prefers the singular to the plural, as he has done before with the words *cause* and *power*, when treating of God.[10] However, in spite of the impossibility of purging language of an inevitably anthropomorphic element, Berkeley says that if we would describe divine action, we should prefer metaphors from human desire and quest for happiness to metaphors of the passive contemplation of "Ideas" delineated in a kind of infinite space (whether an "intelligible world" or "intelligible extension"). Thus, the last objection from Hylas about creation (*Dialogues*, 254) and the correspondence with Johnson about the divine guarantee of this world (*Works*, ii. 292) amount only to the following verbal concessions by Berkeley:

1. Hylas has put the following alternatives to his adversary: either God has executed from all eternity the decree making things perceptible (and how then to escape pantheism?), or else God began to will what he has not willed before (and so there is something new in God, some change which implies imperfection). To this Philonous could content himself with replying that creation is incomprehensible on any hypothesis. The nature of God, he stresses, is altogether transcendent and we imagine the omnipotence of God only through our temporal categories. Without admitting a *before* and an *after* in God, Philonous concedes that the mystery of creation lies in the very necessity of acknowledging a two-fold state of things, without understanding its genesis. "What would you have!" he asks Hylas, "do I not acknowledge a two-fold state of things, the one ectypal or natural, the other archetypal and eternal? The former was created in time; the latter existed from everlasting in the mind of God." (*Dialogues*, 254.)

2. Johnson, in his second letter to Berkeley, is eager to say that the rereading of the *Dialogues* has enlightened him about archetypes: they guarantee the permanence of sensible things when they are not being perceived by finite minds (*Works*, ii. 285). Not discerning how Berkeley has

been on guard against not expressing himself in scholastic jargon, especially in terms of "archetypes," Johnson is now relieved about the extravagances of immaterialism, and he adds that, from the *Dialogues*, he has been happy to infer "that there is exterior to us, in the divine mind, a system of universal nature whereof the ideas we have are in such a degree resemblances as the Almighty is pleased to communicate to us" (*Works*, ii. 285-86). Then he insists: the divine ideas must be conceived as models of *our* ideas, for there is no other guarantee of the identity of our ideas through time, nor of my ideas with my neighbor's. Therefore, in Johnson's reading, divine ideas, in the *Dialogues*, are archetypes in the most traditional sense. To this Berkeley lost no time in answering: "I have no objection against calling the ideas in the mind of God [in the broad sense of the word *idea* seen above] archetypes of ours. But I object against those archetypes by philosophers supposed to be real things, and to have an absolute real existence distinct from their being perceived by any mind whatsoever, it being the opinion of all materialists that an ideal existence in the Divine Mind is one Thing, and the real existence of material things another" (*Works*, ii. 292).

It is true that the materialists, in a way, have their "two-fold state of things," as Philonous has his. The difference is that, with the materialists as imagined by Berkeley, "an ideal existence in the divine mind" is a cautious supposition intended to reassure theologians, whereas "real existence" is elsewhere, in Gassendi's or Newton's studies and laboratories. Hence, this "two-fold state of things" is a pretence that ought to fool nobody. By contrast, Philonous's conceding a two-fold state of things has given rise to many a commentary. It does not deserve such respect.

In Berkeley, it has been generally recognized that, anterior to the creating Will, there is not in God any "Wisdom," any "Wisdom as a plan to be followed. What has been disputed is whether or not to admit in God "decrees" or "resolutions."[11] Such an idle dispute loses sight of two important facts: 1) that Berkeley had firmly insisted on the impossibility of speaking of God otherwise than by anthropomorphic metaphors and, more generally, on the near impossibility of speaking of spirits literally; and 2) that Berkeley's interest in archetypes is above all a concern about the sceptical threat arising from a confused supposition of material archetypes.

Université de Technologie de Compiègne
France

NOTES

1. On the difficulties of Malebranche's two definitions of intelligible extension (the idea upon which God has formed bodies and the immensity itself of the divine being, in so far as participable by corporeal creation), see Henri Gouhier, *La Philosophie de Malebranche* (Paris: J. Vrin, 1926), part 3, chap. 5.

2. Berkeley, *Philosophical Commentaries*, Notebook A, 823 (*Works*, i. 98): "Ideas of Sense are the Real things or Archetypes. Ideas of Imagination, Dreams, etc are copies, images of these."

3. Berkeley, *Works*, viii. 41, letter to Percival of 27 November 1710: "As to what is said of ranking me with Father Malebranche and Mr. Norris . . . I have this to answer: that I think the notions I embrace are not in the least coincident with, or agreeing with, theirs, but indeed plainly inconsistent with them in the main points, insomuch that I know few writers whom I take myself at bottom to differ more from than them."

4. *Mémoires de Trévoux*, May 1713, article 80: "Mr. Berkeley, Malebranchiste de bonne foi, a poussé sans ménagement les principes de sa secte for au-delà du sens commun [dans un . . .] *Traité des Principes de la connaissance.*"

5. Some passages of the *Principles* and of the *Dialogues* do not allow us neatly to sort out archetypes as "material things" from archetypes "divine ideas" (*Principles*, 45, 99; *Dialogues*, 211, 240-41). John Norris, in his *Essay Towards the Theory of the Ideal or Intelligible World* seems to have been concerned to point out the amiguity with which the words *ideas* and *archetypes* are used. See especially Part 1, chap. 2: "The Reality of the Distinction justifi'd . . ." Norris uses the well known image of the seal and the wax to describe the intelligible world as "form": "An ideal World . . . was the primary Mould, Form, Model, or (as *Philo* expresses it) the *Seal* of this. For so that Platonic Writer very emphatically Styles the Intelligible world, calling it ἡ ἀρχέτυπος σφραγὶς, the *Archetypal* or *Original Seal* . . . And such a *Seal* there must be, or we shall never be able to give an account of the *Impression.*"

6. *Dialogues*, 239, 254-55.

7. *Philosophical Commentaries*, Notebook B, 47 (*Works*, i. 12): "Did

ever any man see any other things besides his own ideas . . . ?"
Principles, 4: "What do we perceive besides our own ideas or sensations . . . ?" *Dialogues* (*Dialogues*, 214): "It is evident that the
things I perceive are my own ideas . . ."

8. *Principles*, 25, 57, 137, 141; *Dialogues*, 197, 213, 216, 131.

9. *Philosophical Commentaries, Notebook A,* 780 (*Works*, i. 94): "Nihil
    dat quod non habet or the effect is contained in the Cause is an
    axiom I do not Understand or believe to be true"; 830 (p. 99): "Why
    may we not conceive it possible for God to create things out of
    Nothing. Certainly we our selves create in some wise whenever we
    imagine."

10. *Philosophical Commentaries, Notebook B,* 282 (*Works*, i. 35):
    "Bodies etc do exist whether we think of 'em or no, they being taken
    in a twofold sense. Collections of thoughts & collections of powers to
    cause these thoughts. These later exist, tho perhaps a parte dei
    [mei? rei?] it may be one simple perfect power."

11. J. D. Mabbott, 'The Place of God in Berkeley's Philosophy,' *Journal
    of Philosophical Studies,* **6** (1931); Emmanuel Leroux, 'Note concer-
    nant l'influence de Malebranche sur Berkeley,' *Revue de Métaphy-
    sique et de Morale,* **45** (1938); Martial Gueroult, 'Le Dieu de Berke-
    ley,' in *Berkeley: Quatre Etudes sur la perception et sur Dieu* (Paris:
    Aubier, 1956). To the suggestion of Mabbott that we interpret
    "divine perception" by an image with a pedagogical function – my
    resolve to arrange my papers every Saturday as distinct from the
    order my papers are actually put into each Saturday – Gueroult
    puts the following question (p. 146): "Comment les archétypes ser-
    aient-ils actifs puisque Dieu ne les veut pas, ne les crée pas, mais y
    conforme sa volonté? . . . Y verra-t-on, comme certains inter-
    prètes, des 'intentions'?" To criticize the use of the notion of
    "intention," Gueroult uses language from human description of
    human actions, without taking into account Berkeley's pains to
    make the point that there is something in God that is inexpressible.
    Preferable is Charles McCracken's prudent and careful exegesis of
    the passages in which Berkeley speaks of divine "decrees," in
    "What *Does* Berkeley's God See in the Quad?' in *Archiv für Ges-
    chichte der Philosophie,* **61** (1979). See also Geneviève Brykman,
    Berkeley: Philosophie et apologétique (Paris: J. Vrin, 1984), ch. 8:
    "La Protection de la realité: L'Absence d'unicité de l'univers et la
    question de la 'sagesse' de Dieu."

PART FOUR

EPISTEMOLOGY:
GOD AND MATTER

M. R. Ayers

DIVINE IDEAS AND BERKELEY'S PROOFS
OF GOD'S EXISTENCE

In 1931 J. D. Mabbott doubted whether Berkeley really believed in Divine
Ideas (1968:364-79). More recently, in rather similar vein, Jonathan Bennett has argued that Berkeley hardly cared whether God maintains the
continuity of the tree in the quad by perceiving it when we do not. In particular, the famous argument which purports to deduce God's existence
from the continuous existence of sensible things is represented by Bennett
as no more than a two sentence hiccup in the course of the *Three Dialogues
between Hylas and Philonous* (Bennett 1968 and 1971).

Bennett's interpretation has had its critics. E. J. Furlong and Ian
Tipton both argue convincingly that the problem of things' continuity while
unperceived by finite minds was always of nagging importance to Berkeley
(Furlong 1968; Tipton 1974:321-49). His failure on occasion to give a
definite answer to it does not indicate lack of concern. Tipton also suitably
rebuts Bennett's attempt to find a God-free phenomenalism embedded in
the *Philosophical Commentaries,* with relics in the published works. Yet
both writers make significant concessions to Bennett's view of what he calls
"the Continuity Argument," accepting in effect both his account of its form
and his estimate of its significance. Furlong does very briefly suggest that
Berkeley may not have kept the argument distinct from his main proof
(called by Bennett "the Passivity Argument"): in which case it is to be
found in other passages than the single paragraph to which Bennett restricts it (1968:406f). Yet Tipton does not take up this hint, accepting Bennett's extreme and intrinsically implausible judgement that the Continuity
Argument is "a momentary aberration" (1974:323). In the present paper I
will suggest that none of these commentators has given an adequate account of the form of Berkeley's argument, and that their failure has pre-
vented them from seeing the extent to which it dominates long passages of
both the Second and Third Dialogues. When a correct account of its form is
given, moreover, it does not seem that "the Continuity Argument' is really
the best name for it. Finally, its intimate connection with the Passivity
Argument in Berkeley's dialectical presentation of both in the *Three Dialogues* is so ordered as to support the judgement that it is the senior rather
than the junior of the two-arguments, if not always for Berkeley, then at
least as they appear in that work.

The so-called Passivity Argument first occurs in *A Treatise concerning the Principles of Human Knowledge,* 28-32. Since our ideas of sense are

115

E.Sosa (ed.), Essays on the Philosophy of George Berkeley, 115–128.
©*1987 by D. Reidel Publishing Company*

involuntary, and so evidently not caused by us, they must be caused by an external active substance. This external cause must be spirit, since spirit (as has just been proved) is the only active substance, volition being the only conceivable action. The evidently purposive and humanly useful character of the "regular train or series" of the ideas of sense "sufficiently testifies the wisdom and benevolence of its Author."

As for the so-called Continuity Argument (which does not get directly expressed in the *Principles*) the only passage upon which all commentators are agreed occurs early in the Third Dialogue. The crucial move runs as follows:

> When I deny sensible things an existence out of the mind, I do not mean my mind in particular, but all minds. Now it is plain they have an existence exterior to my mind, since I find them by experience to be independent of it. There is therefore some other mind wherein they exist, during the intervals between the times of my perceiving them: as likewise they did before my birth, and would do after my supposed annihilation. (*Dialogues*, 230f.)

Bennett offers roughly the following part-analysis of Philonous' argument (cf. 1968:380; 1971:169):

(a)   No sensible thing can exist when not perceived by some spirit.

(b)   Sensible things sometimes exist when not perceived by any finite spirit.

(c)   There is therefore an infinite spirit which perceives sensible things at those times.

He then asks why Berkeley feels entitled to the second premise, (b), and rightly sees that a reason is offered in this very passage, in the sentence, "Now it is plain they have an existence exterior to my mind, since I find them by experience to be independent of it." This reasoning Bennett explains as a confusion or conflation involving an ambiguity of the word "independent."

Here Bennett's interpretation rests on an analysis of all occurrences of "depend" and its derivatives in the *Principles* and *Dialogues*. According to him these works contain two main or relevant "uses" of the word. These are the "ownership" use, by which "an idea's independence of a mind is its not occurring in that mind," and the "causation" use, by which "an idea's 'independence' of a given mind is its not being caused, or willed into existence, by that mind." Bennett then purports to find two other passages in which Berkeley has confused the two uses of "depend," a claim which lends plausibility to his suggestion that premise (b) of the Continuity Argument rests on a similar conflation. Berkeley has allegedly arrived at that premise by an unacknowledged slide from my experience of the causal independence of "sensible things" to an assumption of their (as we may put it) ontological independence, i.e. existence out of my mind.

Against this account it can first be said that Bennett's interpretation of the other two passages to which he appeals is itself far from convincing. The first of them *(Principles, 146)* is a restatement of the Passivity Argument. Because "the far greater part of the ideas or sensations perceived by us" are not produced by our will, there "is therefore some other spirit that causes them, since it is repugnant that they should subsist by themselves." Here is an illegitimate slide, Bennett claims, in the reverse direction from the one we have been considering: i.e. this time from the principle that every idea is *owned* by a mind, to the principle that every idea is *caused* by a mind. For, as a general rule (as Bennett rightly says), when Berkeley talks of the incapacity of ideas to subsist by themselves he means that they cannot exist unowned. For Berkeley ideas, to that extent like the traditional accidents with which he sometimes identifies them (cf. *Principles*, 73), need a substance in which to subsist. Despite that general rule, however, the present passage (from *Principles*, 146) is exclusively concerned with the need for a cause, and in this it is just like *Principles*, 29 of which it is explicitly the summary. Such a use of the expression "subsist by themselves" to connote *causal* independence may be unique in Berkeley's works,[1] but it was not at all unusual when Berkeley wrote. It was after all a common thought that, because only God is *causa sui*, only God fully satisfies the traditional definition of a substance as something that subsists by itself. Perhaps a hard distinction between causal and ontological dependence is seldom easily drawn in seventeenth-century philosophy. But in any case it is beyond reasonable doubt that the last clause quoted from *Principles*, 146 simply means that it is repugnant to reason that any idea should lack a cause.

The second passage, *Principles*, 56, is Berkeley's account of the origin of the general prejudice that sensible things have "an existence independent of, and without the mind." It arises, Berkeley says, because men perceive ideas of sense "as not being excited from within, nor depending on the operation of their wills." Bennett thinks that Berkeley's failure here to point out the ambiguity of "depend," "even when actively engaged in criticising a fallacy which it may have helped to engender, irresistably suggests that Berkeley is totally unaware of it." Again Bennett's argument is inordinately thin. For one thing, it is hardly plausible that Berkeley would have been inclined to ascribe the error which is his equivalent of the Cartesian "prejudices of the senses," shared as it is supposed to be by peasants and princes, to a recondite fallacy of equivocation. But it is in any case a prior mistake to find *ambiguity* in Berkeley's own usage. Berkeley holds that ideas have different *kinds* of dependence on spirits. He is here claiming that experience of one kind of independence leads people to assume the other. Talk of "ambiguity" or "conflation" is beside the point. Berkeley's diagnosis has roughly the structure of such a claim as this: "When people know that a woman is financially independent of her husband, they tend to assume that she is emotionally independent of him too." If different *senses* of "independent" were involved in this claim, it would be improper (or a kind of pun) to say such a thing as "A is both financially and emotionally dependent on B." If "conflation" is involved in all this, it is Bennett's conflation of a difference between *kinds* or *species* of dependence with a difference between *senses* or *uses* of "depend." That conflation is endorsed by both Furlong and Tipton.

So much for the view that the Continuity Argument "exploits the ambiguity of 'independent'" (Bennett 1971:170). What it does is in fact rather close to what Berkeley accuses us all of doing in the passage just discussed *(Principles,* 56; cf. 74). He accuses us of the following movement of thought: *Sensible things are causally independent of my mind; therefore they exist outside the mind* (i.e. mind in general, all minds). The move which Berkeley himself makes in the Third Dialogue is subtly different: *Sensible things are causally independent of my mind; therefore they have an existence exterior to my mind.* There is obviously no contradiction in believing both that the former move is invalid and that the latter is valid.[2]

The objection might here be raised that, if a "sensible thing" or idea is *perceived by me,* it thereby, for Berkeley, *exists in my mind* and so in no one else's. That is, it might be objected that "x is perceived by me but has an existence outside my mind" should on his account be a simple contradiction. Such a point is implicit in Bennett's claim that, in the "ownership" use of "depend," "an idea's independence of a mind is its not occurring in that mind." Yet that is to misunderstand Berkeley's employment of the expression "in the mind." Here it is helpful to recall the traditional models for intentionality which supplied some of the material for his philosophising. As Descartes had put one such model, the idea of the sun is the sun itself as it exists in the understanding. For Descartes, of course, the sun also has an existence in reality ("in the sky," as he misleadingly says at one point). Existence in the mind (or in my mind) is on this model no barrier to external existence. As Descartes elsewhere reminds us, there is another important way of thinking about the ideas, namely as modifications of the mind, and to that other notion I will return.[3] Yet if we do identify my idea of the sun with the sun (as I think of it) and also identify the sun which exists in my mind with the sun which exists in reality (as is necessary if the latter is to be an object of knowledge at all), then it follows that (in this sense of "idea") my idea of the sun can in a way have external existence. Thus in the present passage Berkeley is to this extent agreeing with the realist tradition: the involuntariness or causal independence of my sensation or sensory idea of the sun implies that it (i.e. the sun, the object of my perception

or the thing "in my mind") has an existence exterior to my mind (i.e. real
existence of reality).[4] What he expressly denies is that the idea thereby
has an "absolute" existence exterior to, or independent of, mind in general.
For he holds that it is not the kind of thing which *could* exist out of "all
minds."

     What has all this to do with continuity? Furlong remarks paren-
thetically that the argument from one kind of independence to the other is
from "what Hume will call 'distinct' existence to 'continued' existence"; but
that suggestive comparison is a little off-target. For Hume explicitly includes three components under the "distinctness" of objects: "their *external*
position as well as the *independence* of their existence and operation." In
these terms Berkeley's argument is concerned with just two elements of
Humean "distinctness": i.e. he argues from "independence of operation" (or
what is roughly its equivalent in his system) to "independence of existence." Neither sort of independence, for Hume, includes continuity, although he holds that distinctness and continuity are "intimately connected
together." Hume treats this connection as a tightly rational one:

> For if the objects of our senses continue to exist, even when
> they are not perceiv'd, their existence is of course independent
> of and distinct from the perception; and *vice versa*, if their exis-
> tence be independent of the perception and distinct from it, they
> must continue to exist, even tho' they be not perceiv'd.
> (1978:188)

Hume's motive for bothering to distinguish independence from continuity is
explicitly the purposes of his sceptical psychology. For he intends to show
that certain principles of the imagination lead us naturally to believe that
objects have continuous existence, and *so* that they have distinct existence.
Berkeley's argument is in the other direction: once it has been shown that
ideas of sense have an existence exterior to my mind, he feels free to assume that they have a continuous existence, i.e. that they exist whether or
not I perceive them. The last move is less a formal step in argument than
his simply making explicit one of the things involved in ontological independence. What he is spelling out is in effect what Hume will later express by
saying that, as far as distinct and continued existence are concerned, "the
decision of the one question decides the other."[5]

     Now let us consider the long passage, towards the beginning of the
Second Dialogue, about which commentators have been less united (*Dialogues*, 211-15). Bennett states that it is an exposition of the Passivity
Argument. That may seem too obviously a false account of an argument
which Philonous sums up as follows: *"sensible things do really exist: and if
they really exist, they are necessarily perceived by an infinite mind: therefore
there is an infinite mind, or God."* But Bennett evidently sees the reference
to God's perception as no more than a relatively unimportant enrichment of

the Passivity Argument. Every idea must be produced by the will of a spirit *in whose mind the idea exists*. Hence my ideas of sense must exist in the mind which causes them (Bennett 1968:382; 1971:165). Bennett does not remark on the difference between the argument as he expounds it and the argument which occurs at *Principles*, 28-31 (summarized above). But he is right, of course, that it is a Berkeleian principle that what causes ideas must have them (Cf. *Dialogues*, 216,236, 239; *PC*, 812). Thus for Bennett references to God's perception and ideas in the Second Dialogue simply spell out what is left implicit in the Passivity Argument of the *Principles*. The question is whether this proposal does nearly enough to explain them. I take it that it does not.

Let us consider the first formulation of the Second-Dialogue argument. After pointing out that, unlike Hylas, he does not define "the reality of sensible things" in terms of "an *absolute existence* out of the minds of spirits," Philonous continues:

> seeing that they depend not on my thought, and have an existence distinct from being perceived by me, *there must be some other mind wherein they exist*. As sure therefore as the sensible world really exists, so sure is there an infinite omnipresent spirit who contains and supports it.

In maintaining that this is the Passivity Argument Bennett admits to two problems. First, he must hold that the clause "and have an existence distinct from being perceived by me" (which, as he allows, "looks like a reference to ownership") is idle, since on his account it simply *repeats*, in a "careless" way, the point that sensible things "depend not on my thought" or will (Bennett 1971:183). Second, the conclusion, "there must be some other mind wherein they exist," must be taken to be short for ". . . wherein they exist and which causes them"; or rather, to adopt the logical order postulated by Bennett, ". . . which causes them and in which they therefore exist." These contentions, if not positively heroic, are more than a little bold. The second, for example, has to face the difficulty that the argument's conclusion is restated several times within a page, each time without reference to God's role as *cause* of ideas of sense. (The words "contains" and "supports" which occur in the immediately succeeding sentence express only the perceptual relation, the former obviously, the latter by analogy with, e.g., *Principles*, 135, a usage which embodies the general analogy running through Berkeley's philosophy between substance/accident and perceiver/perceived.) To leave so much unsaid for so long would surely be taking carelessness to an extreme.

Fortunately a more satisfying account of Berkeley's reasoning readily appears if we compare it with the Third Dialogue passage just analysed. For it is surely apparent that Berkeley's first move in the earlier passage, as in the later one, is from causal independence to ontological independence or, as he himself calls it (in a phrase which may have influenced Hume's choice of word), to "existence distinct from being perceived by me." The final conclusion too (i.e. that sensible things exist in God's mind) is the same as in the later argument and, as such, is adequately expressed, without ellipsis. What Berkeley does not do in the earlier passage is to spell out the implications of the "distinct" existence of real things, "exterior to my mind," for continuity. Yet, given what Hume calls the "intimate connection" between distinctness and continuity, the latter would seem a very minor enrichment of the argument. That is why the name, "the Continuity Argument," is a misleading title, disastrously misleading if it brings us to suppose, as Bennett seems to have supposed, that where there is no mention of continuity the argument does not occur. To put the point in a way which gives greater credit to Bennett's perceptiveness, the truth behind his paradoxical claims is that essentially the same argument occurs in the Second Dialogue as occurs in the Third, *but without any reference to continuity*. Let us then call that recurring argument "the Distinctness Argument."

After its first exposition in the Second Dialogue, the Distinctness Argument remains the centre of attention for several pages but it picks up various accretions as discussion and restatement proceed. One such deliberate addition is the mention of "archetypes" at the top of p. 213 *(Dialogues)*, a term which looks back to its first occurrence in the discussion of mediate perception in the First Dialogue (p. 204). This second occurrence of the word takes place in a restatement of a lemma of the Distinctness Argument (i.e. "sensible things cannot exist otherwise than in a mind or spirit") as "no idea or archetype of an idea can exist otherwise than in a mind."[6]

The reference to archetypes is retained in the next restatement of the argument *(Dialogues*, 214), but in this passage there is a more significant and striking novelty, namely, Berkeley's building into his proof certain elements of the Passivity Argument:

> It is evident that the things I perceive are my own ideas, and that no idea can exist unless it be in a mind. Nor is it less plain that these ideas or things by me perceived, either themselves or their archetypes, exist independently of my mind, since I know myself not to be their author, it being out of my power to determine at pleasure, what particular ideas I shall be affected with upon opening my eyes or ears. They must therefore exist in some other mind, *whose will it is they should be exhibited to me*. The things, I say, immediately perceived, are ideas or sensations, call them what you will. But how can any idea or sensation exist in, *or be produced by,* any thing but a mind or spirit? (my italics)

What is happening in this passage is that Berkeley, having previously expressed the Distinctness Argument in a pure form, is now feeding into it elements of the Passivity Argument (the clauses italicized) which perform no real function in the argument. The consequent appearance that the Passivity Argument is a sort of natural enrichment of the Distinctness Argument is surely not unintentional. For the significant fact is that Berkeley chooses to enter into the topic of the causality of ideas in and through the question of the ontological dependence of ideas on spirit. He seems to have felt that the substance which supports and produces the sensible world is more evidently, unquestionably spiritual in its perceiving-supporting function than in its role as producer; and that it is somehow more persuasive to locate the "distinct existence" of our ideas of sense in an infinite mind *before* entering on the argument that only that same infinite mind can be their immediate cause. Bennett's exegetical strategy, which is to explain the references to Divine Ideas in the Second Dialogue as a mere enrichment of the Passivity Argument, gets things entirely the wrong way round. The question of spirit as cause (or will) and the question of spirit as support (or understanding) are tied in together, but the latter precedes the former in the order of Berkeley's exposition. The Second Dialogue springs from the First.

Having introduced God-as-cause in this somewhat sidelong fashion, Berkeley then allows Philonous a speech (*Dialogues*, 215) which corresponds to the causal argument of *Principles*, 28-30 and which includes, *for the very first time* in the *Three Dialogues*, the essential premise of the Passivity Argument (if with less than full explicitness): i.e. that our only conception of production derives from experience of our own acts of will. As Philonous soon puts this premise, it is impossible to "conceive any action besides volition." (*Dialogues*, 217) Where this argument differs from the argument of the *Principles*, however, is that there remains clinging to it vestiges of the Distinctness Argument. Ideas of sense are not only "produced by," but "exist in" a spirit. The "things by me perceived" are not only "produced by the will," but are "known by the understanding" of God. There seems therefore to be a very careful intermingling and balance in the exposition of the two arguments at this point in the second Dialogue. The Distinctness Argument has just been re-expressed with forward-looking references to God as cause; the Passivity Argument is now advanced for the first time with glances back to God as perceiver. Only later are these two functions of God directly linked by the principle that what causes ideas must have them (*Dialogues*, 216).

The apparently careful balance involved in the intermingling of the two arguments counts against Furlong's suggestion that Berkeley does not clearly distinguish them. In any case, the pure Distinctness Argument has already been expressed or summarized several times within a few pages in the Second Dialogue (by my count, four times), while the pure Passivity Argument exists in the *Principles*. Even more conclusive is the appearance together of the two arguments, but firmly divided by an oppositive "again," late in the Third Dialogue (this time in the reverse order):

> From the effects I see produced, I conclude there are actions; and because actions, volitions; and because there are volitions, there must be a will. Again, the things I perceive must have an existence, they or their archetypes, out of my mind: but being ideas, neither they nor their archetypes can exist otherwise than in an understanding: there is therefore an understanding. (*Dialogues*, 240)

The two arguments are clearly not conflated by Berkeley, but conjoined as closely as he would wish to conjoin understanding and will. Yet if we take into account the space devoted to each argument thoughout the Second and Third Dialogues, the order in which they are introduced together with, perhaps, the element of subordination in the way in which they are introduced, and finally the sheer number of times each is expressed, summarized or referred to, it seems hardly deniable that, if either receives pride of place, it is the Distinctness Argument.

   To return to the topic of continuity, is it just an accident that the implications of the "distinct" existence of objects for their continuous existence are not so much as mentioned in the several formulations of the Distinctness Argument in the Second Dialogue? Not at all, for in the Third Dialogue Berkeley leads into the issue of continuity with some elaborate (and highly characteristic) care. Bennett passes over this introduction, remarking that, on the usual view of the "Continuity Argument" as important to Berkeley, it appears mysterious why he should be silent on a "beautiful pattern" in his thought. As Bennett interprets each, the Passivity Argument covers the existence of Divine Ideas as long as we perceive "real things," while "the Continuity Argument" covers their existence at the times when we are not perceiving them. That Berkeley notices no such pattern is supposed to be further evidence that the latter is an aberration. Yet, in the long speech of Philonous which leads into the particular restatement of the Distinctness Argument which Bennett calls "the Continuity Argument," Berkeley is indeed concerned with the first part of such a balanced thought, if not quite the "beautiful pattern" which Bennett has in mind.

   What Philonous appeals to in order to establish the existence of "real things" when we perceive them is not the Passivity Argument, but a common-sense trust in the senses backed up by the principle that the existence of sensible things consists in their being perceived: "when therefore they are actually perceived, there can be no doubt of their existence." This latter reliance on the *"esse* is *percipi"* principle would seem rash enough in such a context, since the ideas of a dream would "exist" in *that* sense;[7] but the appeal to the natural authority of the senses is significantly reminiscent of Locke's conception of "sensitive knowledge" and analogous seventeenth-century doctrines (most notably those of Gassendi and Hobbes.)[8] Philonous actually alludes to Locke, reprimanding him for the view that sensitive knowledge "falls short of intuition and demonstration." But another confessed shortcoming of "sensitive knowledge" was that it "reaches no further than our Senses have . . . assured us." With respect to the present, it extends to nothing which is "now quite out of sight" (Locke, *Essay*, IV.ii.14, IV.xi.11). So when Hylas challenges the *"esse* is *percipi"* principle by suggesting that we can suppose our own annihilation without supposing the annihilation of the things we perceive, the stage is well set for a recapitulation of the Distinctness Argument *together with the enriching reference to continuity.* That summary (and its terseness is surely due to its being a summary, not to inattention) makes two points relevant to its immediately antecedent context. First, (contrary, one might add, to Locke's account, but in line with common sense) since I know that the sensible things I perceive have "exterior" existence, I thereby *know* that they exist not only "when . . . they are actually perceived," but also "during the intervals between the times of my perceiving them." Second, so far from undermining the *"esse* is *percipi"* principle, this knowledge leads on to knowledge of the existence of God. The effect is something very like the balanced pattern for which Bennett looks in vain. The character of sensation itself evinces the reality of sensible things as long as we perceive them, while their reality when we do not perceive them is implicit in their "distinct" or "exterior" existence in the mind of God. The ensuing discussion of the nature of the relationship between God (or, more generally, spirit) and sensible things contains still further references to the Distinctness Argument, and even yet another summary of it (*Dialogues*, 240). But only in the present passage is there any particular point in including what is, as it were, a frill: i.e. explicit mention of continuity.

Finally, as something of an appendix, I offer a tentative speculation about "archetypes" and Berkeley's seemingly emphatic refusal to commit himself on the question whether the very same ideas of sense as exist in my mind exist in God's mind, or whether, on the contrary, God's ideas are the archetypes to which mine conform. It may be that Berkeley was simply disinclined to get involved in a metaphysical problem for which he neither had, nor felt he needed, a categorical answer. But it seems equally possible that for him there is no substantive difference between the two accounts. When Johnson proposes, with some personal enthusiasm, a thoroughgoing "archetype" interpretation of Berkeley's theory of reality, Berkeley's reply may seem lukewarm: "I have no objection against calling the ideas in the mind of God archetypes of ours" (*Works*, ii. 292; cf. 274-6, 285f). But what Berkeley may mean to imply is that Johnson's formulation is just one acceptable way of describing a situation which can as well be described in terms of the identity of the "external" and "internal" objects. For he might have seen the possibility within his system of a duality approximating to the duality or ambivalence which Descartes attributed to the notion of an idea. On such a view, it is open to me to count "ideas" on the principle that an idea of mine (like a Cartesian mode) is tied exclusively to me as subject: in which case their reality must be interpreted as a conformity with divine external archetypes. Or we might equally allow my "ideas" (like intentional objects) to "exist in" more minds than one: in which case their reality can be described as their existence exterior to my mind, in God's mind.

Let me try to make this suggestion more plausible. In a rather notorious passage, Berkeley reacts explicitly to the principle that "the same idea which is in my mind, cannot be in yours, or in any other mind," a principle which Hylas combines with the common-sense assumption that different people often see the same thing in a late effort to recover from Philonous the distinction between ideas and things. Philonous's first response seems both deplorable in itself and ill-knit with other Berkeleian arguments. He comes close in effect to suggesting that the whole distinction between idea and thing stems from the ambiguity of "same" as it expresses qualitative or numerical identity:

> some regarding the uniformness of what was perceived, might call it the *same* thing: others especially regarding the diversity of persons who perceived, might choose the denomination of different things. But who sees not that all the dispute is about a word? (*Dialogues*, 247f)

If the reader is shocked by the apparent assumption that two ideas' being of the same particular object is not importantly different from their being qualitatively the same,[9] then it may come as a relief when Hylas points out that the materialist can explain the former as the two ideas' both referring to the same "external archetype." Philonous now seems to change his tune, claiming that he too can "suppose an external archetype" in God's mind.

One problem with this exchange is to connect its two stages. Can Berkeley *really* be saying that the "difficulty" over identity is certainly a merely verbal one, but that, even if it isn't, he has just as good a theoretical solution to it as the materialist's, in the hypothesis of Divine Archetypes? Perhaps, but another possibility is this: Berkeley connects the opposition between the vulgar "We often (directly) perceive the same things" and the philosophical "We never (directly) perceive the same things" with the traditionally recognized equivocation of "idea," so that he is trying in this passage to explain both together (as an equivocation of "same"). On this suggestion, those who, "regarding the diversity of persons . . . , choose the denomination of different things," would be those who tie "the same idea" to one subject (like "the same mode"); whereas their opponents allow the same idea to exist in several minds, explaining it, in line with common speech, as the thing itself, the same thing which all perceive. With this choice of language goes another: the latter party (again like ordinary folk) can make our ideas themselves the subject of real, "external" existence; but the former party, having ruled out that way of talking, must introduce the notion of external archetypes to do the same work. In either case, "external existence" will be external to all minds for the materialist, but external only to finite minds for the immaterialist. That is for Berkeley the important, more than verbal difference of opinion.

If this speculative understanding of Berkeley's thought is near the truth, we can see how for him the question whether Divine Ideas are the same as ours or archetypes of ours is as much a matter of words as the related question whether two people ever perceive the same thing. We can also understand how Philonous's response to Hylas's "difficulty," while it may be sadly inadequate, does not after all fall wretchedly into two dissonant halves.

Wadham College, University of Oxford

NOTES

1. But compare its use in Hylas' attempt at a causal proof of the existence of matter (*Dialogues*, 216). A good text to illustrate the close theoretical link between the notion of accidents' dependence on substance and the notion of causal dependence is, of course, Locke's *Essay concerning Human Understanding*, II.xxiii.1-7. Hylas' speech is a sort of loaded paraphrase of *Essay* II.xxiii.4. The (material) substance is for Locke the postulated "cause of the union" of sensible qualities, which "we cannot conceive, how they should subsist alone, nor one in another."

2. It is precisely the difference between the two which is emphasized by Berkeley in the first sentence quoted, and even more strongly elsewhere: e.g., "The question between the materialists and me is not, whether things have a real existence out of the mind of this or that person, but whether they have an absolute existence, distinct from being perceived by God and exterior to all minds" (*Dialogues*, 235).

3. The notion of an essential two-sidedness of "ideas" was later very well aired by Arnauld in his controversy with Malebranche, with which Berkeley was doubtless acquainted. Arnauld claimed, quite rightly, that he was following Descartes. (Cf. Descartes

1904:8,102f.)

4. Compare Locke's employment of the expressions "real existence" and "real ideas," e.g. in *Essay*, II.xxx, VI.i and IV.iv.

5. It is not absurd to attempt to cast light on Berkeley by considering Hume, despite chronology. For it is arguable that Hume's argument on scepticism of the senses is moulded, both deeply and in many fine details, by his reading of Berkeley. See Ayers 1984.

6. At this point three allegedly crucial premises are carefully and emphatically identified as (i) "the sensible world is that which we perceive by our several senses," (ii) "nothing is perceived by the senses beside ideas," (iii) "no idea or archetype of an idea can exist otherwise than in a mind." There is nothing in all this on the lines of *Every idea requires some active cause*, *All action involves volition*, or *All agents have ideas*, which are lemmas of the Passivity Argument as Bennett sets it out.

7. The same weakness inheres in the ancestral argument against scepticism of *Principles*, 88.

8. It should not be assumed that for Berkeley an appeal to common-sense trust in the senses is something distinct from an appeal to his own arguments or philosophical principles. On Locke's analysis of "sensitive knowledge," what is immediately given or perceived in "actual sensation" is not just the idea, but its arising in us through an external agency, which it therefore adequately signifies or represents. That is what the perception of existence, or of real existence, is for Locke. (Cf. *Essay*, IV.xi.2, IV.iv.4, II.xxxi.2, etc.) For Berkeley too, natural trust in the senses involves a similar short movement from the given external causality of an idea to its reality or distinct existence: but that movement corresponds, of course, to the first step of the Distinctness Argument.

9. The assumption would be less shocking if the question whether "different persons may perceive the same thing" concerned such "things" as *red* or *redness*. Yet although pre-Berkeleian concern with divine archetypes centered on universals, Hylas makes it clear that his objection concerns such particulars as "the garden, the trees, and flowers" which surround him.

BIBLIOGRAPHY

Ayers (1984)   M. R. Ayers, 'Berkeley and Hume: a Question of
                    Influence', in *Philosophy in History*, ed. R. Rorty, J. B.
                    Schneewind, and Q. Skinner. Cambridge University
                    Press.

Bennett (1968)   Jonathan Bennett, 'Berkeley and God', in *Locke and
                    Berkeley*, ed. C. B. Martin and D. M. Armstrong, pp.
                    380-99. New York, Doubleday.

Bennett (1971)   *Locke, Berkeley, Hume: Central Themes*. Oxford, Oxford
                    University Press.

Furlong (1968)   E. J. Furlong, 'Berkeley and the Tree in the Quad', in
                    Martin and Armstrong, *op. cit.*, pp. 400-408.

Descartes (1904)   *Oeuvres de Descartes*, ed. C. Adam and P. Tannery, Vol.
                    VII. Paris, Léopold Cerf.

Hume (1978)   David Hume, *A Treatise of Human Nature*, ed. L. A. Sel-
                    by-Bigge, rev. P. H. Nidditch. Oxford, Oxford University
                    Press.

Mabbott (1968)   J. D. Mabbott, 'The Place of God in Berkeley's Philoso-
                    phy', in Martin and Armstrong, *op. cit.*, pp. 364-79.

Tipton (1974)   I. C. Tipton, *Berkeley: The Philosophy of Immaterialism*.
                    London, Methuen.

A. David Kline

BERKELEY'S DIVINE LANGUAGE ARGUMENT

I. INTRODUCTION

Dean Berkeley wrote *Alciphron* during his somewhat impatient stay in Newport. He wanted to get on with the Bermuda project. Students of Berkeley have been impatient with the *Alciphron* – too much apologetics and too little philosophy. There is one apparent exception. The fourth dialogue, 'The Truth of Theism,' contains a proof of God's existence. But on a closer look many have found an unexciting version of the design argument, a version easily slain by Hume. T. E. Jessop, not one to underestimate Berkeley, puts it bluntly: ". . . the proof is the usual one from effect to cause, not the one peculiar to Berkeley."[1]

In a recent paper, 'Berkeley's Argument from Design,'[2] Michael Hooker has argued persuasively that the inattention to Dialogue IV is undeserved. In this paper the structure of Berkeley's argument will be explored. After an overview of the textual argumentation, three interpretations offered by Hooker will be considered. Out of their critical treatment a new interpretation will be generated. The argument is not the traditional design argument nor a version of the passivity or continuity arguments found in the *Principles* and *Three Dialogues*, respectively.[3] The argument is an inference to the best explanation parallel to the Cartesian argument for other minds.

II. OVERVIEW OF THE ARGUMENT

There are two phases in the discussion of God's existence. In the first, Alciphron, the free-thinker, begins with a methodological prolegomenon. The ontological and cosmological proofs, and appeals to authority and to utility are out. The former, though they may puzzle, never convince; the latter, though perhaps suitable for the cleric or statesman, scarcely deserve mention to the philosopher. Alciphron insists on a proof based on sense perception.

      Euphranor, Berkeley's spokesman, gets Alciphron to admit that men have souls, yet this knowledge is inferred from sense experience. In a

129

E. Sosa (ed.), Essays on the Philosophy of George Berkeley, 129–142.
© *1987 by D. Reidel Publishing Company*

similar manner Euphranor suggests that we can have knowledge of God's existence:

> From motions, therefore, you infer a mover as cause; and from reasonable motions (or such as appear calculated for a reasonable end) a rational cause, soul or spirit? . . . The soul of man actuates but a small body, an insignificant particle, in respect of the great masses of nature, the elements, and the heavenly bodies and system of the world. And the wisdom that appears in those motions which are the effect of human reason is incomparable less than that which discovers itself in the structure and use of organized natural bodies, animal or vegetable. A man with his hand can make no machine so admirable as the hand itself; nor can any of those motions by which we trace out human reason approach the skill and contrivance of those wonderful motions of the heart, brain, and other vital parts, which do not depend on the will of man . . . Doth it not follow, then that from natural motions, independent of man's will, may be inferred both power and wisdom incomparably greater than that of the human soul? (*Alc.*, 146.)

Alciphron admits that there is something to the argument. But he insists that Euphranor's proof of God's existence is much weaker than Euphranor's proof that Alciphron exists. After all, Alciphron stands before him in the flesh.

Euphranor stresses that the argument for another's soul does have the same structure as the argument for God's existence. Alciphron the person, i.e. an individual thinking thing, should not be confused with Alciphron's body. Alciphron's soul is no more nor less given in sense experience than God is:

> . . . in the self-same manner, it seems to me that, though I cannot with eyes of flesh behold the invisible God, yet I do in the strictest sense behold and perceive by all my senses such signs and tokens, such effects and operations, as suggest, indicate, and demonstrate an invisible God, as certainly, and with the same evidence, at least, as any other signs perceived by sense do suggest to me the existence of your soul . . . (*Alc.*, 147.)

The structure of the argument for other minds and the argument for God's existence appear to be analogical. We need not examine the fine structure of these analogical arguments, for, as we shall see, the discussion advances to arguments of an improved form.

The second phase begins with Alciphron's admission that he was initially nonplussed by the previous discussion. But upon further reflection he recognizes that the previous argument was really not successful.

> At first methought a particular structure, shape, or motion was the most certain proof of a thinking reasonable soul. But a little attention satisfies me that these things have no necessary connexion with reason, knowledge, and wisdom; and that allowing them to be certain proofs of a living soul, they cannot be so of a thinking and reasonable one. (*Alc.*, 148.)

Though the previous proofs will not do, Alciphron now asserts what on reflection does justify one's belief in other minds:

> Upon this point, I have found that nothing so much convinces me of the existence of another person as his speaking to me. It is my hearing you talk that, in strict philosophical truth, is to me the best argument for your being. (*Alc.*, 148.)

This argument has the form of an inference to the best explanation. One is not justified in believing in another mind because the other body looks like his or moves like his, etc. One is justified because the other body exhibited linguistic behavior and the only adequate explanation of such behavior is the existence of a mind.[4]

Alciphron challenges Euphranor to produce an argument of similar structure for God's existence – you (Euphranor) wouldn't "pretend that God speaks to man in the same clear and sensible manner as one man doth to another." (*Alc.*, 149.)

Euphranor wants to be sure he understands exactly what needs to be shown:

> '[If] intervention and use of arbitrary, outward, sensible signs, having no resemblance or necessary connexion with the things they stand for and suggest; if it shall appear that, by innumerable combinations of these signs, or endless variety of things is discovered and made known to us; and that we are thereby instructed or informed in their different natures; that we are taught and admonished what to shun, and what to pursue; and are directed how to regulate our motions, and how to act with respect to things distant from us, as well in time and place will this content you? (*Alc.*, 149.)

Alciphron agrees that such a demonstration would satisfy him. Berkeley's central point of the fourth dialogue is that nature constitutes just such a language.

III. HOOKER'S INTERPRETATIONS

Michael Hooker believes that the text can be used to support three interpretations, which he treats as being equally plausible. For facility in discussion I name them as follows: the analogical design argument, the orderliness of sense experience argument, and the sense experience/world
connection argument.

Consider first the suggestion that Berkeley was giving an analogical
design argument (D-argument):

> According to that interpretation, our senses inform us just as
> the spoken language of another informs us, so the data of our
> senses can be viewed as a kind of language. Since tokens of
> spoken language each have intelligent speakers behind them, so
> too must the language of our sense have an intelligent
> "speaker" behind it.[5]

In evaluating the D-argument Hooker rehearses the Humean criticism of
arguments by analogy.

Supposedly on the first interpretation the argument has the following structure:

> Spoken language has the property of being informative and
> having a mind behind it.
> Sense-data have the property of being informative.
> Therefore, sense-data have a mind behind them.

This interpretation suffers from at least two difficulties: (1) The
D-argument is a very weak analogical argument. Analogical arguments will
be stronger as the "objects" of the analogy share more properties. The
D-argument only mentions one property. (2) More importantly, the interpretation does not bring into relief how the theological argument is parasitic
on the argument for other minds, a point emphasized by Berkeley. Furthermore, it undermines their similarity of structure. The linguistic argument for other minds was clearly an argument to the best explanation. Informativeness is only one of the many marks of something being a
language. It is the linguistic behavior of a man that requires explanation by
mind and it is the linguistic behavior of nature that requires explanation by
a Divine Mind. That Berkeley intends his theistic argument to be an inference to the best explanation is evident in his summation of the discussion:
"It [sense-data language] cannot be accounted for by mechanical principles,
by atoms, attraction, or effluvia . . . being utterly inexplicable and unac-
countable by the laws of motion . . . doth set forth and testify the immediate operation of a spirit." (*Alc.*, 159-60.)

The next two interpretations, the orderliness of sense experience argument (O-argument) and the sense experience/world connection argument (C-argument) rest on a distinction between the epistemological and ontological dimensions of the sign relation.[6] The idea is simple: one idea of sense signifying another idea of sense – e.g., the sight of fire signifies the feeling of warmth – is the epistemological sign relation. When an idea of sense signifies an object in the world the relation is ontological.[7]

What follows is Hooker's O-argument interpretation. It is based on the epistemological dimension of the sign relation.

> Viewed from the first perspective an argument to the effect that God preserves the connection between contingent ideas of sense is not straightforwardly an analogical argument from design. What is needed is an explanation of why contingently connected sense data show the remarkably regular co-occurrence that they do. Without the assurance of some ordering force behind the world of sense data, we should not expect the feeling of warmth to accompany the sight of fire. But it does, with remarkable regularity, so there must be an ordering force. By this mode of arguing, then, God is posited as the best explanation of the uniformity of experience.[8]

Hooker correctly points out that on the O-argument Berkeley's view is not unlike the theistic argument of *Principles*. Evaluating the arguments begins by assuring oneself that the phenomenon *needs* explanation, then considering the power of alternative explanations.

Before considering the merits of the O-argument as an interpretation of Berkeley, let us finish the survey by stating the account that rests on the ontological dimension of the sign relation:

> In *Alciphron*, though he refers obliquely to the immaterialist doctrine of his developed philosophy, Berkeley is speaking to the philosophically unsophisticated. His audience will hold a common sense view of our senses as giving us information about a world that is really out there and represented to us by the data of our senses. However, and this is the important point, there is no guarantee in virtue of a necessary connection that our senses do accurately inform us. But because we think we are informed, we must suppose that something exists as the guarantor of the reliability of our cognitive sensory faculties. Hence we conclude that God exists. The analogy to language is just this: In the case of language there is a contingent or conventional connection between words and the things they signify; in the case of the language of nature there is similarly a contingent connection between our experiences and the worldly things they signify. In the case of spoken language it is the

speaker's intention that ensures the reference relationship, and
in the case of the language of nature it is the theophonic deity,
always speaking to us through our senses, who ensures the
reference of our sense experience.[9]

It is clear from the quotation above and other remarks of Hooker's
that on the C-argument interpretation God is invoked to avoid the skepticism generated by Lockean realism. If we assume that real bodies exist
ouside the mind independently of being perceived, what reason is there to
believe that our sense experience, even if it is caused by bodies, accurately
represents them or provides us with information about them? The answer
is that God guarantees that sense experience is informative of the real
world.

It will be useful to begin with this reading and work back to the
O-argument. The C-argument contains some very suspicious assumptions
about the philosophy of language: the referring and informing relation are
the same relation and *a* speaker maintains by *his* intentions the reference
relationship. But we need not pursue those issues, for there is a blunt objection.

How are we to understand "real world?" If we understand the notion in accord with Berkeley's mature philosophy, i.e. as a set of appearances, then the C-argument degenerates into the O-argument. God is pre-
serving connections among sense-data.

Can we understand "real world" in the Lockean sense? Hooker realizes that it is extraordinary to propose that Berkeley is assuming a version of Lockean realism. But Hooker is willing to swallow this on the explanation that Berkeley's audience is the unsophisticated. He supposedly
has put his idealism in the closet and will show the uninitiate the "truth"
about God. There are two things wrong with this: (1) Lockean realism is
not a vulgar doctrine. (2) It is simply preposterous to hold that a thinker of
Berkeley's ability and character would attempt to persuade others by
premises he believed to be false. In the course of the dialogue Euphranor
criticizes Alciphron for being a lazy thinker, only wanting to get the discussion over and not having the intellectual stamina to get matters right. We
should look for a better interpretation than to suppose that Berkeley's discussion of God's existence is not even intended as a sound argument.[10]

We are left with the O-argument. It has at least three problems: (1)
According to the argument God maintains the orderliness of sense-data —
all sense-data. But Berkeley explicitly denies that there is a Divine Language of smell or odor. Yet he insists that the sense-data of smell and odor
are orderly. So if he is giving an inference to the best explanation, it cannot
be the explanation for orderliness simpliciter. The O-argument is not subtle
enough. Berkeley is up to something this argument does not illustrate.

(2) The O-argument does not do justice to Berkeley's lengthy and
complex discussion of other minds. If he is ultimately giving an

O-argument, the preliminaries are at best fat and in effect confusing. One should get on with it. There is orderliness and it needs explanation. A better interpretation would make sense of the preliminaries.

(3) It is very odd that Berkeley would give the O-argument independently of his immaterialist weapons. Standing alone it is not going to convince anyone, especially those in Berkeley's audience. Inferences to the best explanation are evaluated in the context of their competitors. The free-thinkers have an obvious competitor – materialism. Materialism can explain mere orderliness. We have certainly nothing more than a stand-off. An interpretation is needed that would speak less naively to Berkeley's opponents.

IV. THE DIVINE LANGUAGE ARGUMENT

How then should we read the text? The objections to the O-argument provide adequacy conditions for an interpretation: it (i) must illuminate the primacy of a *visual* Divine Language, (ii) must make sense of the other minds discussion, (iii) must give Berkeley something powerful to answer his opponents.

The key is the second adequacy condition. Once it is met the others fall out. Recall that Berkeley rejects what appears to be an analogical argument for other minds, then accepts a certain inference to the best explanation. He, curiously, does not spell out exactly what features of another's linguistic behavior demand explanation by non-materialistic causes. He takes the need for a non-materialistic explanation as obvious. I suspect that the reason he does this is because he is relying on the Cartesian proof of other minds. Berkeley takes that argument as sound and, better yet, he takes his readers as accepting the argument. (It is Alciphron who balks at the analogical argument and suggests the linguistic move.)

This is a very powerful ploy on Berkeley's part. He can build a demonstration of God's existence for free-thinkers on the basis of shared strategy. I do not want to go too far astray with historical details. But a few rough remarks are in order given my claims.

Berkeley was of course familiar with much of Descartes' work. He refers to Descartes (sometimes by name) on numerous occasions. In Dialogue IV when, as we shall see, he criticizes a view on the nature of distance perception, that view is unmistakebly identified with the one defended by Descartes in *Dioptrics*.[11]

Alciphron according to its subtitle is "an apology for the Christian religion against those who are called free-thinkers." As Jessop points out, Berkeley's text is embedded in the "anti-deistic controversy that absorbed much of the attention of the orthodox during the first half of the eighteenth century."[12] Berkeley would not regard Descartes as a free-thinker and deist. But undoubtedly Descartes' emphasis on rationalism and mechanism inspired free-thinking and deism. Berkeley appreciated this historical point.

Free-thinking is a complex and diverse tradition, but two figures Berkeley must have had in mind in composing *Alciphron* were John Toland and Anthony Collins. Toland's *Christianity not Mysterious* received a rejoinder from Peter Browne, the Provost of Berkeley's college.[13] Collins' *Discourse on Free Thinking* was very widely known. It is a clear and urbane work. Now the important point for us is that each of these figures was inspired by Cartesianism.[14] Collins goes so far as to list Descartes among the roll of illustrious free-thinkers.[15]

My claim is that Berkeley knew Descartes and his free-thinking audience well. On many occasions Berkeley had to criticize a Cartesian position in order to make way for his own. In *Alciphron*, "Dialogue IV," matters are different. He will use the Cartesian argument for other minds to build a proof for the existence of God. Given his audience, he expects little resistance on the other minds issue, but then he believes the theistic conclusion will be unavoidable.

In a passage well known to contemporary philosophers, Descartes states that even if a machine looked like a man we could tell that it was not a *real* man:

> . . . they could never use words or other constructed signs, as we do to declare our thoughts to others. It is quite conceivable that a machine should be so made as to utter words, and even utter them in connection with physical events that cause a change in one of its organs; so that, e.g., if it is touched in one part, it asks what you want to say to it, and if touched in another, it cries out that it is hurt; but not that it should be so made as to arrange words variously in response to the meaning of what is said in its presence, as even the dullest men can do.[16]

Descartes makes three important points in this passage: (i) language is composed of *constructed* signs; (ii) linguistic behavior exhibits rich *generative* powers – we are able to combine signs in many diverse ways; (iii) linguistic behavior is *appropriate* to the background environment. Descartes believes that (i) gives an essential property of language and that (ii) and (iii) can only be explained by minds.

If Berkeley is constructing a proof of God's existence in a parallel fashion to Descartes' discussion of other minds, we would expect Berkeley to emphasize similar points about the Divine Language. This is precisely what we find. Berkeley agrees with Descartes that language is a constructed set of signs. The choice of marks or sounds for a given word is arbitrary. And there is no necessary connection between the sign and the thing signified: ". . . God speaks to men by the intervention and use of arbitrary, outward, sensible signs, having no resemblance or necessary connexion with the things they stand for and suggest . . ."

For Berkeley a thing looking little and faint is a sign of its being at a great distance. But there is no necessary connection here. One must by experience make the connection just as by experience one makes the connection between "dog" and dog. Berkeley in Dialogue IV anticipates a Cartesian objection to his thesis and hence repeats some of the basic argument found earlier in *An Essay towards a New Theory of Vision.* Some writers on optics (Descartes for one) held that distance was judged by a kind of natural geometry. According to this view there is a necessary connection between certain "apprehended" angles and the distances of objects. The details are unimportant here. But clearly Berkeley must refute this view in order to maintain that the Divine Language is a *language.* His lengthy effort along these lines is further evidence that he is addressing an audience familiar with the Cartesian moves.

Like Descartes, Berkeley also emphasizes the generative feature of language. Descartes often compares the "language" of brutes with real language. Brutes begin with a small set of primitives. Furthermore, their ability to combine them to form new signs is very impoverished. Man does not suffer this liability. And according to Berkeley neither does the Divine Language. The language of sense-data exhibits "innumerable combinations of these signs." (See also my discussion of the first adequacy condition.)

For Descartes a certain giveaway that a brute is really a simple, albeit gooey, machine is a breakdown in the appropriateness of its behavior. In a humorous example he describes an episode familiar to any cat owner.[17] The beast carefully prepares a hole for its excrement only to miss the hole, but nevertheless carefully covers up the original area. Such behavior is not the mark of a mind. Linguistic behavior in brutes is a more specific version of the general failing. Your parrot may utter "good morning" when you arise for breakfast, but it also gives this cheery greeting when you return from an evening concert. In modern terms the behavior in the cat example and the behavior of "talking" parrots is tropistic.

Can a case be made for the natural language being appropriate? When we speak of an object's behavior being appropriate we must be able to distinguish the object from its environment and then assign goals to the object. If, as the environment changes, the object behaves in accord with its goals we can speak of the behavior being appropriate. Imagine a small shop owner's device to indicate the presence of a customer – perhaps an appropriately located electric eye attached to a buzzer. The object is the electric eye. Its goal is to mark the presence of customers. The device's behavioral repertoire is to buzz or not. If a customer transgresses the space the buzzer sounds.

Modifications of the environment reveal the crudeness of the device. The buzzer sounds when a mailman, a dog, or a falling sycamore leaf approaches. The device gives away its stupidity or mindlessness. Again the issue is to show that natural language, in a way similar to the customer detector, exhibits appropriate behavior but does not break down as the customer detector does, and in fact is so agile that its behavior carries the mark of mind.

The "object" in the natural language case is God. Berkeley tells us His goals – to inform, to teach, to entertain, to direct and to admonish us. The informational goal is primary. (*Alc.*, 149.) For simplicity of discussion I shall restrict God's goals to that of informing us. Relevant behaviors are various natural signs. What constitutes the environment? There is an apparent rub here, especially if we interpret all of nature as God's signs as Hooker does in the O-argument. We need a behavior/environment distinction if the parallel to the customer detector is to be exhibited.

The way clear of the rub is to realize that God's language is a *visible* language and that God's language is informative of the tangible properties of objects.[18]

> Upon the whole, it seems the proper objects of sight are light and colours, with their several shades and degrees; all which, being infinitely diversified and combined, form a language wonderfully adopted to suggest and exhibit to us the distances, figures, situations, dimensions, and various qualities of tangible objects . . . (*Alc.*, 154.)

The visible appearance/tangible property distinction constitutes the linguistic behavior/environment distinction. So the parallel with Descartes' cat and parrot and my customer detector is complete!

Do visible appearances appropriately inform us of tangible properties? Berkeley, quite plausibly, thinks they do. But does natural language, like the customer detector, break down (act inappropriately) and hence reveal not a mind but a dull device? More importantly, does it make sense to test nature? What sort of interference *might* unmask nature as tropistic?

Suppose Fred is chasing a butterfly. We might arrange for various hurdles to plague him – having someone walk in his way, release a playful dog, spray the butterfly with a chemical that excites it to fly faster, etc. The visual language unlike the customer detector does not keep saying the same thing. Nature appropriately speaks anew to Fred, consistent with the goal of informing him. In virtue of that information Fred may successfully negotiate the obstacles, judge the distances and speeds accurately, and grasp the butterfly. So it is conceptually sensible to *attempt* to unmask nature. As it turns out, nature is a sophisticated show.

Berkeley's lengthy discussion of the other minds problem is not just fluff. He, as I have argued, believes the reader to accept or be persuaded by the Cartesian position on other minds. By showing the reader that just those features of human language that cry out for explanation are also features of nature's language, he hopes to force the reader to see the necessity of a Divine Mind.

Returning to the first adequacy condition, we have already seen some evidence for the primacy of visual language, but more can be said. Alciphron having heard Berkeley's argument remains perplexed. He then offers a *reductio* of visual signs forming a Divine Language:

> I cannot help thinking that some fallacy runs throughout this whole ratiocination, though perhaps I may not· readily point it out. It seems to me that every other sense may as well be deemed a language as that of vision. Smells and tastes for instance, are signs that inform us of other qualities to which they have neither likeness nor necessary connexion. (*Alc.*, 157.)

Alciphron's suggestion is that given Euphranor's characterization of nature's language, smell and taste would form a Divine Language. That is absurd, hence the characterization of those features sufficient for a language must be mistaken. One might expect Berkeley to dig in and assert that smells and tastes do form a language. But he does not. His answer is more interesting:

> That they are signs is certain, as also that language and all other signs agree in the general nature of sign, or so far forth as signs. But it is as certain that all signs are not language: not even all significant sounds, such as the natural cries of animals, or the inarticulate sounds and interjections of men. It is the articulation, combination, variety and copiousness, extensive and general use and easy application of signs (all which are commonly found in vision) that constitute the true nature of language. Other senses may indeed furnish signs; and yet those signs have no more right than inarticulate sounds to be thought a language. (*Alc.*, 157.)

I understand Berkeley not to be emphasizing orderliness *simpliciter* in the above. There is a certain orderliness between the cry an animal makes and the animal being in pain or a certain bitter taste and unsweetened chocolate on the palate. These signs do not fail as language because they are necessarily connected with the thing signified or because there is a lack of orderliness in the relation. They fail because of the generative condition. Basic smells and tastes only combine in very limited ways to form new signs. Their limited combining patterns restricts their informative power. But colors and shapes form endless complex and informative new patterns. The impoverishment of the former appearances takes away their license as a real language.

According to the third adequacy condition we should adopt an interpretation that at least *prima facie* gives Berkeley something interesting and powerful to say to his opponents. Neither the D, O or C-arguments do that.

The D-argument is very weak logically. The O-argument is a throwback to the *Principles*. And both the O and C-arguments have obvious materialistic replies. The Divine Language argument being based on the Cartesian proof of other minds is muct more powerful. If Berkeley can persuade his opponent that sense-data form a language, which he has tried to do by emphasizing the Cartesian features of language, there can be little disagreement on how to explain it.

My primary purpose throughout the paper has been to provoke a discussion of the structure of Berkeley's argument. There remains a problem I have side-stepped that demands comment.

The difficulty arises when we consider Berkeley from a contemporary point of view. He assumes that linguistic behavior requires mentalistic explanation. Berkeley does not attempt to defend this claim. (My interpretation explains his silence.) Nevertheless, the received view in philosophy of mind has it that complex performances (e.g., linguistic behavior or problem solving) do not require non-materialistic explanation. The last holdout for any form of non-materialism is not sapience but sentience, e.g., having a certain sensation. The features Descartes and Berkeley draw our attention to were and are explanatorily opaque. The search for an adequate theory is not likely to appeal to seventeenth and eighteenth century minds, but that does not minimize the insight that *simple* mechanical paradigms will not do either.

Iowa State University

NOTES

1.   From Jessop's Introduction to *Alciphron*, p. 13.

2.   Michael Hooker, 'Berkeley's Argument from Design,' in *Berkeley: Critical and Interpretive Essays*, ed. Colin M. Turbayne (Minneapolis: University of Minnesota Press, 1982), pp. 261-70.

3.   These arguments are named and discussed in Jonathan Bennett's well known paper, 'Berkeley and God,' *Philosophy*, **XL** (1965), pp. 207-21.

4.   For a discussion of the logic of inferences to the best explanation, see Gilbert Harman, 'The Inference to the Best Explanation,' *Philosophical Review*, **65** (1965), pp. 88-95; and Peter Achinstein, *Law and Explanation* (Oxford: Oxford University Press, 1971), pp. 119-24.

5.   Hooker, p. 264.

6.   Hooker traces this distinction to Robert Armstrong.

7.   Hooker, pp. 265-66.

8.   *Ibid.*, pp. 266.

9.   *Ibid.*, pp. 269.

10. Furthermore, we should not forget that Hooker has no specific textual evidence for the C-argument, or any of his interpretations for that matter, that goes beyond the passages cited in the overview.

11. See Colin M. Turbayne, ed., *Works on Vision* (Indianapolis: Bobbs-Merrill, 1963), p. xxiii.

12. From Jessop's Introduction to *Alciphron*, p. 4.

13. *Ibid.*, p. 5. For a discussion of Brown and the deists including Toland and Collins, see Paul Olscamp, *The Moral Philosophy of George Berkeley* (The Hague: Martinus Nijhoff, 1970), pp. 184-222.

14. For one example of the Cartesian influence, see John Toland, *Christianity not Mysterious* (London, 1720), p. 58. Ernest Campbell

Mossner, 'Deism,' in *The Encyclopedia of Philosophy*, ed. by Paul Edwards, vol. 2 (New York: Macmillan, 1967), p. 328.

15.   Ernest Campbell Mossner, 'Anthony Collins,' in *The Encyclopedia of Philosophy*, ed. by Paul Edwards, vol. 2 (New York: Macmillan, 1967), p. 145.

16.   Rene Descartes, *Discourse on the Method of Rightly Conducting the Reason*, in *Descartes: Philosophical Writings*, ed. by Elizabeth Anscombe and Peter Geach (London: Thomas Nelson and Sons, 1954), p. 43. Descartes gives another reason (p. 116) which appears to be a generalized version of the first. See Keith Gunderson, *Mentality and Machines* (Garden City, New York: Anchor Books, 1971), pp. 7-17.

17.   Rene Descartes, 'Letter to the Marquis of Newcastle,' in *Materialism and the Mind-Body Problem*, ed. by David Rosenthal (Englewood Cliffs, N.J.: Prentice-Hall), pp. 22-23.

18.   These ideas are not new to *Alciphron*. See *NTV*, 1-28, and *Principles*, 44.

Robert Merrihew Adams

BERKELEY AND EPISTEMOLOGY

Probably the most popular of Berkeley's arguments against the extramental existence of matter is the epistemological argument that we have no reason to believe in such a thing. For Berkeley himself this was by no means the most important argument. In fact, it is not fully developed in the *Three Dialogues*, but only in sections 18-20 of the *Principles*. The reason for the secondary role accorded this argument by Berkeley is indicated by the opening sentence of section 18: "But though it were possible that solid, figured, moveable substances may exist without the mind, yet how is it possible for us to know this?" Berkeley thinks he has proved that the extramental existence of such substances is not even possible. That proof engages his primary interest, and the argument of insufficient evidence comes in only to back it up, for readers who may not have been convinced by the impossibility proof. Nonetheless, Berkeley's epistemological argument is of great interest, both for its own sake and for what it can teach us about the relation between metaphysics and epistemology.

I will first discuss the argument(s) of *Principles*, 18-20, as an attack on what we may call "Evidential Realism." This discussion will lead to reflections on the epistemological situation of metaphysics. Then I will discuss the "Direct Realist" response to Berkeley's epistemological arguments, arguing that it is a weak response, and that there is little reason to prefer Direct Realism either to Idealism or to Evidential Realism.

I. BERKELEY'S ATTACK ON EVIDENTIAL REALISM

Berkeley sets up his argument with a disjunction. If it is possible for us to know that bodies exist outside the mind, then "either we must know it by sense, or by reason."[1] He proceeds to argue that it could not be known by sense, and concludes, "It remains therefore that if we have any knowledge at all of external things, it must be by reason."

This may seem a strange beginning to the argument. Surely any knowledge we might have of the existence of bodies would be founded in sense perception; why then would their existence, if known at all, not be known by sense? The answer to this question is that for Berkeley, "known by sense" means "immediately known by sense." That is explicit in the first Dialogue (*Works*, ii. 174f.), where Berkeley has Hylas say that "in truth

143

E. Sosa (ed.), Essays on the Philosophy of George Berkeley, 143–161.
©*1987 by D. Reidel Publishing Company*

the senses perceive nothing which they do not perceive immediately: for they make no inferences." This suggests the following as at least an approximate understanding of the distinction between sense and reason in *Principles*, 18. Immediate perception is perception not involving any inference. Sense is a faculty of immediate perception, and reason is a faculty of inferring. To deny that extramental bodies could be known "by sense" is not to deny that knowledge of them could be founded in sense perception. It is to deny that they could be immediately perceived in sensation; but that leaves open the possibility that knowledge of them might be indirectly (mediately) grounded in sense perception, by way of an inference. This interpretation is confirmed by the full statement of the conclusion of this introductory portion of Berkeley's argument, which is that "if we have any knowledge at all of external things, it must be by reason, *inferring* their existence from what is *immediately* perceived by sense" (emphasis mine).

What is Berkeley's reason, then, for maintaining that extramental bodies could not be perceived immediately by sense? His argument on this point is very short:

> As for our senses, by them we have the knowledge only of our sensations, ideas, or those things that are immediately perceived by sense, call them what you will: but they do not inform us that things exist without the mind, or unperceived, like to those which are perceived. This the materialists themselves acknowledge.

This is not even a very clear statement of the argument. We may wonder why "those things that are immediately perceived by sense" should not be called extramental bodies, if we may call them what we will. But that is merely a quibble. The gist of the argument is clear. Berkeley is saying that only sensations or ideas, or, more broadly, intramental entities are immediately perceived by sense. And the only justification he sees a need to give for this claim is that it is granted by his opponents.

This is, of course, precisely the claim that is *not* granted by Direct Realists, and we shall have to return to this step of the argument in the second part of the paper. But the claim was so widely accepted in Berkeley's time that it is not surprising that he devotes so little attention to its defense. The opponents he has in view are Evidential Realists, and his epistemological arguments are to be studied principally as an attack on Evidential Realism, a critique of the inference from sense data in the mind to bodies existing outside the mind.

He offers two such arguments, one in section 18 of the *Principles*, which seems to be taken up again in section 20, and one in section 19. In section 18 he argues that the inference from sense data to extramental bodies fails for want of a necessary connection. "But what reason can induce us to believe the existence of bodies without the mind, from what we perceive, since the very patrons of matter themselves do not pretend, there is any necessary connection betwixt them and our ideas?" That there is no such necessary connection, Berkeley argues with considerations quarried from Descartes and Malebranche:

> I say it is granted on all hands (and what happens in dreams, phrensies, and the like, puts it beyond dispute) that it is possible we might be affected with all the ideas we have now, though no bodies existed without, resembling them. Hence it is evident the supposition of external bodies is not necessary for the producing our ideas: since it is granted they are produced sometimes, and might possibly be produced always in the same order we see them in at present, without their concurrence.

Here we might raise questions about the sense or senses of possibility at work in the argument, and about the relevance of dreams and phrensies to possible explanations of our ordinary sense experience, which (as Berkeley himself emphasizes) is rather different in content. But there is no need to dwell on these points. There are well known arguments – Descartes's omnipotent deceiver argument, for one – that support (convincingly, I think) the claim that the production of "all the ideas we have now" without the concurrence of extramental bodies is possible, in some sense not clearly too weak for Berkeley's intentions.

The argument of section 18 is a bad argument for a different reason. It depends on the assumption that the inference from ideas in the mind to bodies outside the mind must be rejected unless the extramental bodies are necessary for the production of the ideas. But this is an unreasonable requirement. In empirical reasoning we do not demand that the evidence be impossible if the hypothesis were false. It is enough that the evidence be less likely to occur if the hypothesis were false.

For instance, impressions in the earth, of a certain size, shape, and pattern, would normally be sufficient evidence for a confident belief that a woman had walked over the ground wearing high-heeled shoes. It would be possible, of course, for this evidence to occur though the belief were false. The apparent footprints might have been made by a chimpanzee wearing high-heeled shoes, by a child playing with its mother's clothes, by a man manipulating a pair of shoes from a helicopter, by a poltergeist, or by the miraculous intervention of God. But in the ordinary context we have in mind, all of these hypotheses are quite improbable. The hypothesis of a woman in high-heeled shoes provides the best explanation of the footprints. It is fair to say that it is unlikely that they would be there if the hypothesis were false.

The inference from the footprints to the woman in high-heeled shoes is thus an example of what is called "inference to the best explanation," and does not depend on a *necessary* connection between the evidence and the hypothesis. This is typical of empirical reasoning. A formal expression of this pattern of thought is Bayes' Theorem in the calculus of probabilities:

$$P(h/e \ \& \ b) = P(h/b) \cdot \frac{P(e/h \ \& \ b)}{P(e/b)}$$

Here $P(h/e \ \& \ b)$ is the probability of the hypothesis h, given the evidence e and background information b; $P(h/b)$ is the probability of h on b alone, "prior" to e; and the fraction, which measures the degree to which e inceases the probability of h, is the ratio of the probability of e, given h as well as b, to the probability of e on b alone. This widely accepted theorem, to which we will have occasion to return, thus says (among other things) that e increases the probability of h to the degree that e would be likelier to be true if h were true than otherwise.

Berkeley seems to acknowledge this point (though of course not in terms of Bayes' theorem) at the beginning of section 19 of the *Principles*, saying,

> But though we might possibly have all our sensations without [external bodies], yet perhaps it may be thought easier to conceive and explain the manner of their production, by supposing external bodies in their likeness rather than otherwise; and so it might be at least probable there are such things as bodies that excite their ideas in our minds.[2]

Responding to this suggestion, Berkeley develops a better argument against Evidential Realism than he had in section 18. His response is that the hypothesis of "external bodies" does not help to explain our sensations,

> . . . for though we give the materialists their external bodies, they by their own confession are never the nearer knowing how our ideas are produced: since they own themselves unable to comprehend in what manner body can act upon spirit, or how it is possible it should imprint any idea in the mind. Hence it is evident the production of ideas or sensations in our minds, can be no reason why we should suppose matter or corporeal substances, since that is acknowledged to remain equally inexplicable with, or without this supposition.

The material hypothesis, Berkeley claims, does not provide the best explanation of the evidence of our senses; indeed it provides no explanation at all because of the notorious difficulty of understanding how mind-body interaction can take place. The evidence of our senses does not increase the probability of the material hypothesis, because we would be no likelier to have that evidence with the external bodies than without them. In Bayesian terms, if h is the material hypothesis, and e is the evidence of our senses,

(Pe/h & b) is not greater than P(e/b).

In philosophical interest and power this is certainly an improvement on the argument of the previous section. It would be nice for us Berkeley fans to think that the bad argument of section 18 was just a dialectical warm-up for the argument of section 19. Unfortunately, section 20 seems to revert to the weaker argument. Berkeley's claim there is that it is "possible" for "an intelligence, without the help of external bodies, to be affected with the same train of sensations or ideas that you are, imprinted in the same order and with like vividness in his mind," and that the "one consideration" that such an intelligence would have "all the reason to believe the existence of corporeal substances, represented by his ideas, and exciting them in his mind, that you can possibly have for believing the same thing . . . is enough to make any reasonable person suspect the strength of whatever arguments he may think himself to have, for the existence of bodies without the mind." The rhetorical effect is smashing, but the substance of the argument is simply an appeal to the fact that it would be *possible* to have the evidence of our senses without any external bodies. In other words, it is the argument whose weakness we would like to think that Berkeley had seen.

Why does Berkeley revert to it? Section 19 is introduced as refuting the suggestion that the material hypothesis "might be at least probable," whereas section 18 is addressed to the question how it would be "possible for us to know" that external bodies exist. It may therefore be conjectured that Berkeley thinks the absence of necessary connection is sufficient to refute claims to *knowledge*, leaving only a much more tentative affirmation of matter to be dealt with in section 19. It is a difficulty for this interpretation, however, that sections 18 and 20 also attack the claim that we have "reason to believe" the material hypothesis. In any event, since an absolutely necessary connection is not required for any degree of certainty that could reasonably be expected on an issue of this sort, it is the argument of section 19 that deserves our attention.

How good is that argument? Surely, one may be inclined to object to Berkeley, there must be some explanation of our sensations – not merely of the fact that we have sensations at all, but especially of the fact that they recur in such patterns as to present us with a stable, orderly world of sensible things. For all its explanatory deficiencies, might not the hypothesis of external bodies be the best explanation available to us for this phenomenon? Can Berkeley provide a better explanation?

Berkeley thinks he can. He does not doubt for a minute that there must be an explanation of the evidence of our senses. He thinks the correct one is provided by a theistic hypothesis. God acts directly on our minds, affecting them with sensations. His goodness and wisdom lead him to give us sensations so patterned as to present us with an orderly world in which we can learn to make decisions that have predictable consequences, and thus to live meaningful lives.

God does this without the aid of external bodies. He has no need of them in causing sensations in us. Indeed the problem of mind-body interaction makes it difficult to see how they would help Him in the project. If we assume, with Berkeley, that theism will be accepted whether or not external bodies are postulated, it seems explanatorily otiose to postulate them. "It is to suppose," as Berkeley says, ". . . that God has created innumerable beings that are entirely useless, and serve to no manner of purpose" (*Principles*, 19). It is a familiar hypothesis that Berkeley came to this line of thought by reflecting on the explanatory uselessness of bodies in the philosophy of Malebranche, according to which our sensory experience is directly caused by God, but extramental bodies serve as "occasions" for God to cause us to have corresponding perceptions.

An occasionalist might think that Berkeley is too hasty in assuming that external bodies are "entirely useless" if God does not need or use them for their own sake. Perhaps indeed it is easier to understand why God would affect us with some of the experiences that we have (particularly some of the disagreeable ones) if He is trying to put us in touch with a extramental world that he values for its own sake. To this Berkeley would doubtless respond that the inertness and qualitative emptiness of matter (at least as it is conceived in modern scientific versions of the material hypothesis) make it impossible to understand why it would be valued for its own sake.

Still, it may be objected, Berkeley's theistic hypothesis can hardly duplicate the astonishing success which the material hypothesis, as developed by common sense and especially by science, has achieved in explaining the detail of our experience. Why do we have sensations as of human and animal bodies, automobiles and computers, functioning with intricate and impressive regularity, as they normally do, if there are not real (though usually unperceived) material structures operating in the ways postulated by science and common sense? In a recent extensive discussion of this objection to Berkeley, J L. Mackie suggests the correct reply to it. Berkeley's theistic hypothesis, according to Mackie, is "open to two different interpretations." On the first, there is no structure in God corresponding to the physical structures elaborated by science and common sense, or at least to the unperceived parts of them; there is only the divine action in causing those particular ideas that we actually perceive.

> According to the other interpretation, God's ideas are in themselves as rich and systematic as the physical world is on the materialist's view, and in the same sort of way. That is, God perceives a three-dimensional Euclidean world or, more probably [up-dating Berkeley a bit], a four-dimensional Einsteinian one, with micro-structure, with electric charges which figure somehow as perceptual objects for him, and so on. Everything that we take to be a correct description of the physical world,

and every scientific advance, is either a correct description of
some of God's ideas or at least a closer approximation to a correct description of them.[3]

On the first of these interpretations, Mackie argues, theistic immaterialism
forfeits the explanatory advantages of the material hypothesis, but on the
second it obtains at least some of them "by making God's ideas mirror so
closely the world that seems to be revealed to common sense and to science."[4]

    This seems right. While Berkeley would surely balk at the sugges-
tion of divine perceptions of electric charges as such, his philosophy of science encourages us to regard successful scientific theories as discoveries of
a real structure of ideas and intentions in the divine mind that causes what
we perceive. Or at least we are to regard the structures postulated by the
best of science as isomorphic with real structures in the divine thought and
will. And if this isomorphism is incorporated in Berkeley's theistic hypothesis, it will offer an explanation of every detail of the experienced world for
which physical science offers an explanation.

    Mackie himself is not convinced by the reply that he proposes on
Berkeley's behalf, finding "at least four serious difficulties for it." Only one
of the four seems to me at all serious. On the theistic view it is "quite mysterious," in Mackie's opinion, why all the details of "the anatomy and
physiology of sense perception" should be a part of the correct account of
things, since they "are utterly irrelevant to the final stage [of the sensory
process], for the sensation is now an idea put directly into our minds by
God, and the apparent causal connections between the sensation and the
various changes earlier in the sequence are illlusory."[5] There are certainly
many questions to which Berkeley has no ready answer about why God
would have set things up as he has; but I think it is clear in a general way
what he would say to this "difficulty." It is a a special case of the objection
he considers in *Principles*, 60-66, why God would affect us with ideas representing such intricate apparent physical causes. His answer, in effect, is
that God does it in order to place us in an appropriate theater for the exercise of intelligence and purpose, in which we can acquire some rational and
voluntary control over the ideas we will experience. And if that is God's
purpose, He obviously has reason to make our sensations a term of some of
the apparent, quasi-causal relations in the world of our experience – and
hence as much reason for establishing the anatomy and physiology of sense
perception as for any other feature of the physical order.

    The other three difficulties proposed by Mackie seem to me even
less compelling. (1) He argues that it will be hard for Berkeley to give a
satisfactory account of human voluntary action without concluding that we
can "bring about changes in God's ideas."[6] His claim that Berkeley "might
be reluctant" to accept this consequence could be backed up by quoting Philonous's statement that "no external being can affect" God (*Works*, ii. 241).

But, as Mackie also acknowledges, Berkeley "could accept" it – at least in the sense that there is no need to saddle Berkeleian metaphysics with a commitment to divine impassibility. (2) Mackie claims that "our sensory data seem to reflect a fully determinate . . . physical world, . . . rather than an indeterminate or incomplete one, which would be at least possible if the corresponding reality consisted in God's having such and such ideas as intentional objects." But, as Mackie concedes, this is not a crucial objection "because the theist could hold that it is a characteristic perfection of God that *his* system of intentional objects is complete as well as consistent." (3) Finally Mackie holds that the detail represented by physical science is ascribed "with less intrinsic plausibility" to God than to a material universe, "just because such detail is not at home in an essentially mental world." Bearing in mind, however, that God's mind is not supposed to share the limits of our minds, I cannot see the slightest reason why such detail would be less at home in a mental than in a material world.

Perhaps the weightiest objection to Berkeley's strategy is simply that it may be thought no easier to understand *how* God produces sensations in our minds than to understand how external bodies would produce them. What mechanism does He use, or how does He operate if he needs no mechanism? Is it not as mysterious how one mind, such as God's, can act on another, such as ours, as how an extramental body can act on a mind? It is not easy to assess the force of this objection. Perhaps Berkeley would say that God's omnipotence is explanation enough of how His will produces its effects.

Rather than trying to obtain a definitive assessment on this point, I want to focus on the epistemological situation at which we have arrived. Our sensations may be regarded as constituting the total empirical evidence we have that is relevant to the nature of sensible things.[7] And we have at least three hypotheses to account for this evidence on the basis of views about what the existence of sensible things consists in: (h_1) the directly causal material hypothesis, according to which bodies that exist independently of being perceived cause our sensations directly, with or without God in the background; (h_2) the occasionalist hypothesis, according to which there are extramental bodies, but they are only occasions for God to cause our sensations; and (h_3) Berkeley's hypothesis, according to which God causes the sensations, with no extramental bodies in the offing. The issue is which of these hypotheses is most probable, given the evidence of our senses.

Let us think about this in relation to Bayes' Theorem:

$$P(h/e \ \& \ b) = P(h/b) \cdot \frac{P(e/h \ \& \ b)}{P(e/b)}$$

Here b represents any relevant background information, as before, and e represents our total body of evidence, our sensations. In this Bayesian context the question whether the evidence of our senses tells more strongly in favor of one of the three hypotheses than the others amounts to the question which of the ratios

$$\frac{P(e/h_1 \ \& \ b)}{P(e/b)}, \quad \frac{P(e/h_2 \ \& \ b)}{P(e/b)}, \quad \text{and} \quad \frac{P(e/h_3 \ \& \ b)}{P(e/b)}$$

has the greatest value. Since we are assessing the hypotheses against the same evidence and background information, as is only fair, the three fractions have the same denominator, and the question reduces to which of the three probabilities $P(e/h_1 \ \& \ b)$, $P(e/h_2 \ \& \ b)$, and $P(e/h_3 \ \& \ b)$ is the greatest – or in other words, on which of the three hypotheses the evidence we have would be likeliest to occur. But since all three are hypotheses to the effect that the evidence we have is caused in a certain way,[8] all of them entail that the evidence e occurs. Hence all three probabilities have the value 1, and the three ratios do not differ in value. This means that our total empirical evidence e does not contribute more to the probability of one of these hypotheses than the others.

It follows that if one of the three hypotheses is more probable than the others, given the available empirical evidence and background information – in other words, if one of the probabilities $P(h_1 /e \ \& \ b)$, $P(h_2 /e \ \& \ b)$, and $P(h_3 /e \ \& \ b)$ is greater than the others – it must be because the corresponding *prior* probability $P(h_1 /b)$, $P(h_2 /b)$, or $P(h_3 /b)$, is greater than the others. This is the result to be expected from Bayes' Theorem, given that the hypotheses are constructed as claims that the evidence is caused in a certain way. The peculiarity of the present case to which I wish to call attention is that as e, the body of our sensations, comprises *all* our available relevant empirical evidence, our assignments of prior probabilities to the hypotheses cannot be based on empirical evidence. They can only be grounded in some sort of a priori judgement or intuition of the intrinsic attractiveness or plausibility of the hypotheses as theories. There is thus a clear sense in which it is not an empirical question which of these hypotheses is the most probable, all things considered.

The significance of this conclusion should not be exaggerated. It does not follow that the overall probability of the hypotheses is in no way affected by experience. Other aspects of the relation of experience to the assessment of plausibility of theories will be discussed in section II below. Here it should be pointed out that the non-empirical character of the question is a consequence of constructing the hypotheses as claims that the evidence is caused in a certain way. If we had e' as our evidence instead of e, the hypotheses would have been constructed as claims that e' was caused in a certain way; and that the difference might have affected their intrinsic or prior plausibility. For this reason the inference from e to any of these hypotheses will still be an *empirical* inference. The judgement that h is the best explanation of e will not be an empirical judgement. But the judgement that the best hypothesis is one that explains e, rather than some other set of facts, is empirical, because it is based on the empirical observation that e is true.

Still it is significant that, given a body of evidence as the total available empirical evidence, the issue can be reduced to a form in which it is clear that one of the hypotheses that explain that evidence cannot be preferred to another except on the basis of an a priori judgement or intuition of their relative attractiveness. This results from the structure of Bayes' Theorem – and, less formally, of inference to the best explanation. For if empirical inference works, not by simple induction, but by leading us to accept the hypothesis that best explains the given evidence, the inference requires, in addition to the evidence, a judgement as to which hypothesis best explains the evidence. And it stands to reason that if we have a case in which the given evidence is the total available empirical evidence, this judgement cannot itself be inferred from empirical evidence.

This point is quite general, and applies to the assessment of scientific as well as metaphysical hypotheses. It is characteristic of metaphysical disputes, however, that it is usually very difficult, if not impossible, to see how to add to the body of available empirical evidence in such a way as to make a significant difference to the epistemological situation, and the disputants are therefore quickly forced to focus on issues that can be decided only by a priori judgements of theory-attractiveness. Empiricists have commonly had a strong aversion to relying on such judgments – at least when it is clearly seen that that is what is being done. This aversion has been a major motive for treating metaphysical hypotheses as "meaningless," and metaphysical issues as "pseudo-questions." That is a desperate expedient, and there is all the less reason to resort to it if we see that the very structure of empirical reasoning requires judgments of theory-attractiveness in addition to the evidence.

Berkeley, at any rate, had no empiricist qualms at this point. He certainly offers a priori arguments for the intrinsic superiority of idealism over the material hypothesis. We have already touched on some of these arguments, in which a prominent place is given to the claim that no intelligible hypothesis has been offered as to how extramental bodies would cause our sensations. I will not turn aside from the epistemological concerns of this paper, however, to say more about this part of Berkeley's case for idealism. Instead I will return to a point that was passed over quickly at the outset of his epistemological attack on the material hypothesis.

II. THE DIRECT REALIST OBJECTION

As was noted above, Berkeley begins this attack with a disjunction: if we know of the existence of bodies outside the mind, we must know it either immediately by sense, or indirectly by reason, inferring their existence from the immediate data of sense. He dismissed the first alternative with very little argument; and precisely that was his mistake, according to the response to his epistemological reasoning that I think is most popular to-day. Many philosophers now maintain that we perceive extramental bodies immediately, and that we do not and need not infer their existence from our sensations, or more broadly, from our knowledge of our own sensory states.

More than one thing has been meant by the claim that we "immediately perceive" bodies existing outside the mind, and by the phrase "Direct Realism" that is used to refer to it. It is one thing to deny that sensations serve as evidence in the justification of beliefs about sensible things; another to deny that the way in which we conceive of sensible things is by having sensations or sensation-like images of them. These logically separable restrictions on the cognitive role of sensation are sometimes not distinguished as sharply as they should be – perhaps because we are mesmerized by pictorial conceptions vaguely associated with the terminology of "direct" or "immediate" perception. As the present paper is entirely concerned with the justification of belief, I will stipulate that by "Direct Realism" here I mean the thesis that in sense perception we form true beliefs in the existence of bodies outside the mind, which are justified without being inferred from or depending on any evidence whatever; and that sensations therefore do not serve as evidence for those beliefs. I do not mean to be implying anything one way or the other about the role of sensation in the formation of conceptions of sensible things, as opposed to beliefs about them.

This Direct Realist thesis seems initially plausible to common sense. If I perceive an object under favorable conditions – holding it in my hand, for example, and at the same time viewing it in good light – what need have I for reasoning or inference? Don't I just know directly that the object is there? And Direct Realists think that if they are right about this, it follows that all of Berkeley's argument against Evidential Realism is beside the point – except insofar as it can be used to educate us about the trouble we will get into if we are so foolish as to think of sensations as evidence. Further reflection, however, may lead common sense to be less satisfied with Direct Realism. Suppose that, standing in the doorway between the kitchen and the dining room, I see an aardvark in the dining room. I say to my wife, who is in the kitchen, "I think there's an aardvark rooting around under the dining room table."

"That's impossible," she says, "Why do you believe it?"

If I reply, "No reason. I don't need a reason," my answer will hardly be acceptable to common sense. The answer that common sense approves, and expects me to give in this situation, is , "Because I see the aardvark." Thus my perceptual experience seems to be not only accepted but demanded by common sense as *evidence* for my belief about the aardvark, contrary to the Direct Realist thesis.

A first reply that direct Realists may offer to this objection is that "Because I see the aardvark" is not synonymous with "Because I have visual aardvark sensations." Seeing an object, as Direct Realists are fond of emphasizing, is not just a matter of having sensations. It is largely a matter of forming beliefs about the object in a certain way. The Direct Realist may be tempted to argue that since seeing an object is largely a matter of forming beliefs about the object, it would be viciously circular to regard the seeing as evidence for those beliefs. How can the fact that I am coming to believe that p be evidence for my belief that p?[9]

This argument must not be accepted, however. The fact that I am coming, or have come, to believe something *in a certain way* is often crucially important for the justification of belief. This is obviously true of testimony in a court of law. We take the fact that a witness believes she acquired a belief in a certain way (namely, by sense perception and memory) as one of the weightiest sorts of evidence for the truth of the belief. Similarly, if I see an aardvark, the fact that I am coming in a certain (sensory) way to believe there is an aardvark there is evidence for the truth of the belief.

Another response the Direct Realist may make is that while it is certainly true that my belief about the aardvark depends for its justification on the fact that I see the aardvark, it is also true, nonetheless, that my visual sensations need not function as a reason or evidence for me, and I do not need any reason or evidence for the belief. This contention may be defended by pointing out that young children and mentally retarded persons can be justified by their perceptual experience in believing things about bodies even though they have no thought of the justification of belief and could not articulate an appeal to their experience as evidence for their belief. The appeal to the evidence of sensation first comes in, on this view, when the belief is challenged or an epistemological issue is raised; and then the evidence is offered, not directly in support of the belief, but in support of the (epistemological) claim that the belief is justified.

There is something right about this response. The claim that sense experience can justify one in holding beliefs about bodies when one does not think about, or even understand, any evidential relation between the sensation and the belief, is plausible. But this provides the Direct Realist no aid or comfort in a dispute with Berkeley (or with an Evidential Realist). For in such a dispute an epistemological issue has been raised, the Direct Realist's views about bodies do confront a challenge from Berkeley or a skeptic or both, and it is assumed that all parties to the discussion are capable of understanding and articulating any evidential relationships that come under consideration. In this context it is impossible to maintain a sharp division between reasons for thinking a belief justified and reasons for accepting or continuing to accept it; and a lack of reasons (if one ought to have them) for thinking the belief justified is bound to cast doubt on the belief itself.

The clear facts of the matter are these: (1) My belief about the aardvark, in the case described, depends for its justification on my visual experience, though not on my understanding of that dependence. If I did not see the aardvark, I would not be justified in believing it was there. (2) All our beliefs about bodies depend ultimately for their justification on our perceptual experience. They depend on it either directly, like my belief about the aardvark, or indirectly, by depending on other beliefs that depend on it directly. (3) An epistemological inquiry into the justification of our beliefs about bodies, if pursued with sufficient tenacity, is therefore bound to lead to perceptual experience as grounds for thinking such beliefs justified, and to the question whether our perceptual experience provides *good* grounds for thinking them justified.

This much the Direct Realist must acknowledge; and when it is acknowledged, little importance is left to the issue whether the perceptual experience is evidence for the beliefs about bodies or only for the claim that those beliefs are justified. Either way, a Realist must defend the claim that if we have certain perceptual experiences, then because we have them, we are justified in believing certain things about bodies. Whatever argument a Direct Realist can produce for this claim, an Evidential Realist can produce an analogous argument for the claim that the perceptual experience is good *evidence* for the beliefs about bodies. And it is hard to see why the Evidential Realist argument would be any more (or any less) vulnerable to skeptical or idealist attack than the analogous Direct Realist Argument.

Consider, for example, the simplest form of Direct Realist defense of the claim that beliefs about bodies are justified by virtue of their connection with perceptual experience – which is that beliefs about bodies that are "immediately" formed in sense perception are so evident to common sense as to need no further justification. As a response to Berkeley, this is very weak. It is not even relevant to the dispute with Berkeley unless the belief that bodies exist independently of being perceived is one of the beliefs that are held to be so evident in sense perception. So understood, this simple Direct Realist defense of belief in matter amounts to no more than saying that (when we have sense experience) it is obvious to common sense that Berkeley is wrong. This may not be a silly thing to say, but it is not much of an argument, and it would be silly to expect Berkeley to be much impressed by it.

Whatever value it may have, however, I see no reason why Evidential Realism could not equally well return a similar answer to Berkeley, saying that when we have sense experience it is so evident to common sense that our sensations are good evidence of the extramental existence of bodies that we need no further justification for so regarding them. In the Bayesian framework discussed in the previous section, the claim would presumably be that it is evident, without argument, that the material hypothesis is the best – antecedently the most probable – of the metaphysical theories that predict the sort of sense experience we have. This seems no worse, and no better, than the corresponding Direct Realist defense. Both, in effect, claim without argument that it is obvious that Berkeley is wrong.

I have long thought that for reasons of this sort, Direct Realism is a remarkably unpromising theory to have obtained the sponsorship of as many first-rate philosophers as it has. But recently I have begun to suspect that this verdict is not entirely fair. Perhaps there is a way in which perceptual experience makes beliefs about bodies convincingly credible, to which the Direct Realist is trying to call our attention, but which is not clearly envisaged in the debate as I have traced it thus far.

In a well known passage of *The Varieties of Religious Experience*, William James says that "Mystical states, when well developed, usually are, and have the right to be, absolutely authoritative over the individuals to whom they come," but that "No authority emanates from them which should make it a duty for those who stand outside of them to accept their revelations uncritically."[10] To anyone other than the subject of such states, James suggests, the experience, or the report of it, is merely evidence, to be sifted in accordance with the usual canons of empirical reasoning, and may or may not be found in the end to provide some support, great or small, for a religious hypothesis. To the mystic who has the experience, however, its epistemological weight is much greater, on James' view; and that seems to me quite reasonable. We need not go so far as to say that mystical experiences ought to be "absolutely authoritative" for those who have them, if that involves accepting any belief "uncritically." But surely it is true that our own experiences have an epistemological value that other people's experiences do not have for us. This is generally recognized to be true of sense experience too. "Seeing is believing," we say.

We cannot get at the peculiar epistemological value of one's own experience simply by thinking of the fact that the experience has occurred as evidence for a hypothesis. For people who have not had the experience can believe as firmly as those who have that the experience has occurred, and can use this fact as evidence for the hypothesis in exactly the same way. What is special about one's own experience is not that one is uniquely able to rely on it as evidence, but that it uniquely affects one's inclinations to believe. It makes the hypothesis seem to one to be true, in a way that merely weighing the evidence of other people's experience does not. Doubting Thomas will not believe until he sees with his own eyes and feels with his own hands. He does not necessarily believe that his own senses are less likely than ten serious friends to deceive him. But sense experience has an impact on his belief that no amount of testimony could have, and we all accept this as reasonable, to some extent, as well as natural.

It will be of interest to inquire how this special epistemological value of one's own experience can be related to Bayes' Theorem:

$$P(h/e \ \& \ b) \ = \ P(h/b) \ . \ \frac{P(e/h \ \& \ b)}{P(e/b)}$$

The crucial point is not that the evidence, e, that the subject of the experience has is different from the evidence that anybody else has. It is true that one normally knows things about one's own experiences that other people do not know; but even in cases where one's own experience has unique value in support of a hypothesis, the facts one knows about one's own experience need not be better evidence for the hypothesis than the facts that other people know. It is rather that having the experience oneself rightly and properly affects the way in which one evaluates the evidence. It increases one's inclination to find the hypothesis a better explanation of the evidence one has than other hypotheses that predict the same evidence.

There is more than one way that this can work in a Bayesian framework. Most obviously, the experience may increase the value one is inclined to assign to P(h/b), the antecedent[11] probability of the hypothesis h. Having a mystical experience, for example, may naturally and rightly cause one to find a religious hypothesis antecedently more probable (that is, intrinsically more plausible) than one otherwise would. Alternatively, the experience may bring one to assign a lower value to P(e/b), and therefore a higher value to the ratio

$$\frac{P(e/h \ \& \ b)}{P(e/b)}$$

by decreasing the plausibility one finds in alternative hypotheses that predict the evidence e. Thus the experience of actually seeing an aardvark in one's dining room may well incline one to find less antecedent or intrinsic plausibility in hypotheses of hallucination or illusion than one would have found in them if one had merely imagined such an experience.

The suggestion that it is often *reasonable* to be influenced in this way by experiences may provoke some to object that the antecedent probability that it is reasonable to assign to any hypothesis is that which it objectively deserves, and that as we are speaking of a probability antecedent to the evidence of the experience in question, its objective value cannot be affected by whether one has had the experience oneself. This objection has a certain rationalistic appeal, but seems to me mistaken. It might be right if we were Olympian beings, capable at all times of a complete and well balanced appreciation of all factors in an epistemological situation. But we are not. In our actual cognitive condition our capacity for improving our intellectual performance depends heavily on our ability to draw from our experience, not only new facts to be treated as evidence, but also a new appreciation of the epistemological relevance and weight of whatever facts we know or might come to know.

If this is right, the following variant of Direct Realism deserves our attention. Perceptual experience, it may be claimed, is not only evidence for beliefs about the world; it also naturally and rightly affects our appreciation and weighing of all the factors in our epistemological situation. In particular, it naturally and rightly inclines us to assign a higher prior or intrinsic probability to the material hypothesis than to alternative hypotheses in which subjective sense experiences such as ours arise without the existence of extramental bodies. On this view, in short, the actual experience of sense perception makes the material hypothesis seem a better theory, and makes idealistic hypotheses seem worse theories, in relation to the same evidence, than they would otherwise have seemed. It may also be claimed that the assignment of prior or intrinsic probabilities which we make under the influence of our sense experience needs no argument to justify it, but is an appropriate starting point in the formation of beliefs.

This is not, strictly speaking, a Direct Realist position, because it allows subjective sensory states to be counted as evidence for perceptual beliefs. What it takes from Direct Realism is the thesis (1) that sense perception contributes something more than evidence to the grounds of our belief, and (2) that this can be used to defend a Realistic view of matter. There is something right about this thesis. Perceptual experience does seem in some way to give intrinsic plausibility to Realism about matter, or to diminish the intrinsic plausibility of theories according to which our perceptual experience occurs without extramental bodies. Realism has a common sense appeal that presents itself as directly rooted in sense experience.

This does not seem to me to be a very powerful argument for Realism, however. Leaving aside many of Berkeley's criticisms of the tenability of the conception of extramental bodies, let us focus only on the question whether this intrinsic plausibility or common sense appeal that is given in perceptual experience carries over from what is often called "Naive realism" to the more "scientific" sorts of Realism that modern philosophers might accept. Surely the view of bodies to which sensation contributes the most initial intrinsic plausibility is not only that they exist independently of being perceived, but also that they have qualities whose nature is perspicuous to us in perception – for example, that they have surfaces that are unbrokenly solid and "covered" with colors that are just like visual appearances of color and are not merely powers to affect us with visual sensations. This is not necessarily a naive view. It was incorporated, for example, in the Aristotelian theory of perception. But it is a view that modern thought seems to have abandoned forever, and for weighty reasons, in giving up Aristotelian physics. This development of modern thought has a price, however, which is that any modern conception of the nature of bodies is going to seem somewhat strange to a common sense that is shaped by our natural reactions to sense experience.

Berkeley adroitly exploits this fact. His *Three Dialogues*, as I have pointed out, do not contain a fully explicit development of the epistemological argument against belief in matter; but one of the strongest impressions they have left with many readers is that they give powerful reasons to doubt that we could justify the belief in matter even if it is intelligible. One source of this impression, I think, is the way in which Hylas begins with a realism about the secondary qualities that does appeal to common sense, and then is forced out of it. By beginning in this way, rather than having Hylas start out with the views of Boyle or Locke on secondary qualities, Berkeley makes, very vividly, the point that common sense views of the nature of bodies that arise in sense perception, if construed as views about the nature of *extramental* bodies, are undermined by arguments and developments of modern thought that few of us are prepared to reject. Other features of modern scientific thought tend in the same direction. Berkeley could have exploited in this context the corpuscularian idea that bodies, though seeming unbrokenly solid, are really discontinuous assemblies of particles separated by empty space. And relativistic physics, with its simultaneity cones and Riemannian space, departs even farther from common sense than any science that Berkeley knew.

Surely, it may be objected, the intrinsic plausibility that perceptual experience contributes to the view that in sensation we are in contact with a reality that exists independently of our perceiving it may remain even though the reliability of common sense views about its qualities is undermined. But Berkeley can agree with this. He no more doubts than his opponents do that there is an independently real cause of our sensations. The question at issue is about the qualities of that cause (cf. *Dialogues*, 239). Berkeley thinks the cause is God, and more particularly ideas and volitions in the divine mind.

I will admit, though Berkeley did not, that his account of the nature of the objects of perception is quite remote from common sense. But is it more remote than viable alternatives? Are ideas and volitions in the mind of God stranger than quarks and quanta? The claim that sense experience enables us to see without argument that modern scientific versions of the material hypothesis are intrinsically better theories, antecedently more probable, than idealistic alternatives has little to commend it. Neither side in this dispute is in a good position to appeal to the impression that perception gives us of sensible things.[1][2]

University of California, Los Angeles

NOTES

1. Unless otherwise indicated, quotations from Berkeley in this and the next six paragraphs are from section 18 of Part I of the *Principles of Human Knowledge*.

2. Here, and in the next paragraph, quotations not otherwise identified are from *Principles*, 19.

3. J. L. Mackie, *The Miracle of Theism: Arguments for and against the Existence of God* (Oxford: Clarendon Press, 1982), p. 76. It is one of the merits of Mackie's book that he sees the essentially theistic character of Berkeley's alternative to the material hypothesis, and

treats it as generating a serious metaphysical argument for theism.

4. *Ibid.*, p. 77.

5. *Ibid.*, p. 77f.

6. All the quotations from Mackie in this paragraph are from pp. 78-80 of *The Miracle of Theism*.

7. This may be an oversimplification. Our total sensory experience certainly constitutes most of our empirical evidence relevant to the nature of sensible things. We have little, if any, relevant evidence that does not come to us through the senses. But perhaps we have some. For example, the problem of evil may suggest that non-sensory suffering is empirical evidence that is relevant to Berkeley's hypothesis, because relevant to its theistic component. It would take a long discussion to evaluate this suggestion, as we would have to consider, not only the issues of theodicy, but also how benevolent a deity is required for Berkeley's metaphysical, as distinct from his religious, aims. In any case, I think my basic epistemological point is untouched. The question, what hypotheses best explain, and hence are best supported by, the *totality* of our experience, is of inescapable importance for epistemology. And, as I shall argue, it is not an empirical question.

8. This is not the only way in which the hypotheses can be understood; but they certainly can appropriately be understood in this way, and doing so brings out the epistemological situation most sharply.

9. D. M. Armstrong begins to argue in this way in *Perception and the Physical World* (London: Routledge and Kegan Paul, 1961), pp. 132f. But in the end he seems to ackowledge the point I am about to make.

10. William James, *The Varieties of Religious Experience* (New York: The Modern Library, no date), p. 414.

11. "Antecedent" here must not be understood temporally, of course. It is also important to this line of thought that in saying that experiencing e may increase the value that one who has the experience is inclined to assign to P(h/b), I do not mean to imply that for such a person P(h/b) thereby becomes a probability "on" e, a probability conditional on e's occurrence. On the contrary, P(h/b) is still a probability independent of e, and in that sense antecedent to the evidence of e. We can think of it as expressing an answer to the ques-

tion, "Suppose there is a universe distinct from ours, about which you know only that b is true; you do *not* know whether e occurs in it; how likely is it that h is true in that universe?" What I am suggesting is that even though P(h/b) is in this way independent of e, the experience of e can appropriately lead us to assign it a higher value. On this view, there is more than one way in which experiencing e may lead us to assign a higher probability to a hypothesis h. It may lead us to believe that the condition laid down in the conditional probability P(h/e) is satisfied. This is the way in which we are most apt to think of the experience of e as increasing the probability of h – the way involved in taking e as *evidence* for h. But my suggestion is that experiencing e may also lead us to believe that the conditional probability P(h/e) is higher than we would otherwise have thought, because the experience affects us so that either the intrinsic plausibility of h (as reflected in P(h/b)), or its advantage in comparison with other possible explanations of e, now seems greater than we would otherwise have thought.

12.   Versions of this paper have been presented to the Berkeley tercentenary conference at Newport, and to philosophical audiences at UCLA and Memphis State and Vanderbilt Universities. I am indebted to many (including a reader for the publisher) for helpful comments.

PART FIVE

PERCEPTION:
VISUALS AND IMMEDIATE PERCEPTION

Phillip D. Cummins

ON THE STATUS OF VISUALS IN BERKELEY'S
*NEW THEORY OF VISION**

INTRODUCTION

This essay is an attempt to ascertain and comprehend the position being
defended in sections 41 through 51 of George Berkeley's *Essay towards a
New Theory of Vision (NTV)*. Discovering the theses presented and the
arguments marshalled in their support is, for these sections, no easy task.
Sections 48 and 49 are especially hard to interpret. Since this part of *NTV*
is very important for Berkeley's presentation of his new philosophical account of vision, a special effort to make sense of these sections seems war-
ranted.
        The one hundred and fifty-nine numbered paragraphs or sections of
the main text of *NTV* fall into four easily discerned divisions. In the first
division Berkeley presents his account of mediately perceiving distance by
sight. At section 52 he switches his attention to seeing magnitude. In sections 88 through 120, on situation, he offers a new explanation of why inverted retinal images do not result in seeing objects upside down. The
fourth division is an extended defense of Berkeley's extraordinary heterogeneity thesis regarding visual and tangible qualities. It is noteworthy that
the first, second and fourth divisions of *NTV* have a special feature, an
addendum or coda, as it were. Each concludes with about ten sections that
introduce a topic or line of thought distinct from, but adjacent to, the main
argument of that division. The final division, for example, concludes with a
brief examination of the question, which extension, visible or tangible, is the
proper object of geometry. The addendum to the second division goes into
detail about minimum visibles and tangibles, which were introduced at section 54. As D. M. Armstrong has observed,[1] the concluding sections of the
first division, sections 41 through 51, do nothing less than shift the

----

* Questions and comments by students in my Berkeley class in the Fall of
1984 sharpened my thinking about the textual materials and issues considered in this paper. I also profited from Richard Fumerton's careful reading of a late draft.

165

E. Sosa (ed.), Essays on the Philosophy of George Berkeley, 165–194.
©*1987 by D. Reidel Publishing Company*

discussion from a technical treatment of how one estimates the distance
from oneself of the everyday objects of perception to a metaphysical account of the proper objects of sight.

In his *Theory of Vision Vindicated and Explained (TVV)*, Berkeley
states that in *NTV* his plan was to analyze "false and popular" suppositions
in search of the philosophical principles of visual perception.[2] One popular
supposition is that humans see distance. Vision is thought to inform one
both of outness and exact distance, that is, one not only sees an object to be
located at some distance or other from oneself, but also sees exactly how
far away it is. Although his initial argument at section 2 of *NTV* seems to
concern exact distance only, Berkeley's position in section 11 is that neither
it nor outness is immediately seen.[3] He does not explain "immediately
seen" or "immediately perceived" in either place, but his comments in sections 9 through 12, 16, and 65 strongly suggest that "immediate seeing" is
seeing, strictly so called, and "mediate seeing" is really judging on the basis
of what is truly seen. Immediate seeing, that is, seeing, is an operation in
which a perceiver becomes aware of an existing object.[4] Such objects of
seeing we shall hereafter call "visuals."[5] Seeing, strictly so called, does not
involve judgement or belief. Mediate seeing, in contrast, is at bottom nothing but a belief or judgement.[6] It too, however, always has an object. As
with other beliefs, the object of mediate seeing need not be the case. The
term "m-visibles" will be used for objects of mediate seeing. As was noted
earlier, Berkeley was convinced that neither outness nor exact distance is
apprehended in immediate seeing. Hence, he asks, how do we mediately see
distance? What in immediate seeing occasions one's judgement about distance and what kind of judgement is it? He proceeds to argue that one does
not judge distance by a geometrical inference, conscious or unconscious,
that derives the actual distance of an m-visible rigorously and necessarily
from some feature of a visual. Instead, he insists, what occurs whenever
one mediately sees how far something is from oneself is an inference which
results entirely from experience and which is in no way founded upon a
necessary connection.[7] It is a conditioned suggestion or learned judgement
founded upon one's experience of contingent factual correlations among visuals, tactile objects, and what might well be called kinesthetic sensations.[8]

In the course of his detailed critique of natural geometry, his opponents' account of mediate seeing, and his all-too-brief presentation of his
own allegedly superior position, Berkeley has little to say about the status
of visuals. He does not say whether he takes them to be mental or physical,
dependent on or independent of perceivers. More importantly, he does not
say whether they are always, sometimes or never spatial objects, that is,
objects located at some distance or other from perceivers. To be sure, retinal images or impressions on the eye sometimes seem to function as the
immediate objects of sight, but only in contexts in which the rival account of
mediate seeing is being castigated.[9] The important point to be grasped is
that an object located at some distance from a perceiver could, so far forth,

be an immediate object of sight, even though neither its outness nor exact distance is immediately seen. Just because Berkeley holds an object's distance from a perceiver is never immediately seen, it does not follow he cannot consistently hold objects at a distance are immediately seen. This is so even on the principle that all of the intrinsic or nonrelational properties of what is immediately perceived must themselves be immediately perceived, since distance from a perceiver is obviously a relational or non-intrinsic property.[10] For these reasons, throughout sections 1 through 40 the question of whether or not visuals do or can exist at some distance from their perceivers remains open. When Berkeley introduces the Molyneux Man in section 41 of *NTV*, the general question of the nature and status of visuals has not yet been answered or even asked.

A. SECTIONS 41 THROUGH 45.

Since William Molyneux introduced the question of what a person blind from birth would see and think when newly blessed with sight, I shall call one in that situation a Molyneux Man (MM, for short).[11] In section 41 of *NTV* Berkeley wrote of MM,

> From what hath been premised it is a manifest consequence that a man born blind, being made to see, would at first have no idea of distance by sight; the sun and stars, the remotest objects as well as the nearer, would all seem to be in his eye, or rather in his mind. The objects intromitted by sight would seem to him (as in truth they are) no other than a new set of thoughts or sensations each whereof is as near to him as the perceptions of pain or pleasure, or the most inward passions of his soul. For our judging objects perceived by sight to be at any distance, or without the mind, is . . . intirely the effect of experience, which one in those circumstances could not yet have attained to.

The specific question being examined is: Would MM at once or almost immediately acquire an idea of distance by sight and so mediately see objects at a distance? Berkeley's answer is "No." He assumes all theorists agree that neither outness nor exact distance is immediately seen. Challenging other theorists, he argues that seeing visuals neither anchors geometrical deductions nor occasions instinctual judgements that providentially satisfy geometrical principles. Instead, he insisted, features of immediate seeing, such as clarity or lack of definition in a visual, and associated kinesthetic sensations are correlated to tangible objects at various distances from the perceiver. The correlating requires numerous visual experiences, which – by hypothesis – MM has not had. So goes Berkeley's negative answer.[1][2] That much is relatively clear.[1][3] What is not at all clear is Berkeley's position about the objects of MM's first visual experiences.

Berkeley writes of MM's visual objects that they would "all seem to be in his eye, or rather in his mind." If Berkeley is claiming that upon gaining sight, MM would *believe* his visuals are in his eye or mind, his position is utterly implausible. What could be the evidential or psychological basis for such beliefs? If, instead, he is claiming MM would *immediately see* his visuals to be in his eye or his mind, his position is incomprehensible. Neither something's being-in-the-eye nor its being-in-the-mind are possible objects of immediate seeing. Berkeley also writes of MM's visuals (objects intromitted by sight) that they "would seem to him (as in truth they are) no other than a new set of thoughts or sensations . . ." If "would seem to him" means "would be believed to be," so that a claim is being made about MM's initial belief upon acquiring sight, it is implausible for the same reason as before. If, instead, it is a claim about what is immediately seen, it is once again incomprehensible, since something's ontological status or membership in a class is also not a possible object of immediate seeing. What exactly is Berkeley struggling to say? My suggestion is that he was offering a compact and confused argument for a thesis about visuals and for some real or supposed corollaries of that thesis.

Let *alpha* be: No visual is external to one who sees it. ("External" means spatially external.) The clue that Berkeley is offering an argument for *alpha* is the parenthetical expression, "as in truth they are," which switches the discussion to the nature or ontological status of visuals. What they are, he claims, are thoughts, sensations, perceptions, passions of the soul. The implicit argument for *alpha* seems to be: Visuals are sensations; no sensation is external to one who perceives it; therefore, no visual is external to one who sees it. Let us next consider a corollary of *alpha*, call it *alpha-a*: No visual is seen to be external to one who sees it. Visuals, recall, are what is immediately seen. A key principle of immediate perception is that an object cannot be immediately perceived to have a property it does not have. Hence visuals are what they are seen to be. Thus, no visual is seen to be external to one who sees it. From *alpha-a* it is but one short – illegitimate – step to *alpha-b*, visuals are seen to be not external, which in turn suggests, *alpha-c*, visuals are seen as inward or in the mind. By interpreting Berkeley as implicitly arguing for *alpha* and its genuine corollary, *alpha-a*, one can make some sense of the startling claims of section 41.

Section 43 contains another argument for *alpha*, but in doing so exhibits signs of confusion. Berkeley's aim, apparently, is answering an argument against *alpha*. It is labelled a prejudice, one from which MM is free. Recall that according to Berkeley's new account of mediate seeing, ordinary adults, having long since experienced the requisite correlations, effortlessly make judgements about the exact distances various objects are from them. So effortless are such judgements that seeing and judging are almost as one. As a result, ordinary adults believe their visuals actually exist at various distances from them. To Berkeley, committed to *alpha*, this is a mistake. It can be overcome, but only after strict inquiry. To hasten the process, Berkeley offers a proof in the form of a reply to an argument against *alpha:*

> At this time it seems agreed on all hands, by those who have had any thoughts of that matter, that colours, which are the proper and immediate objects of sight, are not without the mind. But then it will be said, by sight we have also the ideas of extension, and figure, and motion; all which may well be thought without and at some distance from the mind, though colour should not. In answer to this I appeal to any man's experience, whether the visible extension of any object doth not appear as near to him as the colour of that object; nay, whether they do not both seem to be in the very same place. Is not the extension we see coloured, and is it possible for us, so much as in thought, to separate and abstract colour from extension? Now where the extension is there surely is the figure, and there the motion too. I speak of those which are perceived by sight.

This argument bears a strong family resemblance to one used in section 10 of the *Principles of Human Knowledge* against one version of the primary and secondary qualities distinction. There it functions as an *ad hominem* employed against those who construe secondary qualities as sensations that cannot exist unperceived while simultaneously holding primary qualities, such as extension, figure, and motion, are perception independent sensibles. In that context Berkeley's insistence on the inseparability of color and extension pinpoints a problem for his philosophical opponents.

The *NTV* version is more problematic. To be a genuine proof of *alpha* his argument requires solid evidence that colors are not external to, i.e. not without and at some distance from, those who see them. Instead, Berkeley's claim about colors is introduced with the words, "At this time it seems agreed on all hands, by those who have had any thought of that matter." Hardly compelling. Another problem with the argument concerns the words, "not without the mind." The issue in section 43 is whether colors or any other visuals are without the mind in a spatial sense, that is, whether they are located at some distance or other from those who see them. However, the usual sense in which Berkeley and other philosophers of the period hold colors are not without the mind is that they cannot exist unsensed or cannot occur as states of unperceiving things. Either, then, Berkeley is equivocating on the crucial expression or is relying upon the unstated premise that what cannot exist unsensed or occur as a state of an unperceiving thing cannot be at any distance from one who perceives it.[14] Even one who does not accept Armstrong's claim that the premise is false

must concede it has not been explicitly stated or proven in or prior to section 43.[15]

The first sentence of section 44 reads:

> But for a fuller explication of this point, and to show that the
> immediate objects of sight are not so much as the ideas or re-
> semblances of things placed at a distance, it is requisite that we
> look nearer into the matter and carefully observe what is
> meant in common discourse, when one says that which he sees
> is at a distance from him.

Notice, first, the announcement of an intention to explicate more fully a
point just made. To it is added the announcement of an intention to prove
visuals are not "ideas or resemblances of things placed at a distance." Both
projects are linked to the need to analyze what one means in saying he sees
something at a distance from him. The remainder of 44 comprises two
examples upon which are based what appears to be essentially the same
argument. It is not unfair to say both versions of that argument are obscure. Here is the first:

> Suppose, for example, that looking at the moon I should say it
> were fifty or sixty semidiameters of the earth distant from me.
> Let us see what moon this is spoken of: It is plain it cannot be
> the visible moon, or anything like the visible moon, or that
> which I see, which is only a round, luminous plane of about
> thirty visible points in diameter. For in case I am carried from
> the place where I stand directly towards the moon, it is mani-
> fest the object varies, still as I go on; and by the time that I am
> advanced fifty or sixty semidiameters of the earth, I shall be so
> far from being near a small, round, luminous flat that I shall
> perceive nothing like it; this object having long since disap-
> peared, and if I would recover it, it must be by going back to
> earth from whence I set out.

One's task here is finding an argument in this passage that can plausibly
be linked to the other example, that is an argument for both a thesis developed in the preceding section and the anti-resemblance thesis of section 44,
and that can be framed in terms of what one means when one says he sees
an object at a distance.

My first step towards completing this task is proposing *alpha*, "no
visual is external to one who sees it," as the point Berkeley says needs a
fuller explication. I previously argued that section 43 is best interpreted as
an argument for *alpha*. Since no other general thesis was introduced there,
no further argument for my identification is at present required. My second
step is clarifying the new thesis of section 44, no easy job. The only obvious

thing about the new thesis is that "idea" and "resemblance" are notoriously vague and slippery. For this reason some terminological stipulations and preliminary distinctions are in order. Recall that "visual" was introduced for what is immediately seen and "m-visible" for what is mediately seen. We can employ them to define "replica" and "exact replica," using V for visual and M for m-visible. Let "V is a replica of M" mean: Some nonrelational property of V is the same as some nonrelational property of M. Let "V is an exact replica of M" mean: Each nonrelational property of V is the same as some nonrelational property of M.[16] We next formulate two theses about exact replication for cases in which one correctly judges upon immediately seeing V the distance some object, M, is from him. Strong-*beta* is: No V is an exact replica of the M seen mediately by means of it. Weak-*beta* is: Not every V is an exact replica of the M seen mediately by means of it. My proposal is that Berkeley's new thesis in section 44, "The immediate objects of sight are not so much as the ideas or resemblances of things placed at a distance," is best understood in terms of weak-*beta*. To the obvious question, "why not strong-*beta*?" I can for now only reply: wait.

My third step is reformulating Berkeley's moon travel example in a down-to-earth way. Suppose someone sees Whitehall to be about three hundred meters from him. A visual is seen and has a visual magnitude that can be expressed by 1/S. Our hero approaches Whitehall and subsequently sees it to be about thirty meters from him; the visual's magnitude is S. (Clearly Berkeley believes it is possible to measure the magnitude of visuals by visual means, since he speaks of the visual moon as being thirty points in diameter.[17]) The first question is whether Whitehall, that which is mediately seen on two occasions, is what is immediately seen on both of those occasions? Making the assumption that Whitehall's magnitude has not changed, we now argue that the first visual's magnitude is not the same as the second visual's magnitude, so that one cannot analyze seeing Whitehall at a distance on two occasions as Whitehall's being immediately seen on both of those two occasions. Whitehall cannot both times be both V and M. More generally, what is at issue is the relationship between what is at a distance from the perceiver, the m-visible, and that which is immediately seen, the visual. The argument is that since on some occasions one immediately sees two different magnitudes and thus two different visuals when one has but one m-visible, one cannot systematically and uniformly identify what is (or is believed to be) at a distance with what is immediately seen.[18] The visual, which is seen in the strict and proper sense of "see," is not always the m-visible. This is the argument Berkeley is trying to state in the moon passage quoted earlier.[19] It is an argument for *alpha* in that it is an attempt to detach visuals from the external objects mediately seen by means of them. It is a weak argument because even if it could establish that one's visual is never[20] the same as the m-visible mediately seen by means of it, it does not prove that one's visual cannot be at some distance from oneself.[21] The possibility of a visual which is at some unperceived distance from its perceiver and which occasions the belief in there being some different object at some other distance from the perceiver is sufficiently bizarre for us to hold Berkeley simply and rightly ignored it.

Let us return to the example and consider an extension of the argument. If it is now conceded that one's visual when one sees Whitehall in the distance is not Whitehall, it might well be asked whether that visual is an exact replica of Whitehall. Berkeley's moon argument, if applied to our example, would appear to support a negative answer. At issue is whether one can systematically and uniformly analyze mediate seeing in terms of a visual that is an exact replica of the m-visible, at least for cases of correct perception. The key point remains that the visual seen initially differs qualitatively, specifically, in magnitude, from the visual seen later. Not both of them can be exact replicas of the single unchanging object (Whitehall) that is mediately seen on both occasions. This explication of the argument serves to answer the question of why we concentrated on weak-*beta*. Since Berkeley is trying to refute the position that correct mediate seeing of distance always involves a visual that is an exact replica of what is mediately seen, he only needs to force the concession that in at least one case there cannot be exact replication.[22] That is one of the two conclusions of his moon-travel argument and my Whitehall argument. The other, I have argued, is *alpha*.

What, finally, has this to do with Berkeley's question, what is meant in common discourse when one says that which he sees is at a distance from him? Suppose for the sake of discussion that our perceiver in the Whitehall example said on the first occasion, "I see Whitehall is three hundred meters from me." The issues we have been considering can be understood in terms of the question, what is it that is held to be three hundred meters from the perceiver? This question can be understood in terms of another: what is the most perspicuous paraphrase of the above statement, which for convenience I shall label H? Some candidates follow:

H_1 I immediately see Whitehall is three hundred meters from me.

H_2 I immediately see Whitehall and believe it is three hundred meters from me.

H_3 I immediately see an object, V, and believe that Whitehall, of which V is an exact replica, is three hundred meters from me.

H_4 I immediately see an object, V, and believe that Whitehall, of which V is a replica, is three hundred meters from me.

From the standpoint of everyday life, we can be said to know that on some occasions claims such as H are true. I take Berkeley to be examining alternative analyses or paraphrases of such ordinary claims in the light of certain facts or alleged facts about seeing. Some analyses render ordinary claims false or unknowable; they are to be rejected. Consider, for example, H_1. Recall that at the beginning of *NTV* Berkeley announces that all agree distance is not immediately seen. If that is so, one cannot do what in H_1 the perceiver claims to do. It, therefore, is not taken seriously as an analysis of H. What about H_2? If H is true and H_2 is the correct analysis of H, then *alpha* is false. That is why discrediting H_2 is a way of defending, if not explicating, *alpha*. That the argument of section 44 is meant to discredit H_2 as the correct analysis of H should be clear, since it is designed to show that on the correct uniform systematic analysis of mediate seeing what is judged to be at a distance, Whitehall, in our example, cannot be what is immediately seen.

It should also be obvious that the argument of 44 for weak-*beta* is an argument that H_3 is not the correct analysis or paraphrase of H. The correct analysis of H presupposes a general form of analysis for all claims of the same type as H. If H_3 were the most perspicuous paraphrase of H, then all judgements expressing mediate visual perceptions of distance would involve the claim that V, the visual, is an exact replica of M, the object that is or is believed to be at a distance from the perceiver. But the argument of 44 is supposed to prove that this general requirement cannot be met. It is worth noting, perhaps, that the argument of 44 in no way discredits H_4. Is this significant? This is to be linked to Berkeley's introduction and defence of the heterogeneity thesis. According to it, no quality of a visual is ever the same *kind* of quality as a quality or property of a tangible that is named by the same word.[2][3] If this is indeed the case, both replication and exact replication would be impossible for visuals and tangibles. There is just no evidence to establish in full Berkeley's intellectual motives, so about all one can do is pose the question of whether the heterogeneity doctrine was meant, at least in part, to rule out the possibility that V's are sometimes replicas of M's.

Section 45 of *NTV* is one of the most important paragraphs in Berkeley's philosophical *corpus*. Nevertheless one might well wonder why it or some of its parts were not inserted earlier in the text of *NTV*. In the final sentence of 45 Berkeley defines "idea" as "any the immediate object of sense or understanding." Surely this definition would have been more useful in section 1, where "idea" is first used. Furthermore, most of 45 is devoted to sketching analyses of the perceptual judgements used in mediately seeing objects at a distance. This material would have been very helpful had it been added to sections 20 or 25, where Berkeley insisted that visual judgements of distance are founded on experience alone, but provided no analysis or description of such judgements. Despite these connections to earlier sections, it can be shown why the bulk of the paragraph fittingly follows section 44. Consider the following excerpt:

> Looking at an object I perceive a certain visible figure and col-
> our, with some degree of faintness and other circumstances,
> which from what I have formerly observed, determine me to
> think that if I advance forward so many paces or miles, I shall
> be affected with such and such ideas of touch. So that in truth
> and strictness of speech I neither see distance it self, nor any-
> thing that I take to be at a distance. I say, neither distance nor
> things placed at a distance are themselves, or their ideas, truly
> perceived by sight. This I am persuaded of, as to what concerns
> myself: and I believe whoever will look narrowly into his own
> thoughts and examine what he means by saying he sees this or
> that thing at a distance, will agree with me that what he sees
> only suggests to his understanding that after having passed a
> certain distance, to be measured by the motion of his body,
> which is perceivable by touch, he shall come to perceive such
> and such tangible ideas which have been usually connected
> with such and such visible ideas.

Note, first, the emphatic claim that one's immediate object of sight does not
include distance, is not at a distance and is not taken to be at a distance.
Once Berkeley speaks of what one sees: "I neither see distance it self, nor
anything that I take to be at a distance." Once he speaks of the external
thing: "I say, neither distance nor things placed at a distance are themselves, or their ideas, truly perceived by sight." Thus Berkeley reaffirms
alpha, one of the main claims of 43 and 44. In the second sentence, Berkeley also denies ideas of things placed at a distance are truly perceived by
sight; some version of *beta* is apparently being endorsed. In the light of
these commitments one can understand why in this section Berkeley offers
his own analysis or analyses of claims to see objects at a distance. Since
H_1, H_2, and H_3, have been rejected, a new analysis of H, "I see Whitehall
is 300 meters from me," is needed. What I am suggesting is that in section
45 Berkeley offers his answer to the question posed in 44, what is meant in
common discourse, when one says that which he sees is at a distance from
him?
    What, then, is Berkeley's answer? Actually, he seems to offer two
new analyses. Early in the section, after he has given the conditions for
mediate perception, Berkeley says they determine him to think, "if I advance forward so many paces or miles, I shall be affected with such and
such ideas of touch." Applying this approach to H, we get H_5, if I advance
300 meters, I shall be affected with ideas of touch such as roughness, cold-
ness, etc., i.e. those ideas of touch constituitive of Whitehall. It should be
noticed that the antecedent condition is stated in terms of objective spatial
relations and motions. This analysis of H might be thought unproblematic,

since in *NTV* material things and their enduring independent spatial relations were never explicitly denied. However, it might be argued that the analysis is vitiated by circularity, since "300 meters" occurs in both the expression to be explicated and its analysis.[24] Another way of putting the difficulty is that Whitehall is replaced in the explication by potential immediate objects of touch, but the relation of the perceiver to Whitehall, which is no more objective than Whitehall, remains intact. A peculiar, though perhaps not vitiating, asymmetry has been introduced. Later in section 45 Berkeley again indicates how claims about seeing objects at a distance should be understood. It is possible to interpret his later account as a mere re-wording of his original position, but it also is possible to take it to be hinting at a more phenomenalistic analysis. Formulating his account in terms of the third-person, Berkeley described the crucial judgement as follows: ". . . After having passed a certain distance, to be measured by the motion of his body, which is perceivable by touch, he shall come to perceive such and such tangible ideas which have been usually connected with such and such visible ideas." What corresponds to the antecedent clause of the earlier conditional now specifies distance in terms of motions of the perceiver's body, which in their turn, are linked to what is immediately perceived by touch when one moves. The objective specification of distance has been replaced by a subjective one or at least by a specification in terms of what a perceiver would or could sense. One can easily see how H_5 would be modified to yield H_6, a phenomenalistic analysis of H. All that one has here, of course, is a hint.[25] Certainly, nothing more is done with this proto-phenomenalistic version of claims to see objects at a distance anywhere in *NTV*. But given that it is very difficult to find passages in either the *Principles of Human Knowledge* or *Three Dialogues between Hylas and Philonous* where Berkeley explicitly sets forth a purely phenomenalistic analysis of perceptual judgements, the passages in 45 that I have been examining gain considerable significance for the development of his philosophy.[26]

B. SECTIONS 46 THROUGH 49.

According to Berkeley, just as distance can be seen mediately, that is, inferred on the basis of what is seen, so it can be heard mediately. Sounds, which strictly speaking are the only objects of hearing, never are at any distance from those who hear them and never appear to be such. Nevertheless, normal humans in ordinary circumstances are able to tell how far from them various objects and events are upon hearing specific sounds. The latter are not inherently distance-revealing; rather, one's ability to judge distances on the basis of them is founded upon experience of correlations between them and certain immediate objects of touch and, derivatively, sight. Accordingly, a Sonyneux Man, one deaf from birth who is suddenly

made to hear, would initially not hear things at a distance. The theory of
distance hearing just sketched would seem to underlie two claims Berkeley
emphasized in section 46 of *NTV*. The first is that neither the immediate
object of seeing nor the immediate object of hearing is ever numerically the
same as the object that at the same time is or is believed to be at some distance from the perceiver. The second is that neither the immediate object of
seeing nor that of hearing is ever numerically the same as those immediate
objects of touch with which they are correlated. Berkeley writes:

> Sitting in my study I hear a coach drive along the street; I look
> through the casement and see it; I walk out and enter into it;
> thus, common speech would incline one to think I heard, saw,
> and touched the same thing, to wit, the coach. It is nevertheless
> certain, the ideas intromitted by each sense are widely different
> and distinct from each other; but having been observed con-
> stantly to go together, they are spoken of as one and the same
> thing. By the variation of the noise I perceive the different dis-
> tances of the coach, and know that it approaches before I look
> out. Thus by the ear I perceive distance, just after the same
> manner as I do by the eye.

One would greatly appreciate a more detailed treatment of this account of
how numerically distinct items are spoken of as one and the same thing. If
for no other reason, one might be curious about the sources of Hume's position that mistakes regarding numerical identity underlie belief in the external world.[27] Unfortunately, Berkeley adds no more about how belief in
a single perceptual object is reached. All we have is his emphatic claim that
no immediate object of sight or hearing is ever the same as any object of
touch.

In the next section Berkeley not only concedes, he stresses that the
close analogy between seeing and hearing distance does not seem obvious to
all. Many, perhaps most, would not grant the processes are parallel. One
is less likely to say he hears distance than to say he sees it. One is easily
convinced that external things are not actually objects of hearing; not so
with seeing. The immediate objects of hearing are not so easily and systematically confounded with the immediate objects of touch, Berkeley
claims, as are the immediate objects of sight.[28] He ends section 47 with
these words:

> But then one is with more difficulty brought to discern the dif-
> ference there is betwixt the ideas of sight and touch: Though it
> be certain a man no more sees and feels the same thing than
> he hears and feels the same thing.

Sections 48 and 49 comment on and develop the line of thought presented in the passage just quoted. They are difficult to fathom. Here is 48 in its entirety.

> One reason of which seems to be this. It is thought a great absurdity to imagine that one and the same thing should have any more than one extension and one figure. But the extension and figure of a body, being let into the mind two ways, and that indifferently either by sight or touch, it seems to follow that we see the same extension and the same figure which we feel.

Since what is nominally the final sentence of section 47: "Though it be . . . the same thing," is not an independent clause, "which" in the first sentence of section 48 apparently refers back to "one is with more difficulty brought to discern the difference there is betwixt the ideas of sight and touch." In 48 Berkeley explains one's difficulty by offering an argument against their difference that presumably one might find convincing. In 49 he rebuts the argument and reaffirms the claim made in the concluding words of section 47: "A man no more sees and feels the same thing than he hears and feels the same thing." The argument of section 49 develops as follows:

> It must be acknowledged that we never see and feel one and the same object. That which is seen is one thing, and that which is felt is another. If the visible figure and extension be not the same with the tangible figure and extension, we are not to infer that one and the same thing has two divers extensions. The true consequence is that the objects of sight and touch are two distinct things.[29]

Let us use the expression, "the numerical diversity thesis," for the position that no particular thing or particularized quality, e.g., extension, is ever an immediate object of both sight and touch. Applied to mediate seeing, this position yields the view that one's visual is never numerically the same as one's m-visible. The numerical diversity thesis is stated, somewhat loosely, in section 121 of *NTV*, ". . . there is no one self same numerical extension perceived both by sight and touch."[30] Returning to section 49, we notice that its final sentence, the conclusion of the argument of the section, is: "The true consequence is that the objects of sight and touch are two distinct things." Earlier Berkeley asserts: ". . . We never see and feel one and the same object." It *appears*, then, that section 49 is an argument *for* numerical diversity.

The main mystery remains: What exactly is being argued in 48? The first problem concerns the apparent conclusion, "we see the same extension and the same figure which we feel." Even after the logical ellipsis is filled by "on at least some occasions," one must concede the above claim is not equivalent to "we see and feel the same thing," since it can also be construed as the denial of Berkeley's heterogeneity thesis. The latter is expressed forcefully in section 127 of *NTV*, where Berkeley writes:

> The extension, figures, and the motions perceived by sight are specifically distinct from the ideas of touch called by the same names, nor is there any such thing as one idea or kind of idea common to both senses.[3] [1]

The interpretive question for section 48 is this: Should the expression, "we see the same extension and the same figure which we feel," be understood as a denial of Berkeley's numerical diversity thesis or of his heterogeneity thesis?

Here is an argument for the first alternative. The aim of 48 is explaining why many persons fail to discover the numerical diversity of the immediate objects of sight and touch. The explanation is framed in terms of an argument (that of 48) which is persuasive even though it proves to be inconclusive. Since the key expression is the conclusion of this argument, if it is interpreted as a denial of the heterogeneity thesis, the argument is rendered irrelevant. It is irrelevant because it is unrelated to what is being explained. There being an argument, specious or sound, against the heterogeneity thesis is no reason to deny the numerical diversity thesis, since the falsity of the former does not entail the falsity of the latter. Consequently, someone's being convinced of the argument against heterogeneity in no way explains his rejecting numerical diversity.

Plausible though it is, one must resist this argument and reject its conclusion. It rests upon a mistaken or, at least, questionable interpretation of section 47. Recall that "One reason of which seems to be this," the clause in 48 which introduces the argument under examination, refers back to the penultimate sentence of 47, which reads, "But then one is with more difficulty brought to discern the difference there is betwixt the ideas of sight and touch." The interpretation I'm opposing construes this as having to do with numerical diversity. Notice, however, that nothing is said in the sentence about the numerical diversity of the immediate objects of sight and touch. Notice, too, that its vagueness may go unremarked because the next and final sentence in 47, "Though it be certain a man no more sees and feels the same thing than he hears and feels the same thing," *seemingly* returns to the theme of numerical diversity. Now one can use that construal of the final sentence to interpret the next-to-last, but there is a clear alternative. It rests on the supposition that Berkeley in 47 chose to broaden the discussion from numerical diversity to heterogeneity in order to develop a new argument for the former in 48 and 49. He began 47 by noting that whereas few are able to distinguish immediate objects of sight from their accompanying immediate objects of touch, many do so in the corresponding case of hearing. I suggest that without explicitly indicating his intention, Berkeley broadened the discussion by considering the issue of common sensibles, i.e. nonrelational properties perceived by both sight and touch. We know he thought most people wrongly believe that there are qualities, specifically, extension, figure, and motion, that are immediate objects of both seeing and feeling. Few, if any, believe these qualities are common to both hearing and touch. My proposal is that we regard the final two sentences of 47 as claims about this difference. Berkeley should be understood as claiming that only with difficulty can one realize no sensible qualities are common to both sight and touch even though such is the case. On this interpretation the argument of 48 is an argument against the heterogeneity thesis that uses the denial of the numerical diversity thesis as its main premise. The counter-argument of 49 turns the tables. It utilizes heterogeneity as a ground for denying numerical identity.

Here, again, is the argument of 48, followed by the counter-argument of 49:

> It is thought a great absurdity to imagine that one and the same thing should have any more than one extension and one figure. But the extension and figure of a body, being let into the mind two ways, and that indifferently either by sight or touch, it seems to follow that we see the same extension and the same figure which we feel.

> But if we take a close and accurate view of things, it must be acknowledged that we never see and feel one and the same object. That which is seen is one thing, and that which is felt is another. If the visible figure and extension be not the same with the tangible figure and extension, we are not to infer that one and the same thing has divers extensions. The true consequence is that the objects of sight and touch are two distinct things.

Let us consider these arguments in terms of a situation in which, from the standpoint of common language and thought, someone simultaneously sees and feels something to be round. The following set of propositions is examined.

1. What is seen at t_1 (=one time) is numerically the same as what is felt at t_1.

2. What is seen at t_1 is round.

3. What is felt at t_1 is round.

4. "Round" is minimally equivocal with respect to sight and touch, that is, roundness as seen is not the same quality as roundness as

felt even though both are shapes.

5. If 1, 2, 3, and 4, then what is seen and felt at t_1 has two different shapes at the same time.

6. It is impossible for one and the same thing to have two different shapes at the same time.

The argument presented in 48 is best understood as an abbreviation of the claim that since propositions 1 through 6 are a logically inconsistent set, proposition 4 is to be rejected. The claim is offered as the unarticulated reason the acceptance of which explains why so few accept the heterogeneity thesis.

Berkeley's counter-argument, on this interpretation, is that one need not and must not eliminate the inconsistency of 1 through 6 by the means suggested. Rather one should embrace 4 and reject 1. Once one realizes that visual figure and extension are not the same qualities as tangible figure and extension, one should conclude that the particular object immediately perceived by sight, one's visual, is never numerically the same as what is immediately perceived by touch. The reversal that is at the heart of the argument in 49 is extremely interesting, since it implies there is a strong systematic connection between Berkeley's heterogeneity thesis and his numerical diversity thesis. He is claiming that given certain unexceptional principles (2, 3, 5, and 6), heterogeneity entails numerical diversity. If you accept the numerical identity of any immediate object of touch with any immediate object of sight, then you cannot accept the heterogeneity of visual and tangible figure. If you accept the latter, you must deny the former. There is no middle ground.

The interpretation just presented both makes sense of the otherwise baffling sections 48 and 49 and reveals a powerful systematic commitment on Berkeley's part. If only one could add that the arguments of 48 and 49 are cogent, a truly powerful case could be made. Such, however, is not the case. Both arguments fail for the same reason, that the premise to be rejected is 6. Suppose it is agreed that no surface one touches can be both square and round at the same time. Why must it be agreed that no object one both sees and touches at the same time can be both visually round and tangibly round, when they are considered as different qualities? Why suppose they are incompatible or contrary properties in the way that square and round are. To put it differently, once one concedes "round" is minimally equivocal with respect to qualities perceived by sight and touch, one should also concede "shape" is minimally equivocal with respect to sight and touch, so that the principle, "no object can have two different shapes at one and the same time," cannot be applied until it is restated as "no object can have two different visual shapes at one and the same time and no object can have two different tangible shapes on one and the same time."[3][2] So formulated it does not preclude an object's simultaneously having both a visual and tangible shape. If these criticisms hold, then there is no system-atic connection between Berkeley's numerical diversity thesis and his het-erogeneity thesis, the latter does not entail the former, so the arguments of both 48 and 49 collapse. These peculiar cousins of the familiar perceptual variations arguments[33] can safely be dismissed.

One might be tempted to reassert the connection between the het-erogeneity and numerical diversity theses by the following argument.[34] Suppose one has the experience commonsensically called seeing and touch-ing a round surface. On the heterogeneity thesis the roundness seen is not the roundness felt; therefore, what one sees is not seen to be tangibly round. Invoking the principle[35] that if an object immediately seen is not seen to have a nonrelational property, then it does not have that property, one concludes the object immediately seen is not tangibly round. Invoking Leibniz' Law (here the Diversity of the Discernible), one concludes that the object immediately seen is not the same as the object immediately felt. Af-ter all, the latter is tangibly round. The argument fails. The principle of immediate perception relied upon to reach the initial conclusion need not be accepted. Unless one assumes that what is seen is numerically different from what is touched, thus begging the main question, one cannot fend off obvious counterexamples. What reason has one to deny that an object immediately seen can be warm just because its warmth is not immediately seen. If, as it should be, immediate perception is considered solely in terms of a perceiving subject's being directly aware of an existent, nothing in immediate perception precludes the possibility of a visual having nonrela-tional properties that are not seen. Berkeley holds the principle of immedi-ate perception under examination, but does so because he also held that visuals are sensations[36] that cannot exist unperceived and the Principle of Idealism, which holds that whatever cannot exist unperceived cannot have nonrelational properties it is not perceived to have. Together these commit-ments, which were used in section 41 to secure *alpha*, allow one to argue from the heterogeneity thesis to the numerical diversity thesis, unlike the arguments considered so far.

C. SECTIONS 50 AND 51.

The main theme of sections 41 and 49 is the status of visuals and their relationship to m-visibles. Section 50 contains Berkeley's principal conclu-sions on this subject, which are:

> There are two sorts of objects apprehended by the eye, the one
> primarily and immediately, the other secondarily and by inter-
> vention of the former. Those of the first sort neither are, nor
> appear to be, without the mind, or at any distance off; they

may indeed grow greater or smaller, more confused, or more clear, or more faint, but they do not, cannot approach or recede from us. Whenever we say an object is at a distance, whenever we say it draws near, or goes farther off, we must always mean it of the latter sort, which properly belong to the touch, and are not so truly perceived as suggested by the eye in like manner as thoughts by the ear.

Familiar enough by now. What catches the informed eye or ear are two phrases, first, ". . . they do not, cannot approach or recede from us," and, second, "in like manner as thoughts by the ear." In the first Berkeley makes explicit a position merely implied earlier. It is that visuals *cannot* be at any distance from their perceivers. The second echoes the passage in section 41 in which visuals were called "thoughts or sensations." The two phrases are closely related. Using the Principle of Idealism one can argue from visuals being sensations or thoughts to their not having any (nonrelational) properties they are not seen to have. Since the truth of *alpha* is being founded on the nature of sensations and the Principle of Idealism, its truth might seem to be noncontingent. In 41 Berkeley did argue for *alpha* by claiming visuals are sensations. No wonder in 50 he feels justified in saying they *cannot* be external to us.

The second phrase provides a thematic bridge to section 51, where Berkeley introduces an analogy that becomes more and more important as *NTV* progresses. Here are the first few sentences of 51:

> No sooner do we hear the words of a familiar language pronounced in our ears, but the ideas corresponding thereto present themselves to our minds: in the very same instant the sound and the meaning enter the understanding: So closely are they united that it is not in our power to keep out the one, except we exclude the other also. We even act in all respects as if we heard the very thoughts themselves. So likewise the secondary objects, or those which are only suggested by sight, do often more strongly affect us, and are more regarded than the proper objects of that sense; along with which they enter into the mind, and with which they have a far more strict connexion, than ideas have with words.

Berkeley proceeds to develop the point that because the connection between visuals and m-visibles is so close and established so early, they are easily conflated and only with difficulty distinguished. What I want to consider is a peculiarity in Berkeley's way of presenting the analogy between hearing a sound as a word and mediately seeing an object at a distance.

In Berkeley's account of mediate perception there are three logically distinct elements, two of which are in the limelight, the third of which is needed to connect the other two. They are *(a)* the visual, what is seen in the strict and proper sense, *(b)* the m-visible, the object believed to be at some distance from the perceiver, and *(c)* the belief in the m-visible that is occasioned by seeing the visual. It might seem that the proper characterization of hearing a word in a familiar language would be closely analogous, involving *(a')* the sound, *(b')* the object meant, and *(c')* the thought of the object. In mediately seeing distance, seeing a visual occasions a belief in an external object; there may or may not be an object at the distance it is believed to be from the perceiver. In perceiving a sound as a word, hearing a sound occasions a thought of an object. In some instances, such as that of "unicorn," the object of the thought, what the word signifies, does not exist. Note the apparent points of analogy. Corresponding to *a* is *a'*, to *b*, *b'*, and to *c*, *c'*.

Why elaborate on the analogy in this much detail? Because Berkeley's presentation of the analogy between mediate seeing and hearing a word appears to pair the elements of the two processes in a quite different and rather puzzling way. Note, first, that at the end of section 50, objects at a distance are said to be "suggested by the eye in like manner as thoughts by the ear." Thoughts! Note, too, that in 51 Berkeley says that in hearing a word in a language one knows, "the ideas corresponding thereto present themselves to our minds." He adds later, "we even act in all respects as if we heard the very thoughts themselves." He continues, "So likewise the secondary objects, or those which are only suggested by sight, do often more strongly affect us, and are more regarded than the proper objects of that sense . . ." Since Berkeley used "secondary objects" in connection with m-visibles, mediate objects, in 50, he seemingly in 51 is pairing m-visibles with the thoughts occasioned by the sounds. Otherwise, why does he use such terms as "thoughts" and "ideas"? In short, he appears to be presenting *c'* as the analogue of *b*, the thought of an object occasioned by the sound as the analogue of the object seen at a distance. This is puzzling. What have m-visibles to do with thoughts of objects suggested by sounds? There is no obvious similarity of function. Moreover, if, as is often held, m-visibles in *NTV* are independent, enduring, material things, they seem to be ontologically different from thoughts as well.[37] In short, the analogy apparently being proposed is opaque.

What is happening here is that Berkeley's terminology creates an illusion. To see how this works one needs to recall that Berkeley consistently uses "idea" for objects that are perceived, imagined, recalled, and known. Sometimes its application is restricted to immediate objects of thought and perception, but frequently it is used broadly for whatever is an object of mind. In sections 50 and 51 "idea" is being used in the second, very broad sense. Berkeley is really developing the analogy by pairing *b* and *b'*, using "idea" and "thought" for what is designated by the word, not for the mental concept or image that accomplishes the designating.[38] Hence the items in the analogy are really paired as one would expect: *a* and a', b and b', c and c'. This interpretation, though not strictly provable, has one major advantage: on it Berkeley's discussion makes sense. But why, one might ask, was Berkeley so careless about such important matters. Why does he use "thought" for what obviously may be a nonmental referent of a word? Two explanations suggest themselves. One is that since what is mediately seen and what is meant by a word need not exist to be seen or meant, respectively, Berkeley uses "idea" and "thought" for them to indicate that they are intentional objects. The other is that throughout his philosophical writings, Berkeley systematically conflates objects of mental states with the mental states by which they are apprehended or thought, so that it is no surprise that he is willing to use "idea" and "thought" for both b and c, b' and c'. Trying to decide between these two alternatives would take us far beyond the confines of an already long paper.

Department of Philosophy, University of Iowa

NOTES

1. David M. Armstrong, *Berkeley's Theory of Vision: A Critical Examination of Bishop Berkeley's 'Essay towards a New Theory of Vision,'* (Melbourne, Australia: Melbourne University Press, 1960), p. 23. He devotes his second chapter 'The Central Doctrines of the *Essay*,' to sections 41-51. The careful reader of his excellent study will discern that Armstrong's primary interest is isolating, analyzing, and criticizing certain metaphysical and epistemological doctrines defended by Berkeley and not examining the text of *NTV* in minute detail.

2. See, first, section 38, and also 35.

3. *NTV*, 2, reads: "It is, I think, agreed by all that distance, of itself and immediately, cannot be seen. For distance being a line directed end-wise to the eye, it projects only one point in the fund of the eye, which point remains invariably the same, whether the distance be longer or shorter." I do not pretend to understand how a line projecting a point on the fund of the eye relates to seeing distance immediately, but I am confident Berkeley's argument that distance is not immediately seen is that the resources available in immediate seeing do not permit one to discriminate visually among different distances and so immediately see exact distance. Note, for contrast,

NTV, 11, in which Berkeley states: "Now from Sect. 2 it is plain
that distance is in its own nature imperceptible, and yet it is perceived by sight." Here he seems to be denying outness is immediately seen. David Hume makes an interesting point about seeing
objects as beyond our bodies that might be relevant to the question
of whether what is immediately seen is seen as being at some distance or other from the perceiver. See his *A Treatise of Human
Nature*, L.A. Selby-Bigge and Peter H. Nidditch, editors, second
edition, (Oxford: Clarendon Press, 1978), Book I, Part IV, Section 2,
pp. 190-91.

4. As the second passage quoted in the preceding note demonstrates,
    Berkeley in *NTV* was willing to use "see" for suggestions occasioned
    by what is seen in the strictest sense of "see." Thus he spoke of
    seeing distance mediately. This illustrates his using common speech
    and thought as his starting point. Analysis gradually reveals that
    mediate seeing is a kind of judging, inferring, or believing on the
    basis of what is truly seen. In *TVV* Berkeley is unwilling to allow
    mediate seeing, that is, refuses to allow that what is only suggested
    to the mind by an immediate object of sense is itself an object of
    sense or sensible thing. See, in particular, *TVV*, 9-12. One possible
    reason for this terminological shift is that Berkeley's anonymous
    critic uses "object of sense" for "whatever it is without that is the
    cause of any idea within," a usage Berkeley castigates in *TVV*. See
    'A Letter from an anonymous Writer to the Author of the *Minute
    Philosopher*,' *Works*, i. 277-9, especially paragraph 1 on p. 277.
    Compare *TVV*, 9. I do not mean to imply that the terminological
    change occurs only in *TVV*; see Berkeley, *Three Dialogues between
    Hylas and Philonous*, 174-5, for the restricting of "sensible thing" to
    what is immediately perceived. Berkeley wrote, ". . . The senses
    perceive nothing which they do not perceive immediately: for they
    make no inferences." See, also, *Dialogues*, 204.

5. By "a visual" I mean what is an immediate object of seeing on some
    occasion. On this usage something's being a visual does not preclude
    its being at a distance from its perceiver, its also being an immedi-
    ate object of touch, hearing, or any other mode of perceiving, or its
    being independent of or dependent upon its perceiver.

6. Compare *NTV*, 28, and *TVV*, 9 and 14.

7. "Inference" is my term. At times Berkeley restricts its application
    to cases involving necessary connections, thus equating inference
    and deduction, or cases involving conscious reasoning. He then uses
    "suggestion" to signify mediate perception. For such strictures on

the use of "infer," see *TVV*, 11-13. However, one can use "inference" in a broader sense, leaving open the question of what kind of thought process it involves. Thus, when Berkeley investigates how we mediately see distance in *NTV*, 2-40, he is considering the nature of the inference, in the broad sense, involved in mediate seeing. See, in particular, section 3, and the final quotation of note 5, above.

8. See *NTV*, 16, 17, and 27, for texts that support my use of the term "kinesthetic sensations," by which I mean what one feels when one rolls one's eyes, tracks an object from left to right, squints, and so on.

9. One might initially suppose, upon reading *NTV*, 29-36, that for Berkeley retinal images are immediately seen. For a corrective, compare sections 111-19, especially 119. On inverted retinal images, see Armstrong, *op. cit.*, 45-52, and C. M. Turbayne, 'Berkeley and Molyneux on Retinal Images,' *Journal of the History of Ideas*, **16** (1955), 339-55.

10. It is possible to state in at least a crude way several principles of immediate sensory awareness, that is, principles governing what Berkeley calls seeing, strictly and properly speaking. The first is that if someone immediately sees an object on some occasion, that object exists. In section 88 of his *A Treatise concerning the Principles of Human Knowledge, Works,* ii, Berkeley writes: "I can as well doubt of my own being, as of the being of those things which I actually perceive by sense: it being a manifest contradiction, that any sensible object should be immediately perceived by sight or touch, and at the same time have no existence in Nature, since the very existence of an unthinking being consists in *being perceived.*" A similar statement can be found in *Dialogues*, 230. Note that here Berkeley seems to hold this principle of immediate perception on the basis of a commitment to idealism. I would argue that idealism is not required for the first principle of immediate perception stated above. Immediate perception is a state or relationship that implies the existence of its object; its intentionality is founded on the existence of its object. See the discussion of E-relations in my 'Reid's Realism,' *Journal of the History of Philosophy*, **12,** (1974) 317-40, especially pp. 319-21, 323-25, and 330-33. A second principle of immediate perception is that if someone immediately perceives an object has some property or quality on some occasion, the object has that property or quality on that occasion. In the *Three Dialogues* Berkeley endorses it, having Philonous say of one whose perceptual judgement goes awry, "But his mistake lies not in what he per-

ceives immediately and at present (it being a manifest contradiction to suppose he should err in respect of that) . . ." *Dialogues*, 238. Now let us consider a third principle, the converse of the second: If some object has a property and is immediately perceived by somebody, that person immediately perceives the object has that property. One would expect Berkeley to hold this principle for at most nonrelational properties; he cannot consistently hold it for relational properties. To see why the latter is so, recall that for Berkeley God or some other spirit is the cause of any immediate object of sense. *(Principles,* 26-30). Consequently, every visual and every other immediate object of sense has the relational property of being caused by a spirit. Spirits, however, are not immediately perceived; nor can one be said to know by immediate seeing that visuals have the relational property in question. Hence Berkeley must allow that immediately perceived objects may have a relational property even though no one immediately perceives that they have it. The implication of this for distance is that a visual may have the relational property of being 30 meters from its perceiver even though it is not immediately perceived to have that property, at least insofar as the nature and principles of immediate perception are concerned.

11.   The question associated with Molyneux is not that raised by Berkeley in section 41 of *NTV*. Instead it concerns the relationship between visible and tangible extension and shape as well as the nature of concept formation as it relates to them. The question that Locke made famous by posing it in his *An Essay concerning Human Understanding* thus directly has much more to do with the heterogeneity issue discussed later in this paper than to the question of when one can mediately see distance. See Locke, *Essay*, Peter H. Nidditch, editor, (Oxford, Clarendon Press, 1975), Book II, Chapter ix, section 8.

12.   In section 42 of *NTV* Berkeley notes that on the "common supposition that men judge of distance by the angles of the optic axes," MM would mediately see distance with little or no delay. The reason is that on the common theory he would apply geometrical principles to the optical angles experienced in visual perception. Reaffirming his own position Berkeley writes "But that this is false has, I think, been sufficiently demonstrated." My reading is that "this" refers to the common supposition. Berkeley's argument is: If the common supposition about mediately seeing distance were correct, my negative answer to the question of whether MM would mediately see distance would stand refuted, since the affirmative answer follows logically from the common supposition. However, I have shown the common supposition is false (incorrect), so the affirmative answer is

unproven and my answer remains unrefuted. Berkeley, of course, is not entitled to infer the affirmative answer is false on the grounds that the common supposition is false, since that would commit a blatant fallacy. As for the alternative interpretation that "this" refers to the affirmative answer, one need only note Berkeley has offered no evidence against it, let alone a demonstration of its falsity. In contrast, earlier in *NTV* he offered what he took to be powerful objections to the common theory.

13. What may not be wholly clear is how Berkeley construed his negative answer and thus his positive account of mediate seeing of distance. The negative answer is thought of as a "manifest consequence" of his account. This leaves two genuine alternatives. The first is that his negative answer is an empirical touchstone for his account; the second is that it is a truth known to be such because deduced from a fully established doctrine. On the first it is a deductive consequence the testing of which against clinical data will either invalidate or partially confirm the theory whose consequence it is. On the second it is a truth that it is known because it is deducible from a body of demonstrative truths in the Cartesian-Lockean sense of that term. Unfortunately Berkeley neither answered nor even posed the question raised here. Answering it would require a careful survey of passages in *NTV* and *TVV*. One might note that sections 79, 92-100, 106, 110, 132-3, and 135 of *NTV* also concern the Molyneux Man's abilities and inabilities. In section 100 Berkeley is very guarded about what he has shown; contrast it to 106, 110, and 135. See, too, *TVV*, 71, particularly the final sentence, where Berkeley discusses the Chesselden experiments. Useful, perhaps, are *Principles*, 41, and *Dialogues*, 202. On the Cartesian-Lockean view of demonstrative knowledge, see Locke, *Essay concerning Human Understanding*, Book IV, Chapter ii, section 2-9.

14. We know, of course, that in section 41 Berkeley does link a visual's not being external to its being a sensation. The paradigms for sensations are feelings of pleasure or pain. Visuals in section 41 were said to be as near one as one's perceptions of pain or pleasure. A categorial property commonly denied sensations is the capacity to exist unsensed or as a state of a nonsentient being. Another property they seem to lack is being external to one who feels them. It seems not even sense to ask how far one's pleasure is from oneself. As for the non-externality of thoughts and passions, see section 94 of *NTV*, where Berkeley writes of MM, "All those things that are intangible and of a spiritual nature, his thoughts and desires, his passions, and in general all the modifications of the soul, to these he would never apply the terms upper and lower except only in a me-

taphorical sense." In *Dialogues*, 201-202, lights and colors are called sensations and Philonous says of the Molyneux Man that he would not ". . . have any notion of distance annexed to the things he saw; but would take them for a new set of sensations existing only in his mind." Here, too, Berkeley does seem to use the premiss that visuals are sensations to establish *alpha*. On sensations, see my 'Berkeley's Ideas of Sense,' *Nous*, **9** (1975), 55-72.

15.   Armstrong, *op. cit.*, p. 27: "We shall try to show, however, that whatever Berkeley's opinion on the matter, the view that the immediate objects of sight are two-dimensionally ordered *only*, and the doctrine that the objects of sense-perception do not exist without the mind, stand in the logical relation of indifference." If I understand Armstrong, his position is that Berkeley argued from what I have termed *alpha* to the conclusion that visuals are in the mind, i.e. cannot exist unsensed. *Loc. cit.*, "Contrariwise, in the *New Theory*, as we saw, he asserts that the fact distance is *not* immediately seen shows that the immediate objects of sight *are* in the mind." This involves putting tremendous weight on a few phrases in *NTV*, 41. Note that here Armstrong asserts the key premiss is what I dubbed *alpha-a*, no visual is seen to be external to one who peceives it. *Alpha-a* has so little apparent connection to the in-the-mind thesis that I assume he really meant to say Berkeley argued from *alpha* to the in-the-mind thesis. My view is that Berkeley argues from visuals are sensations to visuals are not external. Also, contrary to Armstrong, I believe that *if* visuals were sensations, they would not be external.

16.   One could modify the definition in such a way that exact replication is a symmetrical relation, so that V is an exact replica of M if and only if M is an exact replica of V. However, one who wants to defend the thesis that in correct mediate perception of distance V is always an exact replica of M might well want to hold M has some nonrelational properties that V lacks.

17.   Berkeley frequently uses the language of points to discuss the perceived magnitude of visuals. I believe this is tied to his doctrine of minimum sensibles. See *NTV*, 54, and 79-87, especially 54 and 79. It is perhaps worth noting that in section 81 of *NTV* Berkeley argues against unperceived parts of minimum visibles on the grounds that they are immediate objects of sight and that no such object exists "without the mind of him who sees it." In assessing this passage one should keep in mind that a consequence of the more plausible version of the third principle of immediate perception discussed in note 10 is the thesis that if someone immediately perceives an

object and does not immediately perceive it to have some nonrelational property, the object does not have that property. Could it be
that this is what Berkeley is getting at in section 81?

18.   To hold that on some, but not all, occasions one and the same object
       is both V and M, is to concede that there is no uniform systematic
       analysis of correctly mediately perceiving objects at a distance.
       Berkeley's argument in section 44 fails against the former position,
       which is compatible with the facts cited in the argument. (This point
       holds generally for perceptual variation arguments; their function
       seems to be that of discrediting certain kinds of claims to systematic
       unity or uniformity in analysis.) The closest Berkeley comes to con-
       sidering the possibility of non-uniform analyses of perceptual states
       is in the *Dialogues*, 184-86, where the problem of ascertaining
       which apparent color of an object is actually the real one is held to
       be insoluble. See, too, pp. 189-90.

19.   Sometimes Berkeley writes as if he holds that a visual persists over
       time and undergoes qualitative change, thus being able to change its
       magnitude. Notice the words that follow "every step I take" in the
       following, which is Berkeley's second example in section 44: "Again,
       suppose I perceive by sight the faint and obscure idea of something
       which I doubt whether it be a man, or a tree, or a tower, but judge
       it to be at the distance of about a mile. It is plain I cannot mean
       that what I see is a mile off, since that every step I take towards it
       the appearance alters, and from being obscure, small, and faint,
       grows clear, large, and vigorous. And when I come to the mile's
       end, that which I saw first is quite lost, neither do I find any thing
       in the likeness of it." See, too, *NTV*, 55. For a corrective, compare
       Dialogues, 201: "Sight therefore doth not suggest or any way
       inform you, that the visible object you immediately perceive, exists
       at a distance, or will be perceived when you advance farther on-
       ward, there being a continued series of visible objects succeeding
       each other, during the whole time of your approach." Here, obvi-
       ously, Berkeley is using "visible" for what is immediately seen. This
       presents no problem if it is recalled that in introducing "visual" I
       made no claim it is a term used by Berkeley. It is worth reflecting
       on how my reconstruction of Berkeley's argument in section 44
       would be altered if one took seriously the possibility of a visual's
       literally changing as one approached or receded from some object.
       On this interpretation the key to establishing that V is not always
       M is showing that V changes, but M does not.

20.   "Never" here means: cannot be systematically and uniformly ana-
       lyzed as. See note 18.

21. Suppose it is agreed that V is not the same as M and that M is 300 meters from me. Even when it is understood that V is immediately seen, it does not follow from these facts alone that V is not some distance from me. This is so even though I cannot immediately see what its distance from me is, since distance from me is a relational property. Berkeley obviously held that if what is immediately seen is not the same as the object that is mediately seen to be a distance from me, then it is at no distance from me. For Berkeley, it seems, the apparent conclusion of the argument of section 44, what is immediately seen is not the same object mediately seen at a distance, is compelling evidence for *alpha*. It does seem odd to distinguish V's from M's, that is, m-visibles, then assert the former are at various distances from their perceivers; that is to assign V's to a spatial limbo or private space. It is worth remarking that if *alpha* is true, then no visual is numerically identical to the m-visible seen by means of it. Suppose MV_1 is mediately seen by S_1 who immediately sees V_1. If *alpha* holds, V_1 is not external to S_1. If S_1 correctly perceives MV_1 to be at some distance from S_1, MV_1 is external to S_1. Hence V_1 is not MV_1. This is significant because it shows that for Berkeley proving visuals are not always identical to the m-visibles seen by means of them is merely a step towards establishing more interesting and controversial positions such as *alpha* and the heterogeneity thesis. For the latter see below.

22. In *Dialogues*, 205-6, Berkeley uses what appears to be an argument against the position I have called weak-*beta*. Note that his argument includes a comment directed against those who hold only one or at most a few visuals are exact replicas of m-visibles. He wants to know how one could ever tell the exact replicas from all the rest. See note 18 above.

23. Berkeley's heterogeneity thesis will be discussed in some detail in section B of this paper.

24. There is circularity in the analysis provided that what is being analyzed is a specification of distance in the ordinary statement. It is not obvious that in *NTV* Berkeley had in mind an eliminative analysis of ordinary distance claims insofar as they are claims about objects of touch. What is odd is that the first analysis seems to eliminate the persisting object of touch, e.g., Whitehall, but not the distance.

25. Armstrong, *op. cit.*, p. 25, apparently does not find any difference between what I have called two different accounts of the judgements employed in mediately seeing objects at a distance. His comments

on p. 31 strongly suggest that he finds no proto-phenomenalism in
NTV.

26.   In *Principles*, 44, there seems to be an attempted analysis of the
      judgements of distance involved in mediate seeing along phenomen-
      alistic lines. Berkeley writes: "So that in strict truth the ideas of
      sight, when we apprehend by them distance and things placed at a
      distance, do not suggest or mark out to us things actually existing
      at a distance, but only admonish us what ideas of touch will be
      imprinted in our minds at such and such distances of time, and in
      consequence of such and such actions." Armstrong, *op. cit.*, p. 31,
      note 16, commenting on this passage, says that Berkeley offers a
      phenomenalist analysis in three other places in the *Principles*, in
      sections 3, 58, and 65. It should be emphasized, however, that in
      none of the other passages are seemingly objective continuants and
      distances analyzed in terms of immediate objects of sense; they
      merely reduce existence claims to conditionals. Note the difference
      between the reductionist flavor of the second analysis in *NTV*, 45
      and the version given in *Principles*, 3: ". . . If I were out of my
      study I should say it existed, meaning thereby that if I was *in my
      study* I might perceive it . . ." (My emphasis.)

27.   Hume, *A Treatise of Human Nature*, I.iv.2, pp. 201-10. My as yet
      unpublished 'How Hume Read Berkeley: Hume's Account of Belief
      in an external World as a Variation on and Refutation of Berkel-
      eyan Immaterialism,' is an attempt to construe Hume's discussion
      of belief in material objects as an alternative to Berkeley's attempt
      to save the truth of common-sense perceptual judgements by anal-
      ysing them as conditional claims about present and future objects of
      immediate perception.

28.   In section 47 Berkeley writes: "I do not nevertheless say I hear
      distance in like manner as I say that I see it, the ideas perceived by
      hearing not being so apt to be confounded with the ideas of touch as
      those of sight are. So likewise a man is easily convinced that bodies
      and external things are not properly the object of hearing; but only
      sounds, by the mediation whereof the idea of this or that body or
      distance is suggested to his thoughts."

29.   Note, too, that the conclusion of the argument introduced by "One
      reason of which . . ." is "we see the same extension and the same
      figure which we feel." It does not seem possible for the argument to
      be a reason in support of the claim made in the final sentence of 47:
      "It be certain a man no more sees and feels the same thing than he
      hears and feels the same thing." I emphasize the points made in the

text for the sake of developing later issues.

30.   It is loosely stated because Berkeley's claim, as it stands, is consistent with his own position only if it is interpreted as a claim about the objects of *immediate* perception. An immediate object of touch definitely can be a mediate object of sight on Berkeley's theory. His official view in *NTV* seems to be that mediate objects of sight in seeing distance are immediate objects of touch on the same or other occasions. See, however, my treatment of section 45 earlier in this paper.

31.   See, too, *NTV*, 121, where Berkeley explicitly distinguishes the issue of numerical diversity from the issue of heterogeneity. The implications of the heterogeneity thesis for a Molyneux Man are stated dramatically in section 135 of *NTV*.

32.   Exactly how the original principle would be reformulated so as to preclude a visual with two or more visual shapes, a tangible with two or more tangible shapes, and so on, is not altogether clear to me. Perhaps it would be a conjunction of sub-principles.

33.   In his early writings Berkeley seems to have used variations in the perception of unchanging objects to develop arguments for four different conclusions: First, for the perception or mind-dependence of sensible qualities and sensible objects; second, for the numerical diversity of a visual and the m-visible perceived by means of it and, thus, for *alpha;* third, for the inadequacy of the exact replica model for mediately seeing distance; and fourth, for the claim that heterogeneity implies numerical diversity.

34.   This argument was proposed by an anonymous referee for this volume whose comments often proved useful.

35.   This principle and immediate perception were originally discussed in note 10.

36.   See my 'Berkeley's Ideas of Sense' (reference in note 14) for evidence that Berkeley's sensible objects are sensations.

37.   It is often held, partly on Berkeley's authority, that *NTV* is but a halfway house to the *Principles*, the point being that in the former the immediate objects of touch are enduring independent material objects and, consequently, radically different in ontological status from visuals. For Berkeley's testimonial see *Principles*, 43. Armstrong vigorously attacks this position. See *Berkeley's Theory of*

Vision, pp. 26-32. My discussion of section 45 of *NTV* earlier in this paper lends some support to Armstrong.

38.   Note that in section 47 of *NTV*, the part quoted in note 28, Berkeley seems to use "idea" for that by means of which a body or distance is suggested to the perceiver rather than that which is mediately seen or heard. It seems to me that at some point in his account of mediate seeing Berkeley must distinguish between the thought or idea of an object at a distance and the object itself; otherwise perceptual error becomes an impossibility.

George S. Pappas

BERKELEY AND IMMEDIATE PERCEPTION

The notion of immediate perception is as crucial and central in Berkeley's philosophy as the kindred notions of direct apprehension or direct awareness are in twentieth century accounts of perception. Unfortunately, Berkeley provided only slightly more light on the best way to understand this important notion than his twentieth century successors did in connection with understanding their related notions. So, if we are to grasp what Berkeley had in mind, some interpretive work is in order; Berkeley's texts, though initially helpful, do not supply all the illumination needed.

In this paper I give an interpretation of the notion of immediate perception. There seem to be three such notions discernible in Berkeley's writings. However, the first two are best seen as different aspects of a single notion of immediate perception, and the third epistemic notion is strictly speaking not a concept of immediate *perception* at all. I also try to explicate what entities, or types of entities, are immediately perceivable on Berkeley's theory. It is on this issue that one important aspect of Berkeley's defense of common sense emerges. It is also in connection with this matter of which entities are immediately perceivable that a central element in the widely rejected Luce-Jessop interpretation of Berkeley is, I claim, found to be quite plausible. Finally, I consider several potential problems with my treatment of Berkeley. The first and second have to do with whether my account is at odds with several key texts, and thus some textual exegesis and adjustment is in order. The remaining problem is philosophical, and if it succeeds the main part and pillar of Berkeley's defense of common sense crumbles. I suggest a way in which this philosophical disaster may be averted.

I. ON NOTIONS OF IMMEDIATE PERCEPTION

At one point in the *Dialogues*, Philonous, speaking for Berkeley, asks Hylas:

> Are those things only perceived by the senses which are perceived immediately? Or may those things properly be said to be "sensible" which are perceived mediately, or not without the intervention of others?[1]

195

E. Sosa (ed.), Essays on the Philosophy of George Berkeley, 195–213.
©*1987 by D. Reidel Publishing Company*

As this passage makes clear, Berkeley thinks that mediate, or what we might term *indirect* perception, requires some perceived intermediary. Thus, if an object O is mediately perceived, then there is some object R which is also perceived, and O would be perceived only if R were perceived. We can illustrate by considering an indirect realist theory of perception of the sort held classically by Locke. On such a theory, an external physical object such as a chair is mediately perceived since, on this theory, all such objects that are perceived at all are mediately perceived. And a chair would be perceived on this theory only if some other object, an idea of sensation, were to be perceived.

Immediate perception can now be easily but only roughly charac-terized since it is directly opposed to mediate perception. Let us speak first of immediate seeing, reserving the more general notion of immediate per-ception for later comment. Then the above remarks give us this:

> D-1   An object O is immediately seen by an observer S at a time t = (1) O is seen by S at t; and (2) it is false that: O would be seen by S at t only if some object R, where R is not identical to O, were to be seen at t by S.

Here we take the term "object" very broadly; events, processes, states and qualities, along with individuals, are to be included as objects. Notice also that the term "seen" is used in the definiens. There is nothing illegitimate about this. Mediate and immediate seeing are types of seeing, and in defining each we rely on an undefined term, "seen," the understanding of which is left at an intuitive level.

The notion of immediate seeing given by D-1 seems to be what Berkeley makes use of in the *Essay towards a New Theory of Vision*, where he argues that as distance is not immediately seen, then the visual percep-tion of distance is dependent on some other perception. He says:

> It is evident that, when the mind perceives any idea not imme-diately and of itself, it must be by the means of some other idea . . . the passions which are in the mind of another are of themselves to me invisible. I may nevertheless perceive them by sight; though not immediately, yet by means of the colours they produce in the countenance. (*NTV*, sect. 9.)

Thus, perception of distance by sight is mediate, a perception accomplished by means of some other perception. Immediate perception, by contrast, is not done by means of and thus is not dependent on some other seeing. It is this feature which is captured in D-1, particularly in its clause (2).

However, further reflection on the *New Theory of Vision* shows that D-1 is not adequate. To see why, consider this passage:

Now, from sec. 2 it is plain that distance is in its own nature imperceptible, and yet it is perceived by sight. It remains, therefore, that it be brought into view by means of some other idea that is itself immediately perceived in the act of vision. (*NTV*, sect. 11.)

This passage indicates that clause (2) of *D-1* is incorrect. A case of seeing is immediate not merely when it lacks dependence on some other *seeing*, but when it is not dependent on any other *perception*. Thus, we should amend clause (2) of *D-1* to read (we here suppress reference to time and observer):

> (2a)   It is false that *O* would be seen only if some object *R*, not identical to *O*, were to be perceived.

That (2a) is a correct reading of section 11 of *NTV* is supported by a consideration of Berkeley's own account of seeing distance. He assumes, with others, that distance is not immediately seen, though it is seen in some sense. Berkeley isolates three other perceptions on which visual perception of distance is dependent: a feeling one gets as the distance between the pupils of the eyes widens or contracts (*NTV*, sect. 16); perception of the degree of confusion in the visual appearance (*NTV*, sect. 21); and the sensation one experiences when the eye muscles are strained as an object is brought closer and closer to the eyes (*NTV*, sect. 27). Of these, only the second is a case of seeing; the other two perceptions involve feeling. Hence, (2a) is preferable to (2).

It is true that when Berkeley comes to actually use his theory of distance perception, he appeals only to the second of the above three operations. For example, his explanation of the Barrow case proceeds along these lines. However, there are still reasons to opt for (2a) over (2). First, in a discussion in which Berkeley juxtaposes his own theory to one proposed by Wallis, he explicitly cites the sensations resulting from straining the eyes as a perception on which visual perception of distance and magnitude is dependent (*NTV*, sect. 77). Moreover, Berkeley elsewhere cites sensations of feeling as those on which, in some cases, visual perception of distance depends (e.g., *Theory of Vision Vindicated and Explained*, sect. 66). Further, Berkeley's theory of perception generally needs (2a). Imagine that a person has a single visual idea X, and that this idea suggests some tangible idea Y. Then by an analogue of clause (2) for touch, Y would be immediately perceived by touch, for its "perception" would not depend on perception of any other tangible idea. Yet we know that this is directly contrary to Berkeley's view; ideas or other entities that are merely suggested in this way are *mediately* perceived.[2] Thus, we need (2a) rather than (2). Even so, there is an important way in which (2a) is not specific enough. Imagine a case in which an observer immediately sees several visual ideas at once, perhaps a cluster of visual shapes. We want to say that he immediately sees both the cluster and the individual ideas that make it up. But clause (2a) causes trouble. For it is true that the observer would see the cluster only if he were to see something other than the cluster, viz., its elements or components. The converse holds as well; the observer would see the several ideas making up the cluster only if he were to see the cluster.

To deal with problems of this sort, we can amend (2a) to:

> (2b)   It is false that O would be seen only if some other object, R, were to be perceived, where R is not identical to O and where R is not an element of or a part of O, or a group of elements or parts of O, nor is O of R.

With (2b)we allow Berkeley to get the desired results; both the cluster of ideas and the constituents of that cluster are immediately seen.

There is another notion of immediate perception (seeing) to be found in Berkeley. For instance, also in the *Essay*, he writes:

> . . . it being already shown that distance is suggested to the mind by the mediation of some other idea which is itself perceived in the act of seeing, it remains that we inquire what ideas or sensations there be that attend vision . . . (*NTV*, sect. 16.)

Here the idea is that mediate or indirect perception is dependent on and is perhaps brought about by an act of suggestion; immediate perception, then, would be that perception that is not dependent on and is not wrought by an act of suggestion. As Philonous says:

> In reading a book, what I immediately perceive are the letters, but mediately, or by means of these, are suggested to my mind the notions of God, virtue, truth, etc. Now, that the letters are truly sensible things, or perceived by sense, there is no doubt; but I would know whether you take the things suggested by them to be so too. (*Dialogues*, 174.)

Is this "no suggestion" notion one which picks out a separate concept of immediate perception? Consider some perception which *is* reached by an act of suggestion. It occurs, as mediate perception, only if some other perception occurs. Thus, mediate perception is that perception that would occur only if some other perception were to occur. By contrast, immediate perception would *not* be dependent on some other perception. The no suggestion notion, then, implies that given in *D-1*. Nevertheless, the former is a richer notion than *D-1*, for it includes, in addition to clauses (1) and (2b) of *D-1*, an idea we might express by a new clause relating just to seeing, thus:

D-2   An object O is immediately seen = clauses (1) and (2b) of $D-1$ are met; and 3) it is false that perception of some thing R, which is not identical to O, suggests O (to the observer).

It is $D-2$, I would claim, that Berkeley actually makes use of, especially in his theory of vision. Since this definition incorporates the earlier $D-1$, we may say that Berkeley does not really have or utilize two distinct notions of immediate perception (seeing). [3]

Two things are worth noticing about this notion of suggestion. First, as Berkeley uses the term, it seems to be restricted to entities which have been associated with each other in some manner. For example, in the *Essay* visual ideas and ideas of touch are said to be associated with one another so that the former often suggest the latter. Association of this sort, in turn, requires that associated entities each be perceived in some manner, perhaps in the past. Thus, it would seem that notions of "God, virtue, truth . . . ," which Berkeley speaks of as suggested by the letters on a printed page (see the last-quoted passage) are not the sorts of things which are perceptually suggestible since none of those things is perceived. Second, suggestion is not a judgmental, cognitive act. Berkeley says in the *Theory of Vision Vindicated and Explained* that:

> To perceive is one thing; to judge is another. So likewise to be suggested is one thing, and to be inferred is another. Things are suggested and perceived by sense. We make judgments and inferences by the understanding. (*TVV*, sect. 42.)

As this passage makes clear, neither perception proper (immediate perception) nor mediate perception reached by suggestion is judgmental or inferential, nor, indeed, a conceptual activity of any sort since it is not discharged by the understanding.

Such a sharp separation between the activity and objects of sense and of the understanding is one we have come to associate with Kant. It also raises, but hardly solves, the vexing question of just how mediate perception can be positiviely characterized given that it is both derivative and non-conceptual (non-judgmental). We need not here try to solve this problem. For us, the important point is that, for Berkeley, perception proper and thus seeing proper is itself non-conceptual and non-judgmental. We thus need to understand $D-2$ along these lines.

Berkeley's use of "immediately perceives" ("immediately sees") is also non-propositional in that the verb takes a grammatical direct object as complemeent rather than some propositional clause. Thus, he is not discussing perceiving *that* something is or is not the case, or perceiving something *as* one thing or another. Moreover, given that immediate perception (immediate seeing) for Berkeley is non-conceptual, as described above, we can also say that the *implicit* or underlying import of the notion of immediate perception is non-propositional as well. The fact that the relevant verb takes a direct object complement, that is, is not merely some surface feature of the way we use the language, one which works to hide some hidden deep propositional structure to immediate perception (seeing).

Given these facts, it is quite plausible to hold that Berkeley's term "immediately sees" is *extensional* in the sense that it supports inferences such as: Person *S* immediately sees object *O*, and *O* is identical to *X*, so *S* immediately sees *X;* as well as, Person *S* immediately sees *O*, and *O* is a part or group of parts of *X*, so *S* immediately sees *X*. Thus, if *S* immediately sees a tree, and that tree is the billionth tree planted in Ohio since the death of Napoleon, then *S* immediately sees the billionth tree planted in Ohio since the death of Napoleon. And, if *S* immediately sees the south side of University Hall, then he also immediately sees University Hall. Inferences of this sort, and related ones, generally fail if the perception verb is propositional and used so that it designates conceptual or judgmental activity.

II. AMENDING *D-2*

Although *D-2* is the notion of immediate seeing that Berkeley actually makes use of, it will not quite serve his interests. One sort of problem case is aimed at clause (2b), while another sort is aimed at clause (3). The former can be brought out by considering a person who sees two non-adjacent visual ideas simultaneously. That is, these ideas are not themselves elements of the same cluster of ideas, perhaps because one is to the left of the visual field and the other is to the right. We want to be able to say that the person immediately sees *both* of these visual ideas and at the same time. But clause (2b) of *D-2* is not satisfied. The ideas in question are distinct and not related to each other as part or element to whole. Nonetheless, the person would not see the one idea if he were to fail to see the other assuming all else is held constant (i.e. he does not close one eye and cut off part of what had been the visual field).

The problem for clause (3) of *D-2* arises when we consider a person who sees two visual ideas and it happens that each suggests the other to him and at the same time. In this case, even if clause (2b) is satisfied, (3) is not and we would have to conclude that neither idea is immediately perceived (seen). But we surely do not want to rule out simultaneous immediate seeing of two ideas, not even when, coincidentally, each suggests the other.[4]

We can solve the problem raised by the first case by thinking of the person's seeing the two visual ideas as one complex perceptual event, one which has simpler perceptual events as components. One simpler component event is the event of seeing the idea to the left; another is the event of seeing the idea to the right. We can speak of objects as *constituents* of events. So, for instance, the idea to the left is a constituent of the relatively simple event of seeing (just) that idea. Both ideas are constituents of the complex event of the two ideas being seen at the same time. What we want to rule out is a situation in which the event of seeing a distinct entity is part of, or included in, the event of seeing *O*. That sort of entity is precisely the sort of intermediary that would lead to *mediate* seeing. On the other hand, we want to allow a case in which the seen entity is *not* a constituent of the event of seeing *O;* that sort of situation is just that of simultaneous immediate seeing of two distinct, non-adjacent entities. Finally, the problem of coincidental suggestion of one immediately seen idea by another can be dealt with by rephrasing clause (3) so that it is subjunctive. Utilizing these two ideas, we can readily amend *D-2* so that the problem cases are overcome. We then have:

> *D-3*   S immediatley sees *O* = (1) *S* sees *O;* and (2) it is false
> that *S* would see *O* only if *S* were to perceive *R*, where
> *R* is not identical to *O*, and where *R* is not a part or
> element or group of parts or elements of *O*, nor is *O* of
> *R*, and where *R* is a constituent of an event which is a
> part of the event of seeing *O;* and (3) it is false that *S*
> would see *O* only if *O* were to be suggested to *S* by *R*.

This definition, I think, captures all of what Berkeley actually meant by the term "immediately sees," as well as what he needs.[5] Moreover, by making use of *D-3*, we have a simple way of defining the more general term "immediately perceives." That is, we assume that analogues of *D-3* can be given for other relevant perception verbs – "immediately hears," "immediately tastes," "immediately smells," and "immediately touches" (or "feels"), and we assume that to perceive is either to see, to hear, to smell, to taste or to touch (feel). Then the notion of immediate perception is easily defined as:

> *D-4*   S immediately perceives *O* = *S* either immediately
> sees, or immediately hears, or immediately tastes, or
> immediately smells, or immediately touches (feels) *O*.

It might be reasonably supposed, however, that something crucial has been overlooked in the discussion thus far, namely, some explicitly epistemic element. Thus, consider this passage:

> HYLAS. . . . how can a man be mistaken in thinking the
> moon a plain lucid surface, about a foot in diameter, or a
> square tower, seen at a distance, round, or an oar, with one
> end in the water, crooked?

PHILONOUS. He is not mistaken with regard to the ideas he actually perceives, but in the inference he makes from his present perceptions. Thus, in the case of the oar, what he immediately perceives by sight is certainly crooked, and so far he is in the right . . . His mistake lies not in what he perceives immediately and at present (it being a manifest contradiction to suppose he should err in respect of that), but in the wrong judgment he makes concerning the ideas he apprehends to be connected with those immediately perceived . . . (*Dialogues*, 238.)

This passage, and others quite similar to it,[6] seem to point to a notion of immediate perception once attributed to Moore, viz.,

> D-5   An object O is immediately perceived by a person S at a time $t = S$'s assertion that he perceives O at t could not be mistaken at t.[7]

Such an interpretation of Berkeley also yields a straightforward account of mediate perception; it would just be that perception about which the relevant assertion could be mistaken. Such a view accords naturally and directly with the ideas expressed in the last-quoted passage.

Although epistemic interpretations of immediate perception for Berkeley, as in *D-5*, are quite common,[8] I think they should be resisted. One reason is that they are not general enough. For Berkeley, all finite percipients immediately perceive some things whenever they perceive at all. Thus, very small children also immediately perceive some entities whenever they perceive. However, such children and more generally anyone who is "conceptually impoverished" would often lack the appropriate concepts necessary for it to be true that their respective assertions (or beliefs) that they perceive something could not be mistaken. Moreover, there is the fact that Berkeley accepts the thesis that ordinary physical objects such as chairs and trees are often immediately perceived (I defend this claim in the next section). Yet, with respect to any such physical object, one's assertion (belief) that it is being perceived certainly could be mistaken. So, the conjunction of *D-5* with the just-mentioned thesis yields the result that no physical object of these sorts (chairs, trees and the like) is ever immediately perceived. This is an unwelcome result.

Still, one might argue that *D-5* does help to bring out something which is both important and endorsed by Berkeley, viz.,

> (1)   If an object O is immediately perceived by a person, then the person's assertion (belief) that he/she perceives O cannot be mistaken.

Further, there is reason to think that Berkeley accepts another important epistemic claim,

(2)   If an object O is immediately perceived by a person, then the person immediately knows that he/she perceives object O.

But, if Berkeley accepts either or both of these statements, then we have a serious problem for the above treatment of D-5. After all, no term designating a physical object and substituted for O in either (1) or (2) will yield other than falsity, one might argue. Moreover, each of (1) and (2) runs afoul of the small children objection raised above for D-5. Hence, the foregoing rejection of D-5 would be regarded as ill-motivated, since it is based squarely on claims that Berkeley is in no position to accept.

To address these issues properly, we need to first have a look at what Berkeley thinks immediately perceived entities might be. Following that, we return to the question of whether Berkeley accepts (1) and (2).

III. IMMEDIATELY PERCEIVED ENTITIES

It is clear that Berkeley accepts the thesis that individual ideas of various sense modalities are immediately perceived. Thus, some ideas are immediately perceived by sight, others by touch and so on. He also allows for *idea-clusters* to be immediately perceived. These would be groups of ideas of the same sense all immediately perceived at the same time, as in the example described in the preceding section. Does he also accept the thesis that

(3)   Some physical objects are immediately perceived.

as I earlier alleged? To see that the answer is *yes*, consider this passage:

> Wood, stones, fire, water, flesh, iron, and the like things which I name and discourse of are things that I know. And I should not have known them but that I perceived them by my senses; and things perceived by the senses are immediately perceived. (*Dialogues*, 230.)

At another point Berkeley says that by the term "body" (here meaning ordinary physical objects) we should mean

> . . . what every plain, ordinary person means by that word, to wit, that which is immediately seen and felt, which is only a combination of sensible qualities or ideas . . . (*Dialogues*, 183.)

Or again, having explained why he has used the word "idea" and what its use comes to, Berkeley says, through Philonous:

> Is this [his explanation] as strange as to say that the sensible qualities are not on the objects: or that we cannot be sure of the existence of things, or know anything of their real natures, though we both see and feel them, and perceive them by all our senses? (*Dialogues*, 236.)

There is also the passage quoted earlier from the *Dialogues* for another purpose where we find Philonous say:

> In reading a book, what I immediately perceive are the letters, but mediately, or by means of these, are suggested to my mind the notions of God, virtue, truth, etc. Now, that the letters are truly sensible things, or perceived by sense, there is no doubt. (*Dialogues*, 174.)

The letters printed on the pages of a book certainly qualify as physical objects, so that this passage, too, works to support (3).

There is, then, ample textual support for the claim that Berkeley endorses (3). Yet, one might ask, how can he do this? After all, the only things Berkeley allows in his philosophy are perceivers and ideas. The answer, of course, is that Berkeley also accepts what I call "ontological phenomenalism," viz., the thesis that

(4)   Each physical object is a collection of sensible ideas.

When we put (4) together with *D-4* we can see how Berkeley is in a position to accept (3). Imagine that a person immediately perceives some ideas that are elements or members of the collection of ideas which constitutes some physical object, e.g., a chair. Then, given that "immediately perceives" is understood along the lines of *D-4*, this will often be enough for the person to immediately perceive the chair. By immediately perceiving some of the constituents of the chair (some sensible ideas) he immediately perceives the chair as well. The analogy here would be to the example cited earlier: by immediately seeing the facing side of University Hall, one also immediately sees University Hall itself.

Not all inferences of this sort work. If University Hall were being razed and all parts of it had been demolished except for the still-standing south wall, then by immediately seeing the south wall one would not be immediately seeing University Hall. The relevant parts have to be attached in the right way. Presumably something similar is required for Berkeley's theory, except that sensible ideas for him are not parts of physical objects. What this similar constraint would be depends on how we explicate his notion of a collection of sensible ideas. Other cases where such inferences fail include those where too small an amount of something is immediately perceived. If I am standing behind a fence and am completely concealed except for one tip of one finger which I have placed in the one hole in the fence, then if you should happen to immediately perceive that finger tip, you would not thereby immediately perceive me. You have not immediately perceived enough of me, despite the fact that what you have immediately perceived of me is attached in the appropriate way. A similar restriction will hold in Berkeley's situation.[9]

These remarks concerning (3) may be taken as lending some support to the Luce-Jessop interpretation of Berkeley as a common-sense realist. That is, one thesis that is essential to common-sense realism, namely the thesis that physical objects are immediately perceived (= statement (3)) is one that Berkeley does endorse, and, indeed, does so plausibly given *D-4* and (4). Of course, this is *not* to say that Berkeley is a realist regarding the *nature* of physical objects; quite to the contrary, he accepts ontological phenomenalism. It is merely to say that he accepts a perceptual claim which is indisputably commonsensical – (3) – and that his doing so is perfectly consistent. Moreover, Berkeley is right to claim that on this point he fares better than any of his competition (Locke, Malebranche, Hobbes, Descartes), for none of his competitors is in a position to embrace (3).

IV. RECONSIDERATION OF AN OBJECTION

Earlier (p. 000, above), I noted that Berkeley seems to accept both (1) and (2), but that if so, he cannot also accept (3) since physical objects are not things about which mistaken belief is impossible or about which one has immediate knowledge. Hence, it is claimed, Berkeley must reject (3).

I think Berkeley would and does reject (1) and (2) instead. The reason is that in the passages from which those claims are culled, Berkeley is speaking of ideas rather than of physical objects. Thus, the following two statements come closer to what he actually endorses:

(5)   If X is immediately perceived by a person, and X is an idea, then the person's assertion (belief) that he/she perceives X cannot be mistaken.

(6)   If X is immediately perceived by a person, and X is an idea, then the person knows immediately that he/she perceives X.

Consider, for example, the passage quoted earlier about mistaken belief (p. 000, above). There Berkeley, through Philonous, is quite explicitly talking about ideas. Or consider this:

> . . . so long as I confine my thoughts to my own ideas divested
> of words, I do not see how I can easily be mistaken. The objects
> I consider I clearly and adequately know. I cannot be deceived
> in thinking I have an idea which I have not. (*Principles*, Intro-
> duction, sect. 22.)

Here again it is clear that reference is to ideas, about which alone is mistaken belief alleged to be impossible. Both of these passages support (5)
rather than (1). As for (6), consider the following:

> . . . when, therefore, they (ideas) are actually perceived, there
> can be no doubt of their existence . . . What a jest it is for a
> philosopher to question the existence of sensible things till he
> has it proved to him from the veracity of God, or to pretend
> that our knowledge in this point falls short of intuition . . .
> (*Dialogues*, 230.)

Here Berkeley seems to be accepting something that implies (6), namely
that if something is immediately perceived then there can be no doubt of its
existence and one has intuitive (immediate) knowledge of its existence. But
again, the entities talked about are ideas. We have also this passage.

> The real objects of sight we see, and what we see we know.
> And these true objects of sense and knowledge, to wit, our own
> ideas, are to be considered, compared, distinguished in order to
> understand the true theory of vision. (*TVV*, sect. 20.)

This passage, too, provides support for (6) rather than for (2).
    We have, then, good reason to think that Berkeley rejects both (1)
and (2); each is stated in too general a form. In fact, however, I believe
Berkeley also rejects (5) and (6) in favor of claims which are both more
cautious and more plausible. To see this, consider the full statement of a
passage I had earlier stated only partially:

> . . . so long as I confine my thoughts to my own ideas divested
> of words, I do not see how I can easily be mistaken. The objects
> I consider, I clearly and adequately know. I cannot be deceived
> in thinking I have an idea which I have not. It is not possible
> for me to imagine, that any of my own ideas are alike or una-
> like that are not truly so. To discern the agreements or disa-
> greements there are between my ideas, to see what ideas are
> included in any compound idea and what not, there is nothing
> more requisite than an attentive perception of what passes in

my own understanding. (*Principles*, Introduction, sect. 22.)

The point to be emphasized about this passage concerns *attentive* perception or awareness. Immediate perception of an idea is not of itself sufficient for immediate knowledge of the idea, or for mistaken belief about the existence of that idea to be impossible. For a person who is inattentive might well make mistakes about an idea he immediately perceives. Thus, what Berkeley actually endorses are:

(7)   If X is immediately perceived by a person who is attentive, and X is an idea, then the person's assertion (belief) that he/she perceives X cannot be mistaken.

(8)   If X is immediately perceived by a person who is attentive, and X is an idea, then the person immediately knows that he/she perceives X.

There is even an excellect reason provided by Berkeley in favor of these two claims. At one point he says:

Color, figure, motion, extension, and the like, considered only as so many *sensations* in the mind, are perfectly known, there being nothing in them which is not perceived. (*Principles*, sect. 87, emphasis original.)

In the same book he also says:

Every particular finite extension which may possibly be the object of our thought is an *idea* existing only in the mind, and consequently each part thereof must be perceived. (*Principles*, sect. 124.)

To steal a line from Henry Price, with respect to individually perceived ideas, "all the goods are in the shop window." Or, in alternative terms, immediately perceived individual ideas are *wholly presented*. The point here is that each non-relational and non-dispositional quality of a wholly presented entity is itself immediately perceived. Given what the foregoing passages support, namely,

(9)   If X is immediately perceived and X is an idea, then X is wholly presented.

we can understand not only why Berkeley would embrace (7) and (8), but also why he would not accept a similar set of claims pertaining to physical objects. Wholly presented ideas, we might say, are "wholly exposed," and attentiveness reveals all there is to be revealed. But no physical object, not even an immediately perceived one, is ever wholly presented.

We have found that the epistemic claims embodied in (1) and (2) are no threat to the contention that Berkeley accepts (3), since, it was argued, Berkeley rejects (1) and (2). It is easy to see, though, that he ought to reject (7) and (8) as well. For the small children case mentioned earlier shows that neither of those claims is true unless modified to include some clause specifying that a concept mastery condition is met. So modified, each of those claims gains in plausibility, while at the same time each serves all the ends Berkeley envisions for it.

V. FURTHER PROBLEMS FACING THE ASCRIPTION OF (3) TO BERKELEY

There are a number of important and powerful objections to the view that for Berkeley physical objects are immediately perceived. We need to consider these before we can reasonably accept the interpretation given in section III.

One objection is that Berkeley often says that nothing is perceived by sight but light and colors, by hearing nothing is perceived but sound, and so on for each of the senses. But surely if anything is immediately perceived it is either immediately seen, heard, tasted, smelled or touched (felt). Thus, Berkeley's own frequently stated words show that he does not accept (3).

A related objection concerns the heterogeneity thesis propounded in the *Essay*. There, it seems, Berkeley's main contention is that no object of sight is ever immediately perceived by touch, and that no object of touch is ever immediately perceived by sight. Indeed, he goes so far as to claim that visual and tactile immediate objects are different in kind. Since we would not want to claim that physical objects are, say, immediately *heard* though neither immediately seen nor touched, the heterogeneity thesis counts heavily against interpreting Berkeley so that he accepts (3).

There is a single way of avoiding both of these objections. We can set out the reply[10] by noting the difference between:

> (10) Nothing is immediately perceived by sight except light and color.

and,

> (11) No ideas are immediately perceived by sight except for those of light and color.

In many passages where Berkeley seems to endorse (10), or its kin for another sense, he explicitly mentions ideas and so endorses (11) instead.[11] A related point holds for the heterogeneity thesis. Sometimes Berkeley expresses this as,

> (12)   No immediate object of sight is immediately perceived by touch. (E.g., *NTV*, sect. 111.)

but more often what he says is,

> (13)   No idea of sight is immediately perceived by touch. (*NTV*, sect. 95.)

The central point of the reply, then, is that it is *at least* as plausible to interpret Berkeley as accepting (11) and (13), based on the relevant texts, as it is to construe him as endorsing the stronger claims made in (10) and (12). The texts alone do not decide the issue.[12]

A non-textual criticism concerns the notion of a collection of sensible ideas. Imagine that a person immediately perceives some sensible ideas, $s_1, s_2, \ldots s_n$ at some time, and that each is a constituent of the collection of sensible ideas which make up some physical object (e.g., a chair). At this time the person immediately perceives only *some* of the constituents of the object. Hence, it is unclear how this person can immediately perceive the object itself; many, indeed most, of its constituents are unperceived.

The response to this objection is to fall back on the analogy used earlier. Thus, consider the ordinary case of seeing University Hall. No person ever sees all or even most of its many parts at any one time, but we do not for *that* reason conclude that people fail to see University Hall. Nor would we conclude, against a direct realist who maintains that University Hall is directly seen, that since some of that building's parts are not directly seen at one time, then neither is the building itself directly seen. Just so in Berkeley's case: failing to immediately perceive all of the constituents of a chair, or even most of them, at one time does not imply that the chair itself is not immediately perceived.[13]

A final objection presents the biggest obstacle. I have said that Berkeley accepts both (3) and (4). If so, then immediately seeing a green chair will typically consist in immediately seeing some green visual ideas which are constituents of the chair. Consider, though, a not quite so typical, though by no means rare sort of case in which the green chair *looks blue*. As we ordinarily think of such cases, the fact that the chair looks blue does not mean that the person does not see the chair. Indeed, he does see the chair; it just happens to look blue at that moment to that observer. If, now, we translate this example into Berkeley's terminology, we say that the person immediately sees some blue visual ideas. We *want* Berkeley to be able to say that, nonetheless, the person immediately sees the green chair.

Otherwise, his claim to be a champion of common sense is jeopardized. After all, it is commonsensical to say that a chair that looks blue is seen even though the chair is green. However, in order to get the desired result we seem forced to say that the *blue* visual ideas are constituents of the collection of sensible ideas which make up the *green* chair. Since this is implausible, we are lead to the conclusion that Berkeley cannot accomodate the sort of case here described.[1][4]

Strictly speaking, this objection is not aimed at (3), but rather at the view that Berkeley is a defender, a serious defender, of common sense. For, if this objection succeeds, his adherence to common sense on this perceptual matter is too slight for him to claim to be a champion of common sense. That, however, would not undermine anything I have claimed in this paper. Even so, this is an important issue that needs to be squarely faced.

A full account of this issue requires a full account of the notion of a collection of sensible ideas, and about this Berkeley says very little. However, what he does say is useful. He emphasizes the law-like relations between members of the collections at issue, for instance in this passage:

> . . . there are spiritual substances, minds, or human souls, which will or excite ideas in themselves at pleasure, but these are faint, weak and unsteady in respect of others they perceive by sense – which, being impressed upon them according to certain rules or laws of nature, speak themselves the effects of a mind more powerful and wise than human spirits. These latter are said to have more *reality* in them than the former – by which is meant that they are not fictions of the mind perceiving them. And in this sense the sun that I see by day is the real sun, and that which I imagine by night is the idea of the former. (*Principles*, 36; emphasis Berkeley's.)

The sensible ideas which constitute a green chair will thus be interrelated in something like a lawful manner. Presumably, the relevant law-statements will include terms which are descriptive of conditions of observation, as well. Berkeley construes an entity such as a green chair as a collection of sensible ideas which are fully describable by some set of laws of the sort just noted.

Imagine that L is the set of true law-like statements descriptive of the interrelations between some sorts of sensible ideas, of various sense-modalities, and of the relations between these sensible ideas and observable conditions. *Primary* constituents of a green chair, then, would be those sensible ideas described by statements in L. We may then say that *derivative* constituents of the collection that makes up the chair are those sensible ideas which themselves are lawfully related to the primary constituents, taken as a group, and to observation conditions. Blue visual ideas are of this *sort*, relative to a green chair. Then we can say that, for Berkeley,

(14)   A physical object (e.g., a green chair) is immediately
perceived just in case some primary constituents of the
chair are immediately perceived, or some derivative
constituents of the chair are immediately perceived.

Something like (14), it seems to me, is what is needed in Berkeley's theory
to accomodate the fact that one might immediately see a green chair when
it looks blue.

It is, of course, odd to find Berkeley purchasing his defense of common sense at the expense of embracing ontological phenomenalism. It is
largely this combination, I think, that gives his philosophy such an air of
hocus-pocus. The lesson to be learned from this combination seems to be
that Berkeley's defense of common sense has to be construed as a *relative*
matter. His philosophy is to be judged on the basis of the *extent* to which it
adheres to common sense in comparison to how the competition fares on the
same point. Since it is reasonable to think that no philosophy, or at least
none in Berkeley's period, adheres completely and strictly to common sense,
Berkeleian advice would be to choose that philosophy which, *ceterus paribus*,
comports best or most with common sense, granting that every competitor
conflicts with common sense somehow. Berkeley claims that he wins this
competition, a claim which I find not altogether implausible.[15] The moral
for this paper, however, is that he is a non-starter in this competition,
given his phenomenalism, if he cannot find a way to plausibly accept (3).[16]

Ohio State University

NOTES

1. *Dialogues*, 174.

2. I here presume that mediate perception, for Berkeley, is actually
    perceiving strictly speaking. There are passages where Berkeley
    says the opposite, however, and a fuller treatment would have to
    take them into account. (E.g., see the first of the *Three Dialogues:
    Dialogues*, 174.)

3. In this I diverge from the insightful account given by George Pitcher
    in his *Berkeley* (London: Routledge and Kegan Paul, 1977),
    pp. 4-24. As I see it, suggestion is Berkeley's positive account of
    just what is involved when the perception of an entity is dependent
    on the perception of an intermediary. That is, the notion of sugges-

tion is supposed to explicate the sort of dependence Berkeley has in mind. The notion of suggestion is thus not brought in to express a different concept of immediate seeing (perception).

4. Coincidental suggestion cases were brought to my attention independently by Tom Downing, Phil Montague and Jim Van Cleve.

5. Actually, *D-3* does not *quite* give Berkeley all that he needs, for there is what I call the "univocality problem" to consider. Dialectically, it is important for Berkeley to mean the same by the term "immediately sees" ("immediately perceives") as his chief opponents mean by the same term. This means that his account of the notion will have to be acceptable to an indirect realist such as Locke, and there is reason to think that *D-3* fails to capture *all* of what a Lockean would mean by "immediately sees." Still, *D-3* comes close enough so that, for present purposes, the univocality problem need not be taken up. For related worries, see James Cornman, *Perception, Common Sense and Science* (New Haven: Yale University Press, 1975), chapter 1.

6. See *Principles*, Intro., 22, as well as *PC*, 693 and 816.

7. N. Malcolm, 'Direct Perception,' in his *Knowledge and Certainty* (Englewood Cliffs, N.J.: Prentice-Hall, 1963), p. 88.

8. Compare G. Warnock, *Berkeley* (London: Peregrine, 1969), chapter 5; G. Stack, *Berkeley's Theory of Perception* (The Hague: Martinus Nijhoff, 1970); and G. Dicker, 'Berkeley and Immediate Perception,' in C. Turbayne, *Berkeley: Critical and Interpretive Essays* (Minneapolis: University of Minnesota Press, 1982).

9. I discuss this more fully in 'Berkeley and Common Sense,' in Turbayne, ed., *op. cit.*

10. I treat this issue in greater detail in 'Berkeley's Heterogeneity Thesis' (unpublished).

11. See, for example, *NTV*, 40 and 129.

12. In fact, I think it is much *more* plausible to interpret Berkeley as holding (11) and (13). I defend this view in the paper cited in note 10.

13. There is also the privacy objection to consider. According to it, each immediately perceived idea is private to the percipient; thus, no

single idea is immediately perceived by two different perceivers. Given that this is so, it is hard to see how two different perceivers might immediately perceive the same physical object since they would never immediately perceive the same constituents of the object. This argument is set out in R. van Iten, 'Berkeley's Alleged Solipsism,' *Revue Internationale de Philosophie*, **XVI**, no. 61-62 (1962). It is considered and rejected in Pappas, 'Berkeley and Common Sense,' and in Cornman, *Perception, Common Sense and Science*.

14.   This objection has been pressed, independently, by Phil Cummins and Nelson Potter.

15.   I discuss this in more detail in 'Adversary Metaphysics,' *Philosophy Research Archive*, **IX** (1983).

16.   Earlier versions of this paper were presented at the Universities of Iowa, Oregon, and Western Ontario. I have received helpful comments and criticisms from Tom Lennon, John Davis, Richard Fumerton, Phil Cummins, George Dicker and George Pitcher.

PART SIX

HISTORICAL SCHOLARSHIP:
INTERPRETATION AND RECEPTION

Bertil Belfrage

A NEW APPROACH TO BERKELEY'S
PHILOSOPHICAL NOTEBOOKS

THE TRADITIONAL APPROACH

Berkeley's *Philosophical Notebooks* consist of sometimes isolated, sometimes incomplete sentences without any normal context. Often, one entry deals with one problem; the following with quite another; the next with a third, etc. As one entry sometimes contradicts another, one cannot possibly maintain without considerable qualification that:

> (1)   All entries in the *Notebooks* are *pieces of one and the same* philosophical puzzle.

(I use the term "puzzle" as it is used for the game in which several pieces are put together in order to create one coherent picture.) A. A. Luce, who was very well aware of this difficulty, sometimes spoke of "the unfairness of indiscriminate and uninformed quotation from" Berkeley's *Notebooks*.[1] He strongly opposed a view of the *Notebooks* that takes them as little more than scrapbooks of disorganized, occasional jottings; he went as far in the other direction as to look upon these entries almost as sections of a sophisticated *tractatus*.[2] But how, according to him, could incompatible entries be parts of a constructive, sober work?

Luce's answer is based on his *Commentary Hypothesis* that, among other things, made him rename the notebooks the *Philosophical Commentaries*. Everyone can see that there are entries in the *Notebooks* that comment on books, other entries, or maybe on some early manuscript. But the Commentary Hypothesis goes much further: when Berkeley started to write the *Notebooks*, he had already written early drafts both of the *Essay on Vision* and the *Principles*, according to the hypothesis. Unfortunately, these early documents are now lost, Luce argues, but if we postulate their existence, they provide us with a context in which these disparate entries of the *Notebooks* become perfectly intelligible: looked upon as commentaries on those early drafts, the inconsistencies in the *Notebooks* remain on the surface. This is the first part of Luce's two-step explanation.[3] The second is that these surface inconsistencies are to be understood by the dialectic method that Berkeley applied.[4] As he had already formulated a version of his main

217

E. Sosa (ed.), Essays on the Philosophy of George Berkeley, 217–230.
©1987 by D. Reidel Publishing Company

doctrine, according to Luce, before he started to write the *Notebooks,* one of his main concerns was now to sharpen his weapons against potential opponents. Therefore, Luce argues, Berkeley sometimes included in his private *Notebooks* what these opponents might be expected to say. But he himself never intended to include these views in his "true" philosophy; he only considered them *tentatively* – just for the sake of argument. Or, in Luce's own words:[5]

> In ancient Greece dialectic was the method of seeking truth by disciplined conversation and ordered discourse as distinct from formal instruction and set speeches. The dialectician asked questions and questioned answers. The entries in Berkeley's notebooks are almost entirely conversational. Scores of them have the formal "Qu:" prefixed; scores more ask questions directly and indirectly. Berkeley is questioning his other self. Berkeley *major* is holding a seminar, so to speak, with Berkeley *minor.* Hence the tension in the notebooks, and the bi-polarity of thought. Hence the shifting standpoints, the oscillation and quick movements to and fro, like that of the shuttle in the loom, as the thinker weaves his reasoned web out of partial, mistaken and conflicting views. Such was the dialectic in the Socratic circle in the streets of Athens long ago, in the classrooms of the Academy and in the earlier dialogues of Plato, when a deep problem was thrashed out by probing questions and provocative answers, and thought rose towards truth on stepping-stones of mistaken and discarded thoughts.

Thus the Commentary Hypothesis explained a great deal of the inconsistencies in the *Notebooks* as being no more than "probing questions and provocative answers" that Berkeley never intended to include as coherent parts of his own work. In other words:

> (2)   Some entries in the *Notebooks* – expressing the view of potential opponents in a dialectic discourse – do *not* have any informative value as far as Berkeley's "true" philosophy is concerned.

Luce also produced an *Error Hypothesis,* according to which Berkeley sometimes failed to realize at once that an idea that perhaps appeared attractive at first, would turn out to be incompatible with some basic doctrine of his *Draft Essay* or *Draft Principles.* As soon as Berkeley realized his error, he corrected himself. Thus some of the inconsistencies in the *Notebooks* are explained as immature failures.[6] As it would be a mistake to include those errors in our interpretation of Berkeley's mature philosophy, we should not forget, according to Luce, that:

(3)   There are entries in the *Notebooks* – expressing imma-
        ture failures – which do *not* inform about Berkeley's
        mature philosophy.

It was against this background that Luce introduced a highly influential
idea in Berkeleian scholarship: the *Black List Hypothesis*. Berkeley needed a
sign to put in the margin opposite mistaken notes or entries expressing
those views that he held only tentatively, and, Luce argued, this was the
plus sign which consigned these entries "to the scrap-heap."[7]
        Luce's view thus includes one positive and one negative element:

(4)   (i) All informative entries are *pieces of one and the same
        puzzle* (Berkeley's "true" philosophy), *but* (ii) there are
        also non-informative "scrap-heap entries," introduced in
        the *Notebooks* by mistake or for the purpose of dialectic
        exercise.

An important task is then to identify those entries which do *not* express
Berkeley's "true" philosophy. In fact, this seems to be the most important
thing of all to do, when Luce goes on to interpret the *Principles* in the light
of the *Notebooks*.[8] I first examine this negative part of Luce's approach to
the *Notebooks*.

THE BLACK LIST HYPOTHESIS

Luce presented the Black List Hypothesis in 1932 as little more than a
plausible suggestion; "I do not pretend that this conclusion is established,"
he said.[9] He argued it in detail in 1944, but even then he added, "I am not
entirely satisfied with it."[10] No further arguments in support of the hypothesis were published. Yet in 1932 he said that if his explanation of the
plus is correct, then:

> . . . the symbol is the most important part of the marginal
> apparatus for students of the development of Berkeley's
> thought. For the large group of entries so marked will consti-
> tute a "Black List" of metaphysical positions tentatively held
> and definitely rejected.[11]

And in 1963, Luce had no longer any doubts about his hypothesis; sometimes the only argument against an alternative interpretation is that it is
compatible with a plus-marked entry.[12] This way of arguing was also
adopted by other scholars. Thus in 1964, S. A. Grave criticized C. M. Turbayne's analysis of Berkeley's concept of mind, because it was based on

plus-marked entries; E. J. Furlong criticized Jonathan Bennett in 1966 on the problem of intermittency, because Bennett's view was reflected in plus-marked entries;[13] *et cetera, et cetera.* In 1967, finally, Luce himself presented the Black List Hypothesis as an established view.[14] But what evidence is there in support of this famous doctrine?

There is only one study in which the evidence is presented in any detail, and that is Luce's Introduction to his 1944 edition of the *Notebooks.*[15] He carefully noted that there are 188 entries marked with "+" and then added the observation that *only 50* of them indicated obvious rejections. As to the remaining 138 plus-marked entries, the hypothesis fails completely in 13 cases; according to Luce these entries express important views "which Berkeley held and continued to hold." This is by itself a disturbing observation for the theory. Some careful attention is needed before putting a sign meaning "reject" opposite an entry. How could he, for example, put a plus by mistake before a short, clearly formulated entry such as *PC,* 369?

> +   By thing I either mean Ideas or that wch has ideas.

This is exactly what we read in section 89 (together with section 2) of the *Principles.* But let us go on, as there are still 125 plus-marked entries left to explain. Ten of them do not have "the true plus sign," Luce says; and as to the remaining 115 entries he produced the *ad hoc* hypothesis that they are "irrelevant to his final argument, or personal, or trivial" – but are they really so? In 1969, I criticized the Black List Hypothesis and, among other things, this *ad hoc* hypothesis.[16] In 1970, Luce accepted my criticism. The list of trivial entries was drastically reduced from 115 to about 30 entries, and the rest of this group of entries was now classified as expressing important views included in Berkeley's works, though not always in the *Principles.* Luce says:[17]

> More than thirty of the plus entries are personal or trivial . . . Some twenty-five are specifically concerned with the *Theory of vision* . . . Not a few of the plus-marked entries . . . have left their mark on the *Three dialogues,* the *De motu* and the *Analyst.*

Luce came to admit that a majority of the plus-marked entries were included in most of Berkeley's major works. As soon as Luce realized that the Black List Hypothesis was wrong, he of course abandoned it.

If we leave out those approximately thirty entries which Luce styled "personal or trivial," then the old Black List Hypothesis only covered one third of the plus entries. In order to explain the remaining two thirds Luce produced a new hypothesis; in these cases, he said:[18]

. . . the plus sign appears to be a 'tick-off', indicating that the
matter has been already handled in the *Commentaries*, in the
'Of infinites', or in a draft of one or other of the published
works.

But a "tick-off" opposite entries used for "one or other of the published
works" is (in those cases) a sign for views *definitely accepted* for those works
– no longer "definitely rejected."

It is true, there are entries in the *Notebooks* expressing views discarded in the published works; and some of these entries do have a plus in
the margin. *Most* of those discarded entries do *not* have a plus, however,
but some other sign or signs opposite them. Therefore, most of the marginal
signs mark some rejected as well as some not rejected entries. As the plus
by no means differs from other signs in this respect, there is no more reason to take a plus for "reject" than an "S," or an "I," etc.

The rather cautious view that Luce presented in the Editor's introduction to his 1944 edition of the *Commentaries* did not warrant the careless interpretation by other scholars who too quickly interpreted the plus
sign as the certain equivalent of "reject." It is simply not supported by the
textual evidence.

Whoever intends to argue from the Black List Hypothesis in future
has a heavy burden of proof, indeed. I cannot see how that could be done
without committing what I call *the Interpreter's Circle:* First to interpret the
Principles; and then to defend this interpretation by reference to a Black
List of entries which – as a consequence of this very interpretation – express discarded views.

THE COMMENTARY HYPOTHESIS

Luce presented one argument according to which we are bound to postulate
the existence of a *Draft Essay*. His argument is based on this cryptic entry:[19]

Query whether the sensations of sight arising from a man's
head be liker the sensations of touch proceeding from thence or
from his legs? (224)

If we read this entry together with sections 101ff. of the *Essay on Vision*,
then it is possible to understand it, Luce argues; but if we don't, it is mere
nonsense to us. His conclusion is:[20]

The entry cannot be understood apart from the book, and
therefore could not have been composed before a draft of the
book was written.

But why could we not understand entry 224 just by reading the entries that
follow in the *Notebook* itself?

The entries that follow (225, 226, 227) reflect, as I see it, a creative
process from a vague idea, obscurely expressed in 224, to the discovery of
one of Berkeley's most fertile thoughts. The cryptic "Query" in 224 leads to
the question how is it that we call *different* ideas "the same" thing (225). As
there is no resemblance between "colours & light" on the one hand and
"hard or soft, hot or cold, rough or smooth" on the other (226), the conclusion is that the connection between visual and tactual data must be the
result of experience (227). Then, the cryptic 224 reappears, now in these
non-cryptic terms:

> . . . How therefore can I before experience teaches me know
> that the Visible leggs are (because 2) connected wth the tangi-
> ble ones, or the Visible head (because one) connected wth the
> tangible head? (227)

Luce said about entry 224: it "cannot be understood apart from the [*Draft
Essay*]." One can equally well say: it cannot be understood apart from entry
227. But is it reasonable, on this ground, to draw the conclusion that
Berkeley wrote these entries backwards: starting from the clear 227,
working himself down through increasing obscurity towards the nonsensical
224? Is not the natural development in a creative process the very contrary: from obscurity to clarity? If we do not accept, however, that Berkeley must have written the clear 227 before the cryptic 224, neither do we
have to accept the same argument when applied to the supposed *Draft Essay*. Hence, Luce's conclusion "therefore [224] could not have been composed before a draft of the [*Essay*] was written," remains a mere conjec-
ture.

If we should one day discover an early *Draft Essay* or *Draft Principles*, then our view will probably change. Until then, I think we have to
confine ourselves to the texts available to us.

THE ERROR HYPOTHESIS

In the Error Hypothesis the criterion is coherence. A coherent part of
Berkeley's view at one time was no "error" from the point of view of his
doctrine at that time – even if he later took another position. But a thesis
that cannot be included as a coherent part of his thought at any stage of his
development must always be disregarded as an immature failure. According to this strong version of the Error Hypothesis:

> (5)   There are immature failures in the *Notebooks* which do
>   not belong to any coherent (Berkeleian) context at all.

Luce's example of such an error is the doctrine of the "Of Infinites." He says:[2] [1]

> Locke's principles that there can be no knowledge where there are no ideas, and that no words should be used without corresponding ideas, were at first accepted as axioms by Berkeley, and they appear as such in the earlier portion of the *Commentaries*. Later in that work they are rejected, for Berkeley came to realize that we know spirit without ideas, and that words often have a purely emotive value.

According to Luce, two things made Berkeley realize that "Locke's principles" were mistaken: emotive terms and our knowledge of spirit. That is to say, as soon as Berkeley became aware of the emotive use of language, and began to investigate our knowledge of spirit, then he at once rejected "Locke's principles." As Berkeley has nothing to say in the *Notebooks* concerning the emotive theory, I concentrate on Luce's second example: our knowledge of spirit.

Our knowledge of spirit is discussed at length in *Notebook A*. It came into focus in a series of entries which perhaps form the most dramatic part of the *Notebooks*. In the first of these entries, Berkeley took one position; rejected it in the next for the very contrary view; and then he turned over the page and began to develop a third view on the concept of mind. The first position is the one in entry 576:

> S   We think we know not the Soul because we have no imaginable or sensible Idea annex'd to that Sound. This the Effect of prejudice. (576)

Probably Berkeley at once rejected this entry and went to the other extreme. Since we have "no imaginable or sensible Idea annex'd to" the term "soul," his conclusion is now:

> S   Certainly we do not know it. this will be plain if we examine w^t we mean by the Word knowlege. neither does this argue any defect in Our knowlege no more than our not knowing a contradiction. (576a)

Thus he went from the one view to the other, but then he tried a middle way. On the pages that follow he began to analyze such concepts as "understanding," "soul," "spirit," "thinking substance," "will," "volition." They are defined in terms of ideas and a variety of aspects of a strict empiricist concept of mind are developed. It is in this context that we find him saying:

> +   Mind is a congeries of Perceptions. Take away Percep-
>   tions & you take away the Mind put the Perceptions &
>   you put the mind. (580)

But was this concept of mind ever a consistent part of Berkeley's doctrine
at any stage of his development? Luce's answer is no; and, therefore, he
rejected it as an error.[22] Was he right in doing so?

I have recently argued that the *Manuscript Introduction* (sometimes
called the *Draft Introduction*) expresses an early philosophy different from
the doctrine that Berkeley published.[23] This creates a new context which
makes it reasonable to ask whether the so-called Humean entries on the
concept of mind are not errors at all, but consistent contributions of an
early philosophy. Did Berkeley then, as Luce maintains, reject the
"Lockean principles," when he began to analyze the concept of mind? Or did
he analyze the concept of mind in the light of "Locke's principles," thus rejecting not them but the view "that we know spirit without ideas?"[24] The
textual evidence strongly supports the latter alternative.

The semantic rule, "No word to be used without an idea" (422), is
emphasized throughout this part of *Notebook A* (see 417, 448, 488, 528,
638, 696), as well as the opinion that "all our knowlege & contemplation is
confin'd barely to our own Ideas" (606, see also 584, 369). That is to say,
we find the so-called Humean entries on the concept of mind in that part of
Notebook A, where Berkeley finds it absurd "to pretend to demonstrate or
reason any thing about" that which we have no idea of (584, see also 421,
551, 595, cf. 720). *The error* in this context is then the uncritical entry 576
"that we know spirit without ideas" (to use Luce's formulation).

Since Luce says, however, that Berkeley "gives a tentative account
of the soul, indistinguishable from Hume's,"[25] he seems to argue that
Berkeley did not really mean what he says in these entries. But is it reasonable to think that Berkeley would write in his private notebook "Say
you," when he actually meant "Say *I*," as he did in this entry:

> Say *you* the Mind is not the Perceptions. but that thing w^{ch}
> perceives. *I answer* you are abused by the words that & thing
> these are vague empty words without a meaning. (581, em-
> phasis added)

This is no isolated standpoint that appears only on this page of *Notebook A;*
some fifty entries later he attacks a similar view:

> Say *you* there must be a thinking substance. Something un-
> known wch perceives & supports & ties together the Ideas.
> *Say I*, make it appear there is any need of it & you shall have
> it for me. I care not to take away any thing I can see the least
> reason to think should exist. (637, italics added)[26]

> *I affirm* 'tis manifestly absurd. no excuse in ye world can be given why a man should use a word without an idea. Certainly we shall find that w^{t}ever word we make use of in matter of pure reasoning has or ought to have a compleat Idea annext to it. i.e. it's meaning or the sense we take it in must be compleatly known. (638, my emphasis)

Berkeley continues:

> Tis demonstrable a Man can never be brought to Imagine any thing shoud exist whereof he has no Idea. Whoever says he does, banters himself with Words. (639)

As we have no idea of "thinking substance," defined as "Something unknown wch perceives & supports & ties together the Ideas," the conclusion should be that "a Man can never be brought to Imagine" that thinking substance should exist – "Whoever says he does, banters himself with Words."

If we go another fifty entries further on in *Notebook A*, we then have this most radical entry on the "Of Infinites" stage:

> I Once more I desire my Reader may be upon his guard against the Fallacy of Words, Let him beware that I do not impose on him by plausible empty talk that common dangerous way of cheating men into absurditys. Let him not regard my Words any otherwise than as occasions of bringing into his mind determin'd ideas so far as they fail of this they are Gibberish, Jargon & deserve not the name of Language . . . (696)

This is not the place to analyze Berkeley's concept of mind. But one thing is clear: at this stage, he does not accept descriptively empty terms in any form. Utterances in cognitive discourse including such terms "deserve not the name of Language," he says. The only way to discuss the concept of mind in this context, therefore, is to define it in terms of ideas, for example:

> + Mind is a congeries of Perceptions. Take away Perceptions & you take away the Mind put the Perceptions & you put the mind. (580)

This entry is no error in any sensible sense of that term. It is, I maintain, a coherent part of the discussion in the first two thirds of *Notebook A*, where Berkeley consistently argues from what Luce styles "Locke's principles." One of the few exceptions is this uncritical remark in entry 576:

> S   We think we know not the Soul because we have no
>   imaginable or sensible Idea annex'd to that Sound. This
>   the Effect of prejudice.

This entry was an error in the context where it appears. And, as we have
seen, Berkeley immediately rejected it. Consequently, Luce's Error Hypothesis fails to explain the inconsistencies between this part of *Notebook A*
and other parts of the *Notebooks*.

This is not only a criticism of the negative part of Luce's approach
to the *Notebooks*, it also affects his "one-puzzle approach." If I am right
that there is in these *Notebooks* a clash between different, seriously meant,
philosophical standpoints, then a totally new aspect of the *Notebooks*
emerges.

A NEW APPROACH

As long as the entries in Berkeley's *Notebooks* are looked upon as phases of
one general philosophical position, a large group of entries have to be rejected as being "scrap-heap entries" – immature failures or provocative
answers just tentatively held for dialectic exercise.[27] This negative approach certainly did not encourage any serious study of those entries la-
beled "Black Listed views." If we take them as seriously intended, I argue,
there will no longer be a large number of "scrap-heap entries" that do not
seem to belong to any intelligible context at all. My explanation of the inconsistencies in the *Notebooks* is that they represent different philosophical
standpoints which were set forth at different times in Berkeley's life. My
point, which is the very contrary of the view expressed in (2) - (5), could
then be summarized as follows:

> (6)   *All* entries are (in principle) to be looked upon as cohe-
>   rent parts of some philosophical puzzle – but there are
>   *pieces of more than one puzzle* in the *Notebooks*.

The positive effect of this view is that it opens those fields for serious study
which were earlier disregarded as errors or non-doctrinal intellectual exer-
cises.
    There is, however, also a negative effect of the view I propose. This
concerns the way in which we may use the *Notebooks* when interpreting
Berkeley's published works. According to the traditional view, we could
equally well quote from the *Notebooks* as from, say, the *Three Dialogues*
when interpreting the *Principles*. If the *Notebooks* contain different philosophical standpoints, however, then some entries do *not* express the philosophy of the *Principles*. Therefore, we cannot automatically include one entry from the *Notebooks* in the context of the *Principles*.

Luce would not disagree with this, of course. The point of disagreement comes when he argues that references to the *Notebooks* are a necessary condition for a successful reading of the *Principles*. Luce says:[28]

> Why not read the *Principles*, and find out for ourselves what Berkeley does teach? That is where the shoe pinches. Without some background knowledge, without some acquaintance with the views discarded, without some appreciation of Berkeley's method of exposition, it is very hard to find out exactly what he does teach.

It is not only "very hard," it seems to be almost impossible to get it all right, because, "Readers of Berkeley's books should know," Luce says, that without this background knowledge (which includes the Commentary, the Error, and, above all, the Black List Hypotheses),[29] "'gross misinterpretation' of some passages in the *Principles* is on first reading *unavoidable*" (my emphasis). But in order to say "That entry expresses a mistaken or discarded view," or "This is a gross misinterpretation of the *Principles*," a standard is needed whereby to judge what is right and what is wrong. What standard could that be except our own interpretation of the *Principles*? This kind of quotation from the *Notebooks* may therefore contribute no more than new examples of the Interpreter's Circle. My point is not that we cannot use the *Notebooks* at all when reading the published works. My point is that the information they provide us with is different from the information we get from published books.

Strictly speaking, the puzzle analogy, so frequently used in this paper, does not apply very well to the *Notebooks* at all. A published book is *the end* of a creative process to which the analogy of a frozen picture may apply – if consistent, its parts could be looked upon as pieces of a puzzle – and our task when reading it is then to find the clear picture that these pieces form when correctly put together. But the *Notebooks* cannot be presented in terms of a frozen picture, I argue; they record a creative process, thus presenting us with a different kind of information than we find in a published *tractatus*. They tell us how Berkeley found his way from one standpoint to another towards the immaterialism of the *Principles* and the *Three Dialogues*. If we follow this development, we may the easier be able to follow his arguments in these books and understand his conclusions. But to pick up one entry here, another there, from the *Notebooks* in support of our interpretation of his published standpoints, that is often perfectly arbitrary.

In order to reconstruct such a creative process, however, it is necessary to establish, if possible, blocks of early and later contributions in the two *Notebooks*. It is, I would maintain, possible to find such blocks,[30] but that is the task of another study.[31]

Bodafors, Sweden

NOTES

1. A. A. Luce, 'Berkeley's *Commonplace Book* – Its Date, Purpose, Structure, and Marginal Signs,' *Hermathena*, **XLVII** (1932), p. 110.

2. See the 'Editor's Introduction,' in George Thomas (ed.), *George Berkeley, Philosophical Commentaries* (Alliance, Ohio: Thomas Edition, 1976), pp. i-v.

3. It was first presented in A. A. Luce, 'The Purpose and the Date of Berkeley's *Commonplace Book*,' *Proceedings of the Royal Irish Academy*, **XLVII**, Sect. C., No. 7 (Dublin, 1943), pp. 275-79.

4. A. A. Luce, *The Dialectic of Immaterialism. An account of the making of the Principles* (London: Hodder and Stoughton, 1963), Chapter 2.

5. Luce 1963 (see note 4), p. 26.

6. Luce 1963 (see note 4), Chapter 1.

7. Luce 1963 (see note 4), pp. 8, 24, 56.

8. Luce 1963 (see note 4), p. 24f.

9. Luce 1932 (see note 1), p. 109.

10. A. A. Luce (ed.), *George Berkeley, Philosophical Commentaries generally called the Commonplace Book* (London: Thomas Nelson and Sons Ltd., 1944), p. xxvi.

11. Luce 1932 (see note 1), p. 110.

12. Luce 1963 (see note 4), pp. 8ff., 24, 82.

13. S. A. Grave, 'The mind and its ideas: some problems in the interpretation of Berkeley,' *The Australasian Journal of Philosophy*, **XLII** (1964), p. 208. E. J. Furlong. 'Berkeley and the tree in the Quad,' *Philosophy*, **XLI** (1966), p. 171.

14. A. A. Luce, *Berkeley and Malebranche. A study in the origin of Berkeley's thought* (1934; reprinted, Oxford: Oxford University Press, 1967), p. x.

15. Luce 1944 (see note 10), pp. xxv-xxvi.

16. Bertil Belfrage, *George Berkeley's Philosophical Commentaries. A presentation of the manuscript* (Lund, 1969, unpublished).

17. A. A. Luce, 'Another look at Berkeley's Notebooks,' *Hermathena*, **CX** (1970), p. 10f.

18. Luce 1970 (see note 17), p. 11.

19. Luce 1943 (see note 3), p. 277.

20. *Ibid.*

21. *Works*, iv. 236.

22. For example in Luce 1932 (see note 1), p. 110.

23. *George Berkeley's Manuscript Introduction.* An editio diplomatica transcibed and edited with introduction and commentary by Bertil Belfrage (Oxford: Doxa, 1986), pp. 32-45.

24. I quote Luce's formulation in *Works*, vol. **4**, p. 236.

25. Luce 1967 (see note 14), p. 105.

26. From the traditional point of view it must be remarkable to find this argument half-way through *Notebook A;* it is mainly the same as the argument against the existence of matter in section 19 of the *Principles:* "[The opinion that matter or corporeal substances exist is] a very precarious opinion; since it is to suppose, without any reason at all, that God has created innumerable beings that are entirely useless, and serve no manner of purpose." It is interesting to note that this argument was at first developed, not against matter, but against the existence of thinking substance.

27. Luce's view is strongly supported by the 80-year old tradition on
     the order and dating of the *Notebooks*. For a critical account of this
     old tradition, see my 'The order and dating of Berkeley's *Notebooks*,'
     in *Berkeley (1685-1985)*, *Revue Internationale de Philosophie*, no.
     154 (1985), pp. 196-214.

28. Luce 1963 (see note 4), p. 24.

29. *Ibid.*

30. For a first step towards this broader project, see my 'The Clash on
     Semantics in Berkeley's *Notebook A*,' in the Berkeley issue of *Hermathena* (1985).

31. I have benefited from helpful comments by David Berman and
     Warren Steinkraus.

Wolfgang Breidert

ON THE EARLY RECEPTION OF BERKELEY
IN GERMANY*

"Berkeley in Germany" is a sad story, in which the scandal of Kant's refutation of idealism was only one of the most important points. In Germany Berkeley's name evokes sometimes a vague image – "there was a bishop" – or the trinity of "Locke, Berkeley, and Hume." Often you will find merely misunderstanding, but more frequently there is great ignorance. Some typical elements of the story are these: the first planned translation of the *Three Dialogues* in Germany proposed by Gottsched is missing, and perhaps it was never carried out[1]; and the beginning of a German edition of Berkeley's philosophical works in 1781 was its end, the first volume, including only the *Three Dialogues*, having been the only one published.

In his famous review of Fraser's edition, C. S. Peirce mentioned Germany as a country "where Berkeley is little known and greatly misunderstood" (*Collected Papers*, 8.36). It may be objected that Peirce was not aware of the intensive discussion evoked by Friedrich Ueberweg and T. Collyns Simon from 1869 till 1871.[2] (I do not know whether Peirce was really acquainted with it.) It any case, Berkeley is not a subject of general education in Germany. For instance, when the Suhrkamp Verlag published the *Dialogues* of Stanislav Lem in 1980, it was not assumed that the readers would have any knowledge of Berkeley. Though the interlocutors are named Hylas and Philonous, and Hylas is characterized as a materialist, and in spite of the fact that Lem himself says in an appendix that the book was begun by a discourse of the bishop Berkeley, the publisher's blurb recommends the book as a "socratic" dialogue. And in Germany it was possible to publish in 1981, without any offence, a history of philosophy comprehending more than thirty chapters, but including no chapter on Berkeley.[3]

One reason may be (I beg your pardon) that there are too many important German philosophers. There are huge works of Leibniz, Kant, Fichte, Hegel, Schopenhauer, Marx, Nietzsche, Heidegger, and many others. So there seems to be no need to read the Irish bishop. If we consider

----

* This paper is based on a more detailed German article, 'Die Rezeption Berkeleys in Deutschland im 18. Jahrhundert,' *Revue internationale de philosophie*, no. 154 (1985), pp. 223-41.

231

E. Sosa (ed.), Essays on the Philosophy of George Berkeley, 231–241.
©*1987 by D. Reidel Publishing Company*

investigators interested in Berkeley outside of Germany, indeed we find a deluge of papers on "Berkeley and Kant" in the bibliographies of Berkeley. But even the non-German authors seem to be primarily interested in Kant, not in Berkeley, other aspects of "Berkeley in Germany" being neglected for the most part. Recent articles on this subject are often written without knowledge of the previous investigations, and only a few publications are worthy of note. I mention only the famous article of Kabitz (1932)[4] publishing the notes of Leibniz on Berkeley, and the instructive paper of Leroy (1953)[5] treating the influence of Berkeley on Kant, Schopenhauer, and Husserl. The excellent dissertation of Eugen Stäbler (1935)[6] is almost never quoted, whereas it is the most detailed presentation of Berkeley's reception in Germany till Hegel. I am indebted to Stäbler for many hints, even if some few notes in his history need to be corrected.

As is generally known, the first German reader of Berkeley known by name is Leibniz, who noted in his copy of Berkeley's *Principles: Multa hic recte et ad sensum meum.* ("A great deal thereof is true and corresponding to my taste.") In a letter of 1715 Leibniz mentioned briefly the Irish author, but without giving the name. The first published writings naming Berkeley in Germany are the review of the *Three Dialogues* in the *Acta Eruditorum* (1717), and the frequently quoted oration on the so-called egoism by Pfaff (1722), which includes a note against Berkeley.[7] Stäbler guessed that Christian Wolff did know Berkeley already in 1724, and indeed Wolff quoted Berkeley by name in a book published in that year, where Berkeley and Collier are entitled the sole exponents of idealism.[8] This quotation was included in the very excited controversy of Wolff and his opponents, first of all Daniel Strähler and Joachim Lange. This controversy was begun by Strähler (1723)[9] in spite of a royal order prohibiting the university teachers at Halle to attack each other by name in publications or lectures. Wolff appealed this order before the royal court, but the theological department of the university also appealed, citing the harmfulness of Wolff's philosophy.

What danger was imputed to Wolff's philosophy? When criticizing Wolff's statement that the sensations, with respect to their existence, were necessary Strähler mentions two dangers.[10] First, he reproached Wolff for sustaining idealism by denying the effect of the body on the soul, and, as Strähler said, idealism was not compatible with the Christian religion; nobody who knew "what idealists hold" would disavow that. The second danger was determinism. This reproach against Wolff was the most important with respect to his expulsion from Halle under penalty of hanging. It is well known that freedom of the will and the corresponding responsibility were considered as fundamental for the government of the state, especially for the military service. But why should so-called idealism be incompatible with religion? It was an often repeated argument that without having an effect on the soul external things would be superfluous with respect to our knowledge and volition, and therefore creation would be not as perfect as possible. This argument lumps together all the monistic philosophies, materialism and idealism, as enemies of religion, because they undermine the perfection of the creation.

As Bracken has convincingly shown, the early reception of Berkeley was more influenced by the reviews than by Berkeley's own published works.[11] Berkeley was just labelled as an idealist and *therefore* he was to be refuted. In Germany there was an additional impediment to a favorable reception of Berkeley's philosophy. The struggle around Wolff caught all the attention of the philosophers, so that Berkeley was only noted in passing as a further representative of the one side. But in consequence of the increasing discussion of so-called idealism during the 18th century the attention on Berkeley increased, too.

The history of the early reception of Berkeley's immaterialism is for the most part a history of rejection at first glance, at best sometimes the attempt at refutation by arguments. Kant's refutation of idealism is only the most famous example out of this collection. In the history of ideas the worst fate of all is to fall into oblivion, and therefore it is not so bad to be refuted, for refutation attracts attention. Followers are uninteresting. For example, the inadequate refutation of Berkeley's idealism offered by Kant in a few pages has occasioned approximately fifty articles, not counting the numerous commentaries on Kant's *Critique of Pure Reason*. Though there are thus more than 500 pages concerning "Berkeley and Kant," the other German 18th century authors who have written on Berkeley – his opponents as well as his followers – are never or hardly ever mentioned in the recent Berkeley research. Indeed, there may be various reasons for this imbalance. Berkeley is perhaps frequently studied by authors encountering difficulties with the German language,[12] but a more serious reason may be the fixation on the "important" philosopher Kant. Either one is trying to show that Berkeley influenced the famous Kant and in this way to reflect a bit of Kant's importance on Berkeley, or one is trying to rehabilitate Berkeley by proving that Kant did not understand or even not know the writings of his opponent. In any case, it is his refutation that has attracted attention. But we should take a look at the other remarkable refutations of idealism and the reactions belonging thereto.

After the publication of the second edition of the *Three Dialogues* (1725), Johann Christoph Gottsched, the critical German translator of Pierre Bayle's *Dictionnaire*, mentioned Berkeley in a dissertation written for the defense of the *influxus physicus* (1727).[13] (Only Kant's later refutation of idealism attracted so much attention as did Gottsched's.) One of his readers wrote a letter to Gottsched expressing a strong inclination *in favor* of idealism, and asking that a copy of Berkeley's *Three Dialogues* be sent to him. The writer was a German and French speaking preacher of the Reformed Church, who was born in Switzerland and became a minister at Bayreuth. His name was Johann Heinrich Meister, called le Maitre. He wrote to Gottsched:[14]

I am convinced that idealism seems only a paradox and hard to digest, because on the one hand we often confuse the ideas of our own mind with those which the idealists attribute only to the ideas founded on the nature of the divinity, and because on the other hand we are generally too much attached to the sub-jection to sensibility and the imagination. I have made great efforts to deliver myself from these prejudices, and after con-sidering the absolute and general dependence of all individual beings . . . after such reflections, I say, I feel less repugnance to represent to myself the reality of the ideas and the illusion of the sensations than I find to imagine the earth turning around the sun.

Obviously Meister uses the term "idealism" in the usual platonic sense and does not yet know Berkeley's sensualism. In Meister's later works I have not found any hint indicating that he had really read any of Berkeley. (It is true that I have not yet compared their sermons.) In any case, Meister had a subtle feeling of the similarity between his own and Berkeley's philo-sophical interest.

Maybe the correspondence with Meister inspired Gottsched to plan a translation of the *Three Dialogues* into Latin (!) and to demonstrate the real existence of a material world without the mind in an additional disser-tation. But since no trace thereof is to be found, probably it was never done.

Sometimes professional philosophers are involved in a disturbing controversy, while the amateurs can look a bit more unemotionally on the problem. An example is the learned and interesting booklet by Friedrich Philipp Schlosser, which was dedicated as a circular letter *(Send-Schreiben)* to the Philosophical and Historical Society of Wittenberg and published in 1730.[15] This treatise is one of the first writings in Germany especially directed against idealism, and the title page promised "some suggestions on how to refute idealism." It is noteworthy that it was at this time that the term "idealism" came into common use. Despite Pfaff's and Wolff's use of the term before 1725, the first edition of Walch's Philosophical Dictionary (*Philosophisches Lexicon*, 1726) does not include the term *Idealisten* ("idealists"), this article having been added in the second edition, which did not appear until 1733. Nonetheless, a paper published in 1970[16] asserts that ". . . the German tradition of Berkeley's 'idealism' . . . began earlier than Wolff, earlier even than Christoph Pfaff . . . However, on the con-trary, Johann Walch was the first author to name Berkeley among the idealists . . . in 1726." (Even if the idealists were mentioned by Walch in 1726, it would not have been earlier than Wolff and Pfaff.)

Schlosser looks upon the idealists as "muddle-headed fellows" who ought to be put "back on the right path." He proceeds from the article "Zeno" in Bayle's Dictionary, refers to the scepticism promoted by Des-cartes, Malebranche, and Fardella, and considers Berkeley in the usual way as a follower of Malebranche. Obviously Schlosser has only a second-hand knowledge of Berkeley obtained from Pfaff's short remarks and from the review of the *Three Dialogues*. Further, he knows of Gottsched's projected translation of the *Three Dialogues* and even his scanty exposition with the reference to the "anonymous idealist of Bayreuth" (i.e. J. H. Meister).

First of all, Schlosser endeavors to do justice to the adversaries, and he takes notice of the differences between the several kinds of so-called idealism. Indeed, he knows that Berkeley is not denying the reality of trees, mountains, rivers and so on, but only fighting against the existence of absolute matter without the mind. I think Schlosser knows more of Berkeley's immaterialistic opinion than, for example, Kant does. He draws up a list of the essentials usually maintained by most of the idealists, which, I think, applies almost exactly to Berkeley (among others). The listed opinions are:

1. There is an infinite spirit.
2. There are finite spirits created by the infinite spirit.
3. These excepted, there is not any other real thing. [Berkeley?]
4. A spirit is a simple immortal being endowed with reason, will, and the faculty of moral resposibility.
5. The so-called bodies do not exist truly without ourselves, but they seem to be so, partly because they are imagined as being without, partly because they occur in steady order.
6. Some of these ideas are more vivacious and are not submitted to our will. These ideas obey the law of sensations, the other ideas obey the law of imagination.
7. The ideas of corporeal things succeed in the same way as other philosophers think that bodies would move.

Corresponding to his fair approach Schlosser concedes that an idealist is not necessarily obliged to be an atheist, but indeed the idealist runs the risk of denying the existence of God. If the idealists were dogmatic, they would be worse than the sceptics. Schlosser agrees with Bilfinger that of course the idealists could cultivate natural sciences, for they were mistaken "not physically, but metaphysically."

Wolff's opponent Joachim Lange had recommended a "philosophy of thrashing" against such miserable persons as the idealists.[17] It would be necessary, he held, to apply the syllogistical argument in "the *ferio* of corporal punishment," using the catch-word *ferio*, here not in its logical, but in its literal physical sense, meaning "I beat." Schlosser remarks that while this argument is a good one in comedy, not so in philosophy, the reference here being to Molière's *Forced Marriage (Marriage forcé)*, where a sceptic philosopher always admonishing his interlocutor to abstain from judgement and to use the reservation "It seems to me" *(Il me semble)* is finally thrashed by his opponent. (The Berkeleians know the somewhat analogous story of Johnson's stone.) The syllogism *ferio*, or the "philosophy of thrashing," has a long tradition and is, I think, not yet finished. But Schlosser stands out against such merely emotional or practical reaction and endeavors to refute the idealists seriously. He emphasizes that the thrashing-argument cannot refute idealism, because it is a dogmatic attitude used to refute another dogmatic attitude, like a child answering the question, "How do you know this?" by saying, "I just know it." *(Ich weiss es eben.)*

Schlosser argues on a relatively high level by refuting some of the pretended refutations of idealism and even by conceding that he is unable to overcome definitely his enemies. He supplies some arguments as weapons for the battle against the idealists:

1. The argument of economy founded on God's wisdom: Given the assumption that there being more implies greater gain, then God's wisdom requires that more be created, for example, matter, too.
2. (which is similar to 1.) The argument of optimism founded on God's design: More of things in harmony would imply greater perfection. If there were not only spirits, but also material bodies, there would be a greated perfection. Therefore, God created the material bodies, too.
3. The argument against voluntarism: The will of God is not a philosophically sufficient reason for the existence of sensations.
4. The argument of logical possibility: Extended material things are logically possible.
5. The argument of analogy: The arguments used by the idealists to prove the reality of other spirits may analogically be applied to the reality of the material bodies. (Note: this argument should not be confused with the argument of analogy to deny spirits in the same manner as Berkeley denies matter. For this can be refuted by considering that all thinking presupposes spirit, but not all thinking presupposes *other* spirits.)
6. The argument of the perfection of the essence of each thing: Each thing is perfect with respect to its essence. Therefore, the soul is perfect. Therefore, it knows the truth. The soul imagines external things. Therefore, they must exist. (The dream is explained by a *partial* imperfection.)

In comparison with Lange's "philosophy of thrashing" and Walch's blunt advice ("One should not engage in any discussion with such people"), Schlosser's moderate reaction is much more reasonable. There are other philosophers, too, who explicitly rejected the "philosophy of thrashing," for example, Georg Friedrich Meier in his *Metaphysik* (1756),[18] and Kant in his metaphysical lectures written down by Johann Gottfried Herder (1762-64).[19] Whereas Meier does not mention Berkeley and primarily considers the Leibnizian idealists, Kant refers to Berkeley's work, namely the *Siris*, but – and this is noteworthy – not to the *Three Dialogues*, though he employs arguments used in the *Dialogues*, but not in the *Siris*.[20] Eschenbach's translation of the *Dialogues* (1756) seems not to have had any remarkable influence except for a review (*Neue Zeitungen von gelehrten Sachen*, 1757). During the fifteen years after this edition appeared, Berkeley's name seems to have been mentioned nowhere in Germany, until Herder defended Berkeley against the attacks of Beattie in a review of Beattie's *Essay on . . . Truth*, which came out in 1772.[21]

Besides Johann Georg Hamann, Herder is the most important German champion of Berkeley. It is a pity that Herder's *Metakritik* on Kant's *Critique of Pure Reason* was not published until 1799.[22] Despite the two early German translations of the *Three Dialogues*, knowledge of Berkeley's original work was still very poor. Though C. Meiners praised Berkeley in 1786 for having argued more conclusively than Malebranche or Leibniz, and though he took Berkeley as evidence of the possibility that idealism does not necessarily lead to dangerous unbelief, and though he sympathized with Berkeley, Meiners thought the *Analyst* and the *Dialogues* were the same book.[23] If we bear in mind this situation in the philosophical circles of Germany during the 18th century, Kant's superficial knowledge about Berkeley cannot be astonishing. Kant focused his refutation of idealism on its Cartesian form, referring only very briefly to Berkeley. Curtly excluding Berkeley's "dogmatic," "mystical,' "gushing" idealism, he confronts his own transcendental idealism connected with empirical realism on the one hand with transcendental realism or empirical idealism, i.e. the Cartesian philosophy, on the other. But whoever would be asked to label Berkeley's philosophy in this way would be compelled to call him a transcendental idealist, on no condition a transcendental realist.

Herder attempts to defend Berkeley against the false and hackneyed reproach repeated by Kant, that his philosophy would "change all ideas into mere effects of the imagination." Contrary to Kant, Herder realizes that in Berkeley's view the ideas were "the *most real* ideas, which he repeatedly and exactly contrasted with empty figments and linguistic abstractions."[24] Herder complains about the ignorance of Berkeley's system, which he thought was more frequently misunderstood than known (p. 296). From Herder's letters we know that he possessed copies of the *Three Dialogues* and of the *Alciphron*, and that he did not see any other of Berkeley's writings earlier than 1798.[25] But corresponding to his intimate knowledge of these books and second-hand information (including such about the *New Theory of Vision*), Herder explicitly demands to call Berkeley's system not "idealism," but rather – if a name is needed at all – '"immaterialism."[26]

Herder was a Berkeley fan. His attitude to Berkeley was a very emotional or personal one. In 1781 he suggested to one of his friends that he enter a bookshop and look into Berkeley's philosophical works, namely the first volume of the proposed German edition. "The works themselves are not for you: a subtle, ideal doctrine; . . . read only the biography placed in front of it. An exceptional man with head and heart, some of his features have quite given pleasure to me."[27] In Herder's fragmentary biographical sketch Berkeley is characterized by his great philanthropism *(Menschenfreundschaft)* and erudition.[28]

Herder was not concerned only with the familiar *Three Dialogues* or the *Theory of Vision*, he was also acquainted with the other Berkeleian works. He translated some entries extracted out of the *Querist*,[29] and in a consideration of cultural evolution (entitled *Tithon und Aurora*)[30] he published a translation of the famous poem on America composed by the "good bishop Berkeley, who was not a poet." All such translations made by Herder are very liberal: this one contains, for example, only five stanzas without rhymes instead of the six rhymed stanzas of the original poem. Obviously Herder attempted to use the poem as an instrument for transmitting his own philosophical ideas. Indeed, already in the introduction to the German edition of the *Three Dialogues* (1781) is included a translation of the poem containing a mistake twisting the meaning of a part into the contrary. Berkeley was painting the "happy climes, where . . . the force of art by nature seems outdone," but the translation says, ". . . where the force of nature by art . . . will be made ashamed."[31] This may be an unwitting alteration, but the changes made by Herder in his translation are obviously intentional. To Berkeley's critical citation of the "pedantry of courts and schools," he added "church and state." The muse turning away from Europe's decay to America is replaced by the muse searching for a younger Europe. And the famous line "Westward the Course of Empire takes its Way" is translated by a question, "O Muse, do you take your way westward?"[32] But I think this translation agrees more with the original than does the translation given in the authorized German edition of Russell's *History of Western Philosophy*, "Westward the Course of Britain takes its Way."[33] But it does not matter in Germany, where – in the words of Peirce – "Berkeley is little known and greatly misunderstood."

Universität Karlsruhe,
Federal Republic of Germany

NOTES

1. *Neue Zeitungen von gelehrten Sachen*, **LXXI,** H (5 September, 1729), p. 656.

2. For references see T. E. Jessop, *A Bibliography of George Berkeley* (London: Oxford University Press, 1934; reprinted, New York, 1968), p. 68, no. 417.

3. Otfried Höffe, ed., *Klassiker der Philosophie.* 2 vols. Munich 1981.

4. W. Kabitz, 'Leibniz und Berkeley,' in *Sitzungsberichte der Preuss. Akademie der Wissenschaften,* Philos.-Histor. Klasse, (Berlin, 1932), pp. 623-636. Cf. A. Robinet, 'Leibniz: Lecture du *Treatise* de Berkeley,' *Études Philosophiques,* 1983 (2), pp. 217-223.

5. A.-L. Leroy, 'Influence de la philosophie Berkeleyenne sur la pensée continentale,' *Hermathena,* **82** (1953), pp. 27-48.

6. Eugen Stäbler, *George Berkeley's Auffassung und Wirkung in der deutschen Philosophie bis Hegel.* (Zeulenroda, 1935). It is quoted, e.g., by E. H. Allison, *Journal of the History of Philosophy,* **11** (1973), p. 44, and by G. J. Mattey, *Kant-Studien,* **74** (1983), p. 163.

7. Christoph Matthaeus Pfaff, *Oratio de egoismo* (Tubingae, 1722), p. 17.

8. Christian Wolff, *De differentia nexus* . . . (Halae Magdeburgensis, 1724), p. 75. Reprinted in Christian Wolff, *Gesammelte Werke,* Series II, vol. 9 (Hildesheim/Zürich/New York, 1983). Berkeley's and Collier's names are missing in the German edition of 1724: *Gesammelte Werke,* Series I, vol. 17 (1980), p. 9.

9. D. Strähler, *Prüfung der Wolffischen Gedancken von Gott, der Welt und der Seele,* Part 1 (Jena, 1723), Part 2 (Leipzig, 1723).

10. *Ibid.,* Part 2, p. 27.

11. H. M. Bracken, *The Early Reception of Berkeley's Immaterialism.* Revised edition (The Hague, 1965).

12. Moreover, it is sometimes difficult to get the older German books.

13. Johann Christoph Gottsched, *Vindicarum systematis influxus physici sectio prior historica* (Lipsiae, 1727), pp. 4-5.

14. J. L. Uhl, ed., *Sylloge nova epistolarum varii argumenti*, vol. IV (Norimbergae, 1764), p. 431. This letter was composed in French.

15. Friedrich Philipp Schlosser, *Send-Schreiben an die Philosophische und Historische Gesellschaft auf der Weltberühmten Academie Wittenberg darinn von einigen Vorschlägen den Idealismum zu bestreiten kürtzlich redet . . .* (Hannover, 1730).

16. D. Park, 'Kant und Berkeley's "Idealism,"' *Studi internazionali di filosofia*, **2** (1970), p. 4.

17. Joachim Lange, *Modesta disquisitio . . .* (Halae Saxonum, 1723), p. 221.

18. Georg Friedrich Meier, *Metaphysik* (Halle, 1755-59), vol. II, no. 374, p. 162.

19. I. Kant, *Gesammelte Schriften* (Berlin: Deutsche Akademie der Wissenschaften, 1910-72), vol. 28, p. 43.

20. G. J. Mattey, "Kant's Conception of Berkeley's Idealism," *Kant-Studien*, **74** (1983), pp. 161-75.

21. *Frankfurter gelehrte Anzeigen*, 1772 (reprinted, Bern, 1970), pp. 665-69, 672-77.

22. Johann Gottfried Herder, *Metakritik*, in *Sämtliche Werke*, vol. III, edited by J. Nadler (Vienna, 1951).

23. C. Meiners, *Grundriss der Geschichte der Weltweisheit* (Lemgo, 1786), pp. 301-2.

24. Herder, *Metakritik*, p. 298.

25. *Von und an Herder. Ungedruckte Briefe aus Herders Nachlass.* Edited by Heinrich Düntzer and Ferdinand Gottfried von Herder. Vol. II (Leipzig, 1861), p. 312.

26. Herder, *Metakritik*, p. 298.

27. "Die Werke selbst sind nicht für Sie: ein subtiles, idealisches Lehrgebäude; . . . lesen Sie bloss das vorangesetzte Leben. Ein

seltner Mann mit Kopf und Herzen, von dem mich einige Züge recht erfreut haben." Letter to Müller, 1781, in Heinrich Gelzer, ed., *Protestantische Monatsblätter für Zeitgeschichte*, **14** (1859), p. 91.

28. *Adrastea*, **VI** (1804), in Herder, *Werke*, ed. Heinrich Düntzer, vol. 14 (Berlin, 1879), p. 787.

29. Loc. cit., pp. 791-99. (The last entries are taken out of *A Discourse Addressed to the Magistrates*.)

30. *Zerstreute Blätter*, Collection 4 (1792). In Herder, *Werke*, ed. Heinrich Düntzer, vol. 15 (Berlin, 1879), pp. 201-16.

31. ". . . in welchen die Stärke der Natur durch die kunst, und . . . beschämt seyn werden." G. Berkeley, *Philosophische Werke, Erster Teil* (Leipzig, 1781), p. 27.

32. "O Muse, nimmst Du westwärts Deinen Flug?"

33. "Gen Westen geht Britanniens Weg." B. Russell, *Philosophie des Abendlandes* (Darmstadt, ³ 1954), p. 536.

Matthew Kapstein

A BIBLIOGRAPHY OF GEORGE BERKELEY
1980–1985

This is the latest in an on-going series of Berkeley bibliographies, the most recent before this having been Colin M. Turbayne's "A Bibliography of George Berkeley 1963-1979" [CMTB hereinafter], which appeared in Prof. Turbayne's *Berkeley: Critical and Interpretive Essays*. The conventions adopted there have been generally retained here as well: Part I lists editions of Berkeley's own writings, ordered according to date of composition, while Part II lists writings on Berkeley, in alphabetical order by authors' names. Though the period covered here is 1980-1985, a small number of works published earlier, which were omitted from Prof. Turbayne's bibliography, have been also been included. I have no doubt that future bibliographers of Berkeley will discover any number of omissions in the present list, particularly of works which appeared in 1985.

The present bibliography does not include the following sorts of works by or about Berkeley: extracts from Berkeley's own writings appearing in, e.g, general college textbooks; published abstracts; reviews; articles on Berkeley appearing in the popular press (of which there were a great many in connection with tercentenary events in 1985).

Research for this bibliography made use of the *Philosopher's Index* database using the *Dialog* Information Retrieval Service, supplemented by the resources of the John D. Rockefeller Library, Brown University. I wish to thank Prof. Ernest Sosa for his many suggestions, and the contributors to this volume for the bibliographical data which they kindly forwarded to me.

I. BERKELEY'S WRITINGS

i. Collections

1. *Works on Vision*. Ed. Colin M. Turbayne. Reprinted, Connecticut: Greenwood Press, 1981. See CMTB for full details on the contents of this collection.

2. *George Berkeley, Philosophical Works including the works on Vision*. Ed. M. R. Ayers. Reprinted, London: Everyman's Library, 1983.

See CMTB for complete details on the contents of this collection.

3. George Berkeley, *Oeuvres Philosophiques*. Ed. Geneviève Brykman, with the collaboration of Dominque Berlioz-Letellier, Michelle and Jean-Marie Beyssade, Michel Blay, Laurent Déchery, Marilène Phillips. 2 vols. Paris: P.U.F. Epiméthée, 1985.

4. *Schriften über die Grundlagen der Mathematik und Physik*. Trans. Wolfgang Breidert. Frankfurt a. M.: Suhrkamp, 1985.

ii. Individual Works

Of Infinites, 1707

5. *Des Infinis*. Trans. Dominique Berlioz-Letellier. In *Oeuvres Philosophiques*, vol. I. See no. 3.

Philosophical Commentaries, 1707-1708

6. *The Notebooks of George Berkeley, Bishop of Cloyne (1685-1753): Tercentenary Facsimile Edition*. Ed. with a Postscript by Désirée Park. Oxford: The Alden Press, 1984.

7. *Notes philosophiques*. Trans. Geneviève Brykman et Jean-Marie Beyssade. In *Oeuvres Philosophiques*, vol. I. See no. 3.

Draft Introduction to the Principles of Human Knowledge, begun in 1708

8. George Berkeley, *Manuscript Introduction*. Edited with an Introduction and Commentary by Bertil Belfrage. Lund, Sweden: Doxa, 1985.

9. *Introduction manuscrite aux Principes*. Trans. Dominique Berlioz-Letellier. In *Oeuvres Philosophiques*, vol. I. See no. 3.

An Essay towards a New Theory of Vision, 1709

10. *Essai pour la nouvelle théorie de la vision*. Trans. Laurent Déchery. In *Oeuvres Philosophiques*, vol. I. See no. 3.

A Treatise Concerning the Principles of Human Knowledge, 1710

11. *Eine Abhandlung über die Prinzipien der menschlichen Erkenntnis.* Trans. Friedrich Überweg. Ed. Alfred Klemmt. Hamburg: Meiner, 1979.

12. *Traité des Principes de la connaissance humaine.* Trans. Marilène Phillips. In *Oeuvres Philosophiques*, vol. I. See no. 3.

13. *Principios del conocimiento humano.* Trans. Pablo Masa. Barcelona: Orbis, 1985.

Three Dialogues between Hylas and Philonous, 1713

14. *Drei Dialoge zwischen Hylas und Philonous.* Trans. Raoul Richter. Ed. Wolfgang Breidert. Hamburg: Meiner, 1980.

15. *Trois dialogues entre Hylas et Philonous.* Trans. Jean-Marie Beyssade. In *Oeuvres Philosophiques*, vol. II. See no. 3.

De Motu, 1721

16. 'Sobre el movimiento. Sobre el principio y la naturaleza del movimiento sobre la causa de la trasmisión de los movimientos (1721).' Trans. Robert Torretti. *Diálogos*, **14** (1979), pp. 119-141.

17. *Du mouvement.* Trans. Michelle Beyssade and Dominique Berlioz-Letellier. In *Oeuvres Philosophiques*, vol. II. See no. 3.

Correspondence with Samuel Johnson, 1729 onwards

18. *Correspondance philosophique avec S. Johnson.* Trans. Geneviève Brykman, *Oeuvres Philosophiques*, vol. II. See no. 3.

The Theory of Vision, or Visual Language . . . Vindicated and Explained, 1733

19. *La théorie de la vision . . . défendue et expliquée.* Trans. L. Déchery. In *Oeuvres Philosophiques*, vol. II. See no. 3.

The Analyst, 1734

20. *L'Analyste.* Trans. Michel Blay. In *Oeuvres Philosophiques*, vol. II. See no. 3.

Defense of Free-Thinking in Mathematics, 1735

21. *Défense de la libre pensée en mathématiques.* Trans. D. Berlioz-Letellier. In *Oeuvres Philosophiques*, vol. II. See no. 3.

II. WRITINGS ON BERKELEY

22. Adam, M. 'Le mot "archétype" chez Berkeley." *Revue Philosophique
de la France et de l'Étranger* (1982), pp. 523-528.

23. Allaire, Edwin B. 'Berkeley's Idealism Revisited.' In Turbayne, Colin
M., ed. *Berkeley: Critical and Interpretive Essays.* Minneapolis:
University of Minnesota Press, 1982, pp. 197-206.

24. Anghinetti, P. 'Berkeley's Influence on Joyce.' *James Joyce Quarterly*,
19 (1982), pp. 315-329.

25. Atherton, Margaret. 'The Coherence of Berkeley's Theory of Mind.'
Philosophy and Phenomenological Research, **43** (1983),
pp. 389-400.

26. Ayers, M. R. 'Berkeley's Immaterialism and Kant's Transcendental
Idealism.' In Vesey, Godfrey, ed., *Idealism Past and Present*,
Cambridge: Cambridge University Press, 1982, pp. 51-69.

27. Ayers, M. R. 'Berkeley and Hume: a question of influence.' In Rorty,
R., Schneewind, J. B., and Skinner, Q., eds. *Philosophy in
History*. Cambridge: Cambridge University Press, 1985,
pp. 303-337.

28. Bar-On, A. Z. 'Berkeley and the Sources of Phenomenology.' (In He-
brew.) *Iyyun* **29** (1980), pp. 44-53.

29. Bar-On, A. Z. 'Husserl's Berkeley.' In Anna-Teresa Tymieniecka, ed.,
Soul and Body in Phenomenology. Dordrecht: Reidel, 1983,
pp. 353-63.

30. Belfrage, Bertil. 'An Obscure Supplement to Volume One of Berkeley's *Works*.' *Berkeley Newsletter*, **6** (1982-83), pp. 17-21.

31. Belfrage, Bertil. 'Dating Berkeley's Notebook B.' *Berkeley Newsletter*, **7**
(1984), pp. 7-13.

32. Belfrage, Bertil. 'Facts concerning Berkeley's Notebooks.' *Berkeley Newsletter*, **7** (1984), pp. 17-22.

33. Belfrage, Bertil. 'The Order and Dating of Berkeley's *Notebooks*.' *Revue Internationale de Philosophie*, **154** (1985), pp. 196-214.

34. Berlioz-Letellier, Dominique. 'Un inédit de Berkeley: *Of Infinites*.' *Revue Philosophique de la France et de l'Étranger*, **172** (1982), pp. 45-57.

35. Berman, David. 'Bishop Berkeley and the Fountains of Living Waters.' *Hermathena*, **128** (1980), pp. 21-31.

36. Berman, David. 'Berkeley's Philosophical Reception after America.' *Archiv für Geschichte der Philosophie*, **62** (1980), pp. 93-99.

37. Berman, David. 'Enlightenment and Counter-Enlightenment in Irish Philosophy.' *Archiv für Geschichte der Philosophie*, **64** (1982), pp. 148-165.

38. Berman, David. 'Beckett and Berkeley.' *Irish University Review* (1984), pp. 42-45.

39. Berman, David. 'Berkeley and the Moon Illusions.' *Revue Internationale de Philosophie*, **154** (1985), pp. 215-222.

40. Berteloot, S. *Contribution à l'histoire de l'empirisme*. Université de Province, 1983.

41. Bieri, Peter. 'Sein und Aussehen von Gegenstanden: Sind die Dinge farbig.' *Zeitschrift für Philosophische Forschung*, **36** (1982), pp. 531-52.

42. Bouwsma, O. K. 'Notes on Berkeley's Idealism.' In Craft, J. L., and Hustwit, Ronald E., eds. *Toward a New Sensibility: Essays of O. K. Bouwsma*. Lincoln/London: University of Nebraska Press, 1982, pp. 170-211.

43. Bracken, Harry M. 'Hume on the "Distinction of Reason."' *Hume Studies*, **10** (1984), pp. 1-108

44. Breidert, Wolfgang. 'On some marginal signs in the *Philosophical Commentaries*.' *Berkeley Newsletter*, **8** (1985), pp. 7-8.

45. Breidert, Wolfgang. 'George Berkeley (1685-1753).' *Fridericiana (Zeitschrift der Universität Karlsruhe)*, **36** (1985), pp. 3-13.

46. Breidert, Wolfgang. 'Die Rezeption Berkeleys in Deutschland im 18. Jahrhundert.' *Revue Internationale de Philosophie*, **154** (1985), pp. 223-241.

47. Brykman, Geneviève. 'Le Cartesianisme dans le *De Motu.' Revue internationale de philosophie*, **33** (1979), pp. 552-69.

48. Brykman, Geneviève. 'Berkeley et l'intérieur absolu des choses.' *Revue Philosophique de la France et de l'Étranger*, **170** (1980), pp. 421-432.

49. Brykman, Geneviève. 'Pouvoir d'abstraire et notions abstraite chez Berkeley.' *Recherches sur le XVIIème siècle*, no. 4. Paris: Éditions du Centre National de la Recherche Scientifique, 1980, pp. 157-166.

50. Brykman, Geneviève. 'Berkeley à Newport: 1729-1979.' *Recherches sur le XVIIème siècle*, no. 4. Paris: Éditions du Centre National de la Recherche Scientifique, 1980, pp. 167-170.

51. Brykman, Geneviève. 'Du commencement introuvable de l'immatérialisme.' *Études Philosophiques* (1980), pp. 385-397.

52. Brykman, Geneviève. 'Microscopes and Philosophical Method in Berkeley.' In Turbayne, Colin M., ed. *Berkeley: Critical and Interpretive Essays*. Minneapolis: University of Minnesota Press, 1982, pp. 69-82.

53. Brykman, Geneviève. 'Philosophy and Apologetics in Berkeley.' *Berkeley Newsletter*, **6** (1982-83), pp. 12-16.

54. Brykman, Geneviève. 'Le Modèle Visuel de la Connaissance chez Berkeley.' *Revue Philosophique de la France et de l'Étranger*, **173** (1983), pp. 427-441.

55. Brykman, Geneviève. *Berkeley, philosophie et apologétique*. 2 vols. Paris: Vrin, 1984.

56. Brykman, Geneviève. 'La notion d'"archétype" selon Berkeley.' *Recherches sur le XVIIème siècle*, no. 7. Paris: Éditions du Centre National de la Recherche Scientifique, 1984, pp. 33-43.

57. Brykman, Geneviève. 'Principe de ressemblance et hétérogénéité des idées chez Berkeley.' *Revue Internationale de Philosophie*, **154** (1985), pp. 242-251.

58. Burnyeat, M. F. 'Idealism and Greek Philosophy: What Descartes Saw and Berkeley Missed.' *The Philosophical Review*, **90** (1982), pp. 3-40.

59. Burnyeat, M. F. 'Idealism and Greek Philosophy: What Descartes Saw and Berkeley Missed.' In Vesey, Godfrey, ed., *Idealism Past and Present*, Cambridge: Cambridge University Press, 1982, pp. 19-50.

60. Burnyeat, M. F. 'The sceptic in his place and time.' In Rorty, R., Schneewind, J. B., and Skinner, Q., eds. *Philosophy in History*. Cambridge: Cambridge University Press, 1985, pp. 225-254.

61. Byrne, P. A. 'Berkeley, Scientific Realism and Creation.' *Religious Studies*, **20** (1984), pp. 453-64.

62. Camporesi, Cristiano. 'Aporie Berkeleyane.' *Rivista di Filosofia*, **73** (1982), pp. 471-73.

63. Cantor, Geoffrey. 'Berkeley's *The Analyst* Revisited.' *Isis*, **75** (1984), pp. 668-683.

64. Cappio, James. 'Aristotle, Berkeley, and Proteus: Joyce's Use of Philosophy.' *Philosophy and Literature*, **5** (1981), pp. 21-32.

65. Clark, Stephen R. L. 'God-Appointed Berkeley and the General Good.' In Foster, John, and Robinson, Howard, eds. *Essays on Berkeley: A Tercentennial Celebration*. Oxford: Clarendon Press, 1985, pp. 233-253.

66. Cummins, Phillop. 'Hylas' Parity Argument.' In Turbayne, Colin M., ed. *Berkeley: Critical and Interpretive Essays*. Minneapolis: University of Minnesota Press, 1982, pp. 283-294.

67. Davidson, Arnold I., and Hornstein, Norbert. 'The Primary/Secondary Quality Distinction: Berkeley, Locke, and the Foundations of Corpuscularian Science.' *Dialogue: Canadian Philosophical Review*, **23** (1984), pp. 281-304.

68. Deprun, J. 'Diderot devant l'idéalisme. *Revue Internationale de Philosophy*, **38** (1984), pp. 67-78.

69. Dicker, Georges. 'Two Arguments from Perceptual Relativity in Berkeley's Dialogues between Hylas and Philonous.' *Southern Journal of Philosophy*, **20** (1982), pp. 409-22.

70. Dicker, Georges. 'The Con.' In Turbayne, Colin M., ed. *Berkeley: Critical and Interpretive Essays.* Minneapolis: University of Minnesota Press, 1982, pp. 46-66.

71. Dicker, Georges. '"An Idea Can Be Like Nothing but an Idea."' *History of Philosophy Quarterly*, **2** (1985), pp. 39-52.

72. Doney, Willis. 'Is Berkeley's a Cartesian Mind?' In Turbayne, Colin M., ed. *Berkeley: Critical and Interpretive Essays.* Minneapolis: University of Minnesota Press, 1982, pp. 273-282.

73. Doney, Willis. 'Berkeley's Arguments against Abstract Ideas.' *Midwest Studies in Philosophy*, **8** (1983), pp. 295-308.

74. Dürrheim, Karl. 'Berkeley und Reininger.' *Wiener Jahrbuch für Philosophie*, **16** (1984), pp. 147-151.

75. Fimiani, Mariapaolo. *George Berkeley. Il nome e l'immagine (Il nuovo codice).* Cosenza: Lerici, 1979.

76. Fimiani, Mariapaolo. 'Thomas Jessop a un anno dalla morte.' *Filosofia*, **33** (1982), pp. 203-208.

77. Flage, Daniel E. 'Berkeley's Notions.' *Philosophy and Phenomenological Research*, **45** (1985), pp. 407-26.

78. Fleming, Noel. 'The Tree in the Quad.' *American Philosophical Quarterly*, **22** (1984), pp. 25-36.

79. Fleming, Noel. 'Berkeley and Idealism.' *Philosophy*, **60** (1985), pp. 309-325.

80. Foster, John, 'Berkeley on the Physical World.' In Foster, John, and Robinson, Howard, eds. *Essays on Berkeley: A Tercentennial Celebration.* Oxford: Clarendon Press, 1985, pp. 83-108.

81. Foster, John, and Robinson, Howard, eds. *Essays on Berkeley: A Tercentennial Celebration.* Oxford: Clarendon Press, 1985.

82. Furlong, E. J. 'On Being "Embrangled" by Time.' In Turbayne, Colin

M., ed. *Berkeley: Critical and Interpretive Essays.* Minneapolis: University of Minnesota Press, 1982, pp. 148-155.

83. Garber, Daniel. 'Locke, Berkeley, and Corpuscular Scepticism.' In Turbayne, Colin M., ed. *Berkeley: Critical and Interpretive Essays.* Minneapolis: University of Minnesota Press, 1982, pp. 174-193.

84. Glauser, Richard. 'Les relations de signification chez Berkeley.' *Studia Philosophia*, **42** (1983), pp. 165-200.

85. Glouberman, M. 'The Dawn of Conceptuality: A Kantian Perspective.' *Idealistic Studies*, **9** (1979), pp. 187-212.

86. Glouberman, M. 'Berkeley and Kant: Archetypes vs. Ectypes.' *Rivista Critica di Storia della Filosofia*, **36** (1981), pp. 139-155.

87. Glouberman, M. 'Berkeley and Cognition.' *Philosophy*, **56** (1981), pp. 213-21.

88. Glouberman, M. 'Abstraction and Determinacy: The Ideological Background of Berkeleianism.' *Idealistic Studies*, **12** (1982), pp. 14-34.

89. Glouberman, M. 'Consciousness and Cognition: From Descartes to Berkeley.' *Studia Leibnitiana*, **14** (1982), pp. 244-65.

90. Hardwick, Charles S. 'Berkeley and Peirce.' In Ketner, Kenneth L., ed. *Proceedings of the C. S. Peirce Bicentennial International Congress.* Lubbock, Texas: Texas Technical Press, 1981.

91. Harper, William. 'Kant on Space, Empirical Realism and the Foundations of Geometry.' *Topoi*, **3** (1984), pp. 143-62.

92. Hausman, Alan. 'Adhering to Inherence: A New Look at the Old Steps in Berkeley's March to Idealism.' *Canadian Journal of Philosophy*, **14** (1984), pp. 421-444.

93. Hoffmann, Yoel. '"Dream-World" Philosophers: Berkeley and Vasubandhu.' In Ben-Ami Scharfstein, *Philosophy East/Philosophy West.* New York: Oxford University Press, 1978, pp. 247-268.

94. Hooker, Michael. 'Berkeley's Argument from Design.' In Turbayne, Colin M., ed. *Berkeley: Critical and Interpretive Essays.* Minneapolis: University of Minnesota Press, 1982, pp. 261-270.

95. Hornstein, Norbert. See Davidson, Arnold I., and Hornstein, Norbert.

96. Hutcheson, P. 'Berkeley's God Perceives.' *Southwest Philosophical Studies*, **8** (1983), pp. 81-88.

97. Kline, A. David. 'Berkeley, Pitcher, and Distance Perception.' *International Studies in Philosophy*, **12** (1980), pp. 1-8.

98. Kuklick, Bruce. 'Seven thinkers and how they grew: Descartes, Spinoza, Leibniz; Locke, Berkeley, Hume; Kant.' In Rorty, R., Schneewind, J. B., and Skinner, Q., eds. *Philosophy in History*. Cambridge: Cambridge University Press, 1985, pp. 125-139.

99. Lambert, Richard T. 'Berkeley's Use of the Relativity Argument.' *Idealistic Studies*, **10** (1980), pp. 107-21.

100. Lambert, Richard T. 'Berkeley's Commitment to Relativism.' In Turbayne, Colin M., ed. *Berkeley: Critical and Interpretive Essays*. Minneapolis: University of Minnesota Press, 1982, pp. 22-32.

101. Lambert, Richard T. 'The Literal Intention of Berkeley's Dialogues.' *Philosophy and Literature*, **6** (1982), pp. 165-171.

102. Lamers, Robert. 'Berkeley and Schopenhauer.' *Schobenhauer-Jahrbuch*, **62** (1981), pp. 120-43.

103. Lascola, Russell A. 'Berkeley: Inconsistencies and Common Sense.' *Idealistic Studies*, **14** (1984), pp. 193-96.

104. Lehman, Craig. 'Will, Ideas, and Perception in Berkeley's God.' *Southern Journal of Philosophy*, **19** (1981), pp. 197-203.

105. Lennon, Thomas M. 'Representationalism, Judgment and Perception of Distance: Further to Yolton and McRae.' *Dialogue: Canadian Philosophical Review*, **19** (1980), pp. 151-62.

106. Leyvraz, Jean-Pierre. 'La notion de Dieu chez Berkeley.' *Revue de Théologie et de Philosophie*, **112** (1980), pp. 241-52.

107. Lloyd, A. C. 'The Self in Berkeley's Philosophy.' In Foster, John, and Robinson, Howard, eds. *Essays on Berkeley: A Tercentennial Celebration*. Oxford: Clarendon Press, 1985, pp. 187-209.

108. Loeb, Louis E. *From Descartes to Hume*. Ithaca/London: Cornell University Press, 1981.

109. Margolis, Joseph. 'Berkeley and Others on the Problem of Universals.' In Turbayne, Colin M., ed. *Berkeley: Critical and Interpretive Essays*. Minneapolis: University of Minnesota Press, 1982, pp. 207-227.

110. Mates, Benson. 'On Refuting the Skeptic.' *Proceedings and Addresses of the American Philosophical Association*, **58** (1984), pp. 21-35.

111. Mattey, G. J. 'Kant's Conception of Berkeley's Idealism.' *Kant-Studien*, **74** (1983), pp. 161-175.

112. Maull, Nancy L. 'Berkeley on the Limits of Mechanistic Explanation.' In Turbayne, Colin M., ed. *Berkeley: Critical and Interpretive Essays*. Minneapolis: University of Minnesota Press, 1982, pp. 95-107.

113. McCracken, C. J. 'What *Does* Berkeley's God See in the Quad?' *Archiv für Geschichte der Philosophie*, **61** (1979), pp. 280-292.

114. McGowan, William. 'Berkeley's Doctrine of Signs.' In Turbayne, Colin M., ed. *Berkeley: Critical and Interpretive Essays*. Minneapolis: University of Minnesota Press, 1982, pp. 231-246.

115. McKim, Robert. 'Wenz on Abstract Ideas and Christian Neo-Platonism.' *Journal of the History of Ideas*, **43** (1982), pp. 665-71.

116. McKim, Robert. 'Berkeley on Human Agency.' *History of Philosophy Quarterly*, **1** (1984), pp. 181-94.

117. Melvil', Y. K., and Suško, S. A. 'The Argument of Dr. Johnson: Samuel Johnson, critic of Berkeley.' [In Russian.] *Voprosy Filosofii, Moscow* (1981), pp. 133-144.

118. Messenger, Theodore. 'Berkeley and Tymoczko on Mystery in Mathematics.' In Turbayne, Colin M., ed. *Berkeley: Critical and Interpretive Essays*. Minneapolis: University of Minnesota Press, 1982, pp. 83-91.

119. Meyer, Eugen. *Humes und Berkeleys Philosophie der Mathematik vergleichend und kritisch dargestellt*. Reprint of 1894 edition. Hildesheim/New York: Olms, 1980.

120. Mill, John Stuart. 'Bailey on Berkeley's Theory of Vision.' In Robson, J. M., ed. *Essays on Philosophy and the Classics. Collected Works of John Stuart Mill, Volume XI.* Toronto/Buffalo/London: University of Toronto Press, 1978, pp. 245-269.

121. Mill, John Stuart. 'Berkeley's Life and Writings.' In Robson, J. M., ed. *Essays on Philosophy and the Classics. Collected Works of John Stuart Mill, Volume XI.* Toronto/Buffalo/London: University of Toronto Press, 1978, pp. 449-471.

122. Mirarchi, Lawrence A. 'A Note on the Language Model of Nature.' In Turbayne, Colin M., ed. *Berkeley: Critical and Interpretive Essays.* Minneapolis: University of Minnesota Press, 1982, pp. 247-260.

123. Monro, D. H. 'Utilitarianism and the Individual.' *Canadian Journal of Philosophy,* **5** (1979, supplement), pp. 47-62.

124. Monro, D. H. 'The Sonneteers History of Philosophy.' *Philosophy,* **55** (1980), pp. 363-375.

125. Moore, James A. 'The Semiotic of Bishop Berkeley—A Prelude to Peirce?' *Transactions of the Charles S. Peirce Society,* **20** (1984), pp. 325-42.

126. Murphy, R. T. 'Husserl's Relation to British Empiricism.' *Southwestern Journal of Philosophy,* **11** (1980), pp. 89-106.

127. Nawratil, K. 'Das Urerlebnis in der Geschichte des abendländischen Denkens. Kleine Studien zur Philosophie Robert Reiningers. III: Neuzeit.' *Wiener Jahrbuch für Philosophie,* **14** (1981), pp. 45-72.

128. Nelson, John O. 'Does Physics Lead to Berkeley?' *Philosophy,* **57** (1982), pp. 91-104.

129. Neri, Luigi. '"Filling the World with a Mite": un Paradosso dell'Infinita divisibilita.' *Rivista de Filosofia,* **71** (1980), pp. 67-97.

130. Newton-Smith, W. H. 'Berkeley's Philosophy of Science.' In Foster, John, and Robinson, Howard, eds. *Essays on Berkeley: A Tercentennial Celebration.* Oxford: Clarendon Press, 1985, pp. 149-161.

131. Nielsen, Harry A. 'A Categorical Difficulty in Berkeley.' *Philosophical Research Archives,* **6** (1980), no. 1422.

132. Nigi, A. 'Il problema della religione in Berkeley I.' *Rivista Rosminiana di Filosofia e di Cultura,* **78** (1984), pp. 236-247.

133. Nigi, A. 'Il problema della religione in Berkeley II.' *Rivista Rosminiana di Filosofia e di Cultura,* **79** (1985), pp. 38-50.

134. Norton, David Fate. 'The Myth of "British Empiricism."' *History of European Ideas,* **1** (1981), pp. 331-344.

135. Odegard, Douglas. 'Berkeleian Idealism and the Dream Argument.' *Idealistic Studies,* **11** (1981), pp. 93-99.

136. Pappas, George S. 'Ideas, Minds, and Berkeley.' *American Philosophical Quarterly,* **17** (1980), pp. 181-94.

137. Pappas, George S. 'Berkeley, Perception, and Common Sense.' In Turbayne, Colin M., ed. *Berkeley: Critical and Interpretive Essays.* Minneapolis: University of Minnesota Press, 1982, pp. 3-21.

138. Pappas, George S. 'Adversary Metaphysics.' *Philosophy Research Archives,* **9** (1983), pp. 571-86.

139. Park, Desirée. 'Prior and Williams on Berkeley.' *Philosophy,* **56** (1981), pp. 231-41.

140. Park, Desirée. '*Notions:* the Counter-Poise of the Berkeleyna Ideas.' *Giornale di Metafisica,* **3** (1981), pp. 243-265.

141. Park, Desirée. 'On Taking Ideas Seriously.' In Turbayne, Colin M., ed. *Berkeley: Critical and Interpretive Essays.* Minneapolis: University of Minnesota Press, 1982, pp. 35-47.

142. Park, Desirée. 'Facts and Reasons concerning Berkeley's reprinted "Works."' *Berkeley Newsletter,* **7** (1984), pp. 14-16.

143. Peacocke, Christopher. 'Imagination, Experience, and Possibility: a Berkeleian View Defended.' In Foster, John, and Robinson, Howard, eds. *Essays on Berkeley: A Tercentennial Celebration.* Oxford: Clarendon Press, 1985, pp. 19-35.

144. Phillips, Marilène. 'Berkeley sur la volonté: quelques "Notes

philosophiques."' *Revue Internationale de Philosophie*, **154** (1985), pp. 252-258.

145. Piper, W. B. 'Kant's Contact with British Empiricism.' *Eighteenth Century Studies*, **12** (1978-79), pp. 174-89.

146. Pitcher, George. 'Berkeley on the Mind's Activity.' *American Philosophical Quarterly*. **18** (1981), pp. 221-227.

147. Popkin, Richard H. 'Berkeley and Pyrrhonism.' In Myles Burnyeat, ed., *The Skeptical Tradition*. Berkeley: University of California Press, 1983, pp. 377-396.

148. Pucelle, J. 'Berkeley a-t-il été influencé par Malebranche?' *Études Philosophiques* (1979), pp. 19-38.

149. Raynor, David. *'Minima Sensibilia* in Berkeley and Hume.' *Dialogue: Canadian Philosophical Review*, **19** (1980), pp. 196-200.

150. Robinet, A. 'Leibniz: lecture du *Treatise* de Berkeley.' *Études Philosophiques* (1983), pp. 217-223.

151. Robinson, Howard. 'The General Form of the Argument for Berkeleian Idealism.' Foster, John, and Robinson, Howard, eds. *Essays on Berkeley: A Tercentennial Celebration*. Oxford: Clarendon Press, 1985, pp. 163-186.

152. Robles, Jose A. 'Perception e Infinitesimales en Berkeley.' *Dianoia*, **26** (1980), pp. 151-77.

153. Robles, Jose A. 'Perception e Infinitesimales en Berkeley II.' *Dianoia*, **27** (1981), pp. 166-85.

154. Robles, Jose A. 'Berkeley y su Crítica a los Fundamentos del Cálculo.' *Revista Latinoamericana de Filosofia*, **10** (1984), pp. 141-50.

155. Rogers, Karen. 'Two Mistakes about Berkeley.' *Philosophy*, **55** (1980), pp. 552-53.

156. Rorty, R., Schneewind, J. B., and Skinner, Q., eds. *Philosophy in History*. Cambridge: Cambridge University Press, 1985.

157. Sanabria, Jose Ruben. 'El Conocimiento en la Filosofia Moderna: II El Empirismo.' *Humanitas (Mexico)*, **21** (1980), pp. 59-80.

158. Sanyal, Shyamali. 'George Berkeley on the Problem of Universals.' *Indian Philosophical Quarterly*, **10** (1983, supplement), pp. 7-12.

159. Sasso, Javier. 'Immaterialismo y Verificacionismo en *Filosofia del Entiendimiento.*' *Revista Latinoamericana de Filosofia*, **8** (1982), pp. 247-54.

160. Schacht, Richard. *Classical Modern Philosophers.* London/Boston/ Melbourne/Henley: Routledge & Kegan Paul, 1984.

161. Scruton, Roger. *From Descartes to Wittgenstein.* London/Boston/Henley: Routledge & Kegan Paul, 1981.

162. Smith, A. D. 'Berkeley's Central Argument Against Material Substance.' In Foster, John, and Robinson, Howard, eds. *Essays on Berkeley: A Tercentennial Celebration.* Oxford: Clarendon Press, 1985, pp. 37-57.

163. Solimini, Maria. 'Realismo e semantica nell'analisi berkeleyana della percezione visiva.' *Annali della Facoltà di Lettere e Filosofia, Bari.* **14** (1969), pp. 441-459.

164. Sosa, Ernest. 'Berkeley's Master Stroke.' In Foster, John, and Robinson, Howard, eds. *Essays on Berkeley: A Tercentennial Celebration.* Oxford: Clarendon Press, 1985, pp. 59-81.

165. Spicker, Gideon. *Kant, Hume und Berkeley.* Facsimile of 1875 Berlin edition. Available on request only. Ann Arbor: University Microfilms International, 1980.

166. Steinkraus, Warren E. *New Studies in Berkeley's Philosophy.* Washington: University Press of America, 1981.

167. Steinkraus, Warren E. 'Berkeley, Epistemology, and Science.' *Idealistic Studies,* **14** (1984), pp. 183-92.

168. Stewart, M. A. 'William Wishart, an Early Critic of *Alciphron.*' *Berkeley Newsletter,* **6** (1982-83), pp. 5-9.

169. Stroud, Barry. 'Berkeley vs. Locke on Primary Qualities.' *Philosophy,* **55** (1980), pp. 149-66.

170. Taylor, C. C. W. 'Action and Inaction in Berkeley.' In Foster, John,

and Robinson, Howard, eds. *Essays on Berkeley: A Tercentennial Celebration.* Oxford: Clarendon Press, 1985, pp. 211-225.

171. Tennant, R. C. 'The Anglican Response to Locke's Theory of Personal Identity.' *Journal of the History of Ideas,* **43** (1982), pp. 73-90.

172. Thrane, Gary. 'The Spaces of Berkeley's World.' In Turbayne, Colin M., ed. *Berkeley: Critical and Interpretive Essays.* Minneapolis: University of Minnesota Press, 1982, pp. 127-147.

173. Tipton, I. C. 'The Philosopher by Fire in Berkeley's *Alciphron.*' In Turbayne, Colin M., ed. *Berkeley: Critical and Interpretive Essays.* Minneapolis: University of Minnesota Press, 1982, pp. 159-173.

174. Tsai, Denis Hsin-An. 'God and the Problems of Evil in Berkeley.' *Philosophical Review (Taiwan),* **6** (1983), pp. 125-36.

175. Turbayne, Colin M., ed. *Berkeley: Critical and Interpretive Essays.* Minneapolis: University of Minnesota Press, 1982.

176. Turbayne, Colin M. 'Lending a Hand to Philonous.' In Turbayne, Colin M., ed. *Berkeley: Critical and Interpretive Essays.* Minneapolis: University of Minnesota Press, 1982, pp. 295-310.

177. Turbayne, Colin M. 'A Bibliography of George Berkeley 1963-1979.' In Turbayne, Colin M., ed. *Berkeley: Critical and Interpretive Essays.* Minneapolis: University of Minnesota Press, 1982, pp. 313-329.

178. Turbayne, Colin M. 'Hume's Influence on Berkeley.' *Revue Internationale de Philosophie,* **154** (1985), pp. 259-269.

179. Urmson, J. O. *Berkeley.* Oxford: Oxford University Press, 1982.

180. Urmson, J. O. *Berkeley.* Trans. Jesús Martín Cordero. Madrid: Alianza Editorial, 1984.

181. Urmson, J. O. 'Berkeley on Beauty.' In Foster, John, and Robinson, Howard, eds. *Essays on Berkeley: A Tercentennial Celebration.* Oxford: Clarendon Press, 1985, pp. 227-232.

182. Valberg, E. 'A Theory of Secondary Qualities.' *Philosophy,* **55** (1980), pp. 437-53.

183. Vesey, Godfrey, ed. *Idealism Past and Present*. Cambridge: Cambridge University Press, 1982.

184. Vermeulen, Ben. 'Berkeley and Nieuwentijt on Infinitesimals.' *Berkeley Newsletter*, **8** (1985), pp. 1-5.

185. Vision, Gerald. 'Hume's Attack on Abstract Ideas: Real and Imagined.' *Dialogue: Canadian Philosophical Review*, **18** (1979), pp. 528-37.

186. Walker, R. C. S. 'Idealism: Kant and Berkeley.' In Foster, John, and Robinson, Howard, eds. *Essays on Berkeley: A Tercentennial Celebration*. Oxford: Clarendon Press, 1985, pp. 109-129.

187. Warnock, G. J. *Berkeley*. Notre Dame University: Notre Dame Press, 1983.

188. Wedberg, Anders. *A History of Philosophy, Volume Two: The Modern Age to Romanticism*. Oxford: Clarendon Press, 1982.

189. Wenz, Peter S. 'The Books in Berkeley's Closet.' *Hermathena*, **128** (1980), pp. 33-40.

190. Wenz, Peter S. 'Berkeley's Two Concepts of Impossibility: A Reply to McKim.' *Journal of the History of Ideas*, **43** (1982), pp. 673-80.

191. Wenz, Peter S. 'Berkeley and Kant on Analytic and Synthetic *A Priori*.' *Berkeley Newsletter*, **5** (1981), pp. 1-5.

192. Wheeler, K. M. 'Berkeley's Ironic Method in the *Three Dialogues*.' *Philosophy and Literature*, **4** (1980), pp. 18-32.

193. Wilson, Margaret D. 'Did Berkeley Misunderstand the Quality Distinction in Locke.' In Turbayne, Colin M., ed. *Berkeley: Critical and Interpretive Essays*. Minneapolis: University of Minnesota Press, 1982, pp. 108-123.

194. 'On the "Phenomenalisms" of Berkeley and Kant.' In Wood, Allen, ed. *Self and Nature in Kant's Philosophy*. Ithaca: Cornell University Press, 1984, pp. 157-173.

195. Wilson, Margaret D. 'Berkeley and the Essences of the Corpuscularians.' In Foster, John, and Robinson, Howard, eds. *Essays on Berkeley: A Tercentennial Celebration*. Oxford: Clarendon Press,

1985, pp. 131-147.

196. Winkler, Kenneth P. 'Berkeley on Abstract Ideas.' *Archiv für Geschichte der Philosophie*, **65** (1983), pp. 63-80.

197. Winkler, Kenneth P. 'The Authorship of "Guardian" 69.' *Berkeley Newsletter*, **7** (1984), pp. 1-6.

198. Winkler, Kenneth P. 'Berkeley on Volition, Power, and the Complexity of Causation.' *History of Philosophy Quarterly*, **2** (1985), pp. 53-70.

199. Woolhouse, R. S. 'Reid and Stewart on Lockean Creation.' *Journal of the History of Philosophy*, **20** (1982), pp. 84-90.

200. Woozley, A. D. 'Berkeley on Action.' *Philosophy*, **60** (1985), pp. 293-307.

201. Yolton, John W. *Thinking Matter: Materialism in Eighteenth-Century Britain*. Minneapolis: University of Minnesota Press, 1983.

202. Young, Theodore A. *Completing Berkeley's Project: Classical vs. Modern Philosophy*. Lanham, Maryland: University Press of America, 1985.

INDEX OF PERSONAL NAMES

SYNTHESE HISTORICAL LIBRARY

Texts and Studies in the History of Logic and Philosophy

Editors:

N. KRETZMANN (Cornell University)
G. NUCHELMANS (University of Leyden)
L. M. DE RIJK (University of Leyden)

1. M. T. Beonio-Brocchieri Fumagalli, *The Logic of Abelard* (transl. from the Italian). 1969.
2. Gottfried Wilhelm Leibniz, *Philosophical Papers and Letters*. A selection translated and edited, with an introduction, by Leroy E. Loemker. 1969.
3. Ernst Mally, *Logische Schriften* (ed. by Karl Wolf and Paul Weingartner). 1971.
4. Lewis White Beck (ed.), *Proceedings of the Third International Kant Congress*. 1972.
5. Bernard Bolzano, *Theory of Science* (ed. by Jan Berg). 1973.
6. J. M. E. Moravcsik (ed.), *Patterns in Plato's Thought*. 1973.
7. Nabil Shehaby, *The Propositional Logic of Avicenna: A Translation from al-Shifa: al-Qiyas*, with Introduction, Commentary and Glossary. 1973.
8. Desmond Paul Henry, *Commentary on De Grammatico: The Historical-Logical Dimensions of a Dialogue of St. Anselm's*. 1974.
9. John Corcoran, *Ancient Logic and Its Modern Interpretations*. 1974.
10. E. M. Barth, *The Logic of the Articles in Traditional Philosophy*. 1974.
11. Jaakko Hintikka, *Knowledge and the Known. Historical Perspectives in Epistemology*. 1974.
12. E. J. Ashworth, *Language and Logic in the Post-Medieval Period*. 1974.
13. Aristotle, *The Nicomachean Ethics* (transl. with Commentaries and Glossary by Hypocrates G. Apostle). 1975.
14. R. M. Dancy, *Sense and Contradiction: A Study in Aristotle*. 1975.
15. Wilbur Richard Knorr, *The Evolution of the Euclidean Elements. A Study of the Theory of Incommensurable Magnitudes and Its Significance for Early Greek Geometry*. 1975.
16. Augustine, *De Dialectica* (transl. with Introduction and Notes by B. Darrell Jackson). 1975.
17. Arpád Szabó, *The Beginnings of Greek Mathematics*. 1978.
18. Rita Guerlac, *Juan Luis Vives Against the Pseudodialecticians. A Humanist Attack on Medieval Logic*. Texts, with translation, introduction and notes. 1979.
19. Paul Vincent Spade (ed.), *Peter of Ailly: Concepts and Insolubles. An Annotated Translation*. 1980.
20. Simo Knuuttila (ed.), *Reforging the Great Chain of Being*. 1981.
21. Jill Vance Buroker, *Space and Incongruence*. 1981.
22. E. P. Bos, *Marsilius of Inghen*. 1983.
23. Willem Remmelt de Jong, *The Semantics of John Stuart Mill*. 1982.
24. René Descartes, *Principles of Philosophy*. 1983.
25. Tamar Rudavsky (ed.), *Divine Onmiscience and Onmipotence in Medieval Philosophy*. 1985.
26. William Heytesbury, *On Maxima and Minima*. Chapter 5 of *Rules of Solving Sophismata*. Translation. 1984.
27. Peter King, *Jean Burridan's Logic*. The Treatise on Supposition. The Treatise on Consequences. 1985.
28. Simo Knuuttila and Jaakko Hintikka (eds.), *The Logic of Being*. 1986.